GLOBAL ENVIRONME
AND INTERNATIONAL
AGREEMENTS

The designations employed and the presentation of the material in this publication do not imply the expression of any opinion whatsoever on the part of the Secretariat of United Nations concerning the legal status of any country, territory, city or area, or of its authorities, or concerning the delimitation of its frontiers or boundaries.

Global Environmental Problems and International Environmental Agreements

The Economics of International Institution Building

Timothy Swanson

University College London and Centre for Social and Economic Research on the Global Environment, UK

and

Sam Johnston

Secretariat of the Convention on Biological Diversity

Edward Elgar

Cheltenham, UK • Northampton, MA, USA

Published in association with UNCTAD

Published by
Edward Elgar Publishing Limited
Glensanda House
Montpellier Parade
Cheltenham
Glos GL50 1UA
UK

Edward Elgar Publishing, Inc.
136 West Street
Suite 202
Northampton
Massachusetts 01060
USA

A catalogue record for this book
is available from the British Library

Library of Congress Cataloguing in Publication Data
Swanson, Timothy M.
    Global environmental problems and international environmental
    agreements : the economics of international institution building /
    Timothy M. Swanson and Sam Johnston.
        1. Environmental law, International.   2. Economic development—
    Environmental aspects.   I. Johnston, Sam.   II. Title.
    K3585.4.S93   1999
    341.7'62—dc21   98–31083
                                                                          CIP

ISBN 1 85898 751 2 (cased)

Typeset by Manton Typesetters, 5–7 Eastfield Road, Louth, Lincs, LN11 7AJ, UK.
Printed and bound in Great Britain by Bookcraft (Bath) Ltd.

Contents

List of figures

List of tables

Acknowledgements

This manuscript was commissioned by Professor John Cuddy of the International Trade Division of the United Nations Conference on Trade and Development (UNCTAD). The idea was to develop an economic and a legal framework for the training of negotiators from developing countries in the principles of international environmental lawmaking. During the time required for the execution of this project the subject matter of the text has become ever more important – giving testimony to the important vision that UNCTAD has displayed in commissioning the work. Now the issues surrounding the negotiation of international environmental agreements are more important than ever before.

In the completion of the text we have received support and encouragement from numerous quarters. Philippe Sands of the Foundation of International Environmental Law and Development was a co-author of some of the material in Part III of this book, and we appreciate his contribution to the project. Edouard Dommen gave extensive comments and criticism to earlier drafts, and they were very useful and encouraging. Our respective institutions have also provided us with support and encouragement. For Sam Johnston, the Secretariat of the Biodiversity Convention has been patient in allowing his involvement, and Calestous Juma has been especially solicitous. For Tim Swanson, Cambridge University and now the University College London and the Centre for Social and Economic Research on the Global Environment (CSERGE) have been supportive. We are grateful to all of these individuals and institutions for their aid and encouragement, especially to Janet Roddy and Susannah Marshall of CSERGE. Finally we are grateful for the assistance received from all those at Edward Elgar who have assisted in bringing the book to print, especially Edward Elgar, Dymphna Evans, Julie Leppard and Ian Garbutt.

Preface

In 1974 the Scientific Committee of the North East Atlantic Fishery Commission (NEAFC) established a sustainable quota for herring at the level of 310 000 tonnes. In theory, all that was required for the continued annual harvesting of this tonnage of herring was for the various states working this fishery to keep their total catch at or beneath this total. In the following two years the half-dozen states operating within this agreement argued acrimoniously concerning their relative quota entitlements. The UK argued in favour of quotas based upon natural proximity. The Soviet Union argued in favour of quotas based upon historical usage rates, and general development status. Denmark argued in favour of quotas based upon current fishing fleets (as Denmark had recently expanded its own). Despite the fact that the quota recommended by the Scientific Committee was only about half of this level, *the individual quotas demanded by the various states aggregated to 572 000 tonnes.* The next year the impact of this overfishing was a severely cut aggregate quota – to 254 000 tonnes – but once again the parties failed to agree on the current distribution. The result was that two parties refused to accept their designated allocations, and the total harvest was 50 per cent greater than the recommended quota once again (365 000 tonnes). By 1976 the herring fishery had collapsed and the NEAFC was out of business.

This book is about these sorts of resource management problem that exist at the interstices between the various governance units that we know as sovereign states. This structure of resource management used to be adequate for most purposes, but it is becoming increasingly stretched by the technologies and scales of human economies. The pressures of increasing interdependencies means that there is the need for new forms of institutions for resource management. This book examines the sources of these pressures, and the institution-building process that is being occasioned as a result.

This book is interdisciplinary because it concerns an area of human activity that exists at the interface between the development process and the institution-building process. The development process continues unabated with its attendant effects on and implications for natural resources and environmental scarcity. The potential limits on and sustainability of this process have been two important subjects of debate over the past couple of decades. Increasingly this debate is occurring in the context of specific resources rather than vague concepts: climate change, ozone layer, biodiversity and marine resources. The discussion of the feasibility of continued development is becoming focused on these various factors and their limiting capacities. One of the most important limiting factors concerning the sustainability of the development process is the capacity of all of the human societies on earth to learn how to cooperate with one another in addressing these problems. All of these resources are now the subject of international agreements and ongoing negotiations over their terms and effects. The capacity for development to continue is becoming increasingly linked to the capacity for these negotiations to conclude.

This book attempts to explain these problems through the examination of the international lawmaking process: the recognition of international interdependence; the negotiation of international agreements; and, the evolution of international resource management. It attempts to explain global environmental problems as being embedded within two processes: the process of economic development and the process of institutional development. In order to understand how and why these problems remain unresolved, it is as important to understand the mechanics of international lawmaking, as it is important to understand the economics of common resources. Therefore this text examines the general problem of global resource management by means of both general principles and a case-study-based approach, by looking at how and why specific negotiations and agreements have failed to achieve the efficient resource management that they pursue. It is only by looking to the mechanics of the process that the full complexity of global environment resource management can be comprehended.

This book is structured as follows: Part I introduces the economics of the development process and its implications for global resources. Chapter 1 reopens the 'limits to growth' debate and examines it for the kernels of truth that remain. It addresses the questions: what is the common characteristic of the resources that lie at the core of global environmental problems? Which resources are inadequately managed by standard decentralised (nation-by-nation) development? Chapter 2 identifies one common aspect of many global management problems – the problem of managing the development process for the maintenance of options for future generations. Every choice that we take regarding resource management has an efficiency and a distributional aspect, and one of the primary constituencies missing from the resource allocation process is that of all future generations. How do we represent them in global development and resource management? Chapter 3 is a case study illustrating the ideas developed in the first two chapters, by reference to the problem of biodiversity management. It addresses the specific question of why would the current development process fail to manage adequately the resource of biodiversity? In sum, these first three chapters provide an introduction to the ideas of global development, its direction when undertaken on an unmanaged basis, and the gaps which exist in the decentralized development process which necessitate global management (and therefore international environmental agreements).

Chapter 4 provides the link between Parts I and II. It describes the uneven process of development as it has occurred across the globe, and how this unevenness drives the development of unique and individual national perspectives on environmental problems. One of the most substantial problems of international environmental agreements is the fact that there is no single or objective viewpoint on natural resource management. Optimal resource management is based upon a weighing of costs and benefits of resource usage, and every state will strike this balance differently depending upon how it weighs up this equation. Since every state views the same environmental impacts differently, the starting point for the negotiation of international environmental agreements must necessarily be disagreement.

Part II builds on this insight to develop and describe the institution-building process that occurs in response to the inefficiencies resulting from the national management of international resources. There is a clear gain to be achieved from movement to a joint management structure in respect to all of these resources, and the potential attainment of this gain is what drives the institution-building process. However, counterbalancing this potential gain is the never-ending debates concerning its distribution – the bargaining problem of international environmental agreements. In Part II this bargaining problem is seen again and again in the context of one resource after another.

Chapter 5 is a general introduction to some of the ideas that were developed in Part I and all of the ideas to be developed in Part II. This allows the more specialized student to move directly to the institution-building material, without the necessity of parsing the entirety of Part I. Chapter 6 is a general introduction to the concepts that have been developed in the literature on international environmental agreements. This develops the basic ideas of free riding, and the difficulty of deciding the distribution of resource rents within a heterogeneous environment. It demonstrates that states may be demanding additional shares either because of the belief in their differentiated status, or because they are able to command a large share of the value of the resource by holding out. It further demonstrates that it is often, if not always, to differentiate between the two different phenomena. This problem lies at the core of the costliness of the institution-building process.

Chapter 7 is an institutional analysis of the holdout problem. It examines several of the major reasons that states demand larger shares of the total value of the common resource. These reasons include: natural characteristics; development status; and, general holdout rents. The various case studies (including the case of NEAFC alluded to above) indicate that states make their arguments in every context on predictable grounds. Nevertheless the near impossibility of differentiating between true entitlements (to sidepayments) and raw free-riding remains.

Chapter 8 demonstrates that this problem remains even after the ink is dry on the agreement. States are not only able to shift resource rents around during the negotiating phase, but they are also able to do so after it is over. Negotiations after negotiations. The capacity afforded to states under international law to retain rights and reject responsibilities, while remaining within international agreements, allows considerable room for ongoing manoeuvres. This chapter discusses reservations, non-implementation and various other techniques used to negate the effect of international environmental agreements.

Chapter 9 illustrates the evolution of one particular regime – the Convention on International Trade in Endangered Species (CITES). It demonstrates how the original meaning of an agreement can be completely revised through the ongoing process of change and revision that the process implies. International environmental law is first and foremost a process – a living and continuing round of negotiations. It is the understanding of this – its organic nature – which allows the student to understand how and why the failures of international resource management are allowed to continue.

Part III provides a summary of the principles of international environmental law for the layperson. It is provided here as a reference, and as a summary of how the various forces described within this book have culminated in some sorts of codifiable principles. The generality of the principles within this area of law indicates the way in which they have developed. The need for more substance is implicit in the failures that continue.

This volume is provided as an introductory text for students interested in the area of global environmental policy making and institution-building. It may also be of interest as a reference to practitioners and policy makers in the area. We hope that it provides an initial framework for understanding the process-based problems in the field, and that this contributes to both better teaching and better institution-building in the future.

Tim Swanson
Sam Johnston

For Gill and Jean
and the kids

PART I

THE ECONOMICS OF GLOBAL ENVIRONMENTAL PROBLEMS: GLOBAL DEVELOPMENT, GLOBAL LIMITS AND GLOBAL SUSTAINABILITY

Timothy Swanson

1 The limits to growth: global development, efficiency and sustainability

1 Global development and global limits: the role of international environmental agreements

In this chapter we examine the natural constraints on global growth and development. Human society has been expanding for many centuries in terms of population, land and other resource use, and general levels of economic activity. This continued expansion raises the question: where are the limits to this process? The work of the classical economists (Ricardo, Mill and Malthus) was preoccupied with this question, but for many decades it seemed that economic expansion occurred without this inquiry. Uncontrolled growth and development were assumed to be the answer to many social problems, rather than the creator of many. In the past couple of decades we have been engaging in the first systematic investigation of the global implications of uncontrolled growth, and the role of planning and management in this process.

The role of international environmental agreements in the global development process is to provide for the regulation that is deemed necessary to channel this process effectively. For this reason it is essential to commence with an investigation of global development, its direction and its implications. We must understand what problems development creates, and which it resolves. In this chapter we address the question raised by the classical economists: Are there limits to growth? Then we move on towards the more recent questions raised by the global development process.

2 The economics of efficient resource management

In order to understand the economic nature of an 'environmental problem' (inefficient resource exploitation), it is necessary to understand the nature of *efficient* resource utilization. Sometimes the two phenomena may give rise to outward manifestations that appear very similar. All exhaustible resources (for example minerals) will necessarily be depleted through human use, and so the mere decline of a resource base cannot invariably equate with inefficient usage. How is it possible to separate between those forms of resource depletion that are efficient and those that are not? The object of this section is to give a short course in natural resource economics in order to define how resources may be depleted, both efficiently and inefficiently. The two following sections then describe the interrelationships between efficient resource depletion and development and inefficient resource depletion and development.

3

2.1   *Natural resources as natural assets*

Economists view all natural resources as a natural form in which society holds some of its capital. Capital is the stock of society's resources (human, man-made and natural) that generate a flow of goods and services (Table 1.1). 'Natural capital' is a flow-generating resource whose form was endowed by nature. For example the capital stock of a given society might consist of a number of people (and their education and health levels), together with its natural resources (for example forests and fisheries) and their man-made capital stock (machinery, tools and buildings). Each of these forms of capital yields a flow of benefits to that society, on which it depends for its subsistence and consumption. The human forms of capital yield labour, communication and innovation. The natural forms of capital yield various goods and services. The most noticeable would be the fish from the fishery and the timber from the forest; however, the natural capital equally yields various 'systemic' forms of services, such as the flow of clean water and pure air on which we depend. Then, of course, there are the forms of capital that economists usually study: the machinery and tools made by man for use in production. These 'man-made' forms of capital did not exist initially (as did the other two forms); they are the result of the productive use of flows from the natural and human forms of capital ('investment').

Table 1.1   Capital stocks and their flows

	Human	Natural	Man-made
Capital:			
	People	Forests	Machines
	Education	Fisheries	Tools
Flows:			
	Labour	Timber	Lumber
	Invention	Wood fuel	Chairs
	Service	Fish	Food

One of the fundamental pathways to development of society is the balancing of that society's capital stock. One of the means by which an optimal capital portfolio is pursued is through *conversion* between asset forms. That is, although society commences with a certain stock of assets in various forms (natural, human and man-made), one of the important choices that it must make is how to reshape that portfolio, shifting assets between the various capital forms. Such shifting of assets occurs through the process of conversion.

Conversion might occur, for example, if a forest is removed and marketed, with the proceeds invested in a hospital or a school. This process would convert the forest (a natural form of capital) into healthy and educated individuals (human forms of capital). Alternatively the proceeds from the sale of the forest might be invested in a new factory, or a financial asset such as a bond.

In any of these cases the 'balance sheet' for that society would be altered to reflect the movement of its assets between the different forms. The portfolio of the society would be reconstructed through such conversions to render the society more dependent upon flows from human (or man-made) capital assets and less dependent upon natural forms of capital. Through undertaking the quantity and quality of the conversions that it desired, the society would effectively determine the precise portfolio of assets on which it would depend.

So, in this sense, natural resources are simply natural forms of assets within a society's capital stock. In an economic framework there is little reason a priori to prefer an asset form, simply because that was the form in which it was endowed naturally. Therefore human development will often result in a substantial reshaping of the natural set of assets through the process of conversion.

2.2   Efficient resource conversion: Hotelling's rule

When are such conversions efficient? The short answer to this question is that an asset should be 'cashed in' so long as it fails to yield the market rate of return. That is, if the market rate of return on capital is 6 per cent, and the forest is only yielding a return of (say) 3 per cent on its cash value, then it would make sense to harvest the forest, convert it to cash and invest it at 6 per cent. Of course, as the number of forests declined, the prices of their goods and services should increase, while the reverse is true of the assets experiencing increasing investment. Through such a process of conversion, an equilibrium between different asset forms should occur, where all asset forms (human, natural and man-made) are all yielding the same (market) rate of return.

There are two general complicating factors in this simple scenario: capital gains and stock externalities. The former implies that resource owners will perceive their natural assets as yielding a higher-than-actual return on account of the prospect for capital gains (future price changes). The latter implies that resource owners will perceive their natural resources as yielding a lower- than-actual return on account of the inability to appropriate the value of certain flows.

An alternative way of looking at conversion is to examine the process by which resources would be depleted efficiently. That is, given a stock of a depletable asset (such as, say, a tin mine), how should the mine owner proceed to mine the ore?

This is the question asked by Harold Hotelling in 1931 in his classic article on the depletion of an exhaustible resource. In this situation, it would appear that there would be little reason not to mine all of the ore as quickly as possible since it renders no benefits while it remains within the ground. That is the choice in the case of a mineral is between the natural asset form (ore in the ground) and another asset form (for example money in the bank). The former yields no return, while the latter yields the prevailing rate of interest. Therefore, at first sight, it would seem to make sense to mine all of the ore and place the proceeds into another asset.

However this analysis ignores the effect that the mine owner would have on the price that he would receive in the process of mining. In the simplest case, where the mine owner has a monopoly over the market, the control over resource price is absolute. We will examine this case in order to make clear how the prospect for capital gains determines the path for resource depletion.

In essence, the monopolist mine owner can determine the rate at which the price escalates by determining the amount of the mineral substance to place on the market in each period. He will definitely place less on the market in each period (as there is no incentive to keep the ore in the mine unless the price is rising). The amount that he places on the market in each successive period will be determined by the price rise that he wishes to achieve. In effect Hotelling showed that a mine owner with control over his price will extract the mineral at that rate that will cause the price to rise at the market rate of interest; the mine owner will be constrained from immediately exhausting the mine by reason of the capital gains he can achieve by releasing it onto the market in a measured fashion. Figure 1.1 demonstrates this process. If the initial price and quantity of the resource is represented by point $Q1$ on the demand curve, then the resource owner will release a reduced quantity ($Q2$) onto the market in the next period, and so on. Such a pattern of resource depletion (and marketing) will result in the gradual escalation of the resource price (at a rate equal to the rate of interest) and the gradual depletion of the resource stock (at a similar rate).

Hotelling's rule is the statement that resource depletion will occur at that rate that will cause the value of the resource stock to equal the market rate of return. In the simplest form (where the only return from the resource derives from its depletion), Hotelling's rule states that depletion will occur at that rate that will cause the price to rise at the rate of interest. This is the form in which the rule is demonstrated in Figure 1.1.

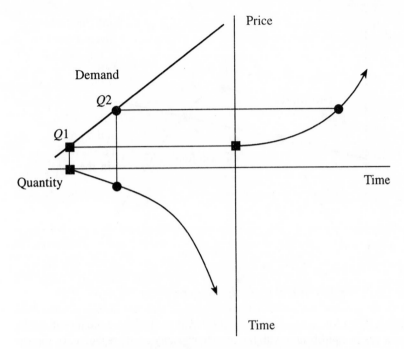

Figure 1.1   Hotelling's rule and optimal resource depletion

2.3   The efficient depletion of renewable resources

Obviously, in the case of certain resources (for example minerals), if human societies are to make use of them, then they will be depleted. These are the *exhaustible resources*: those resources whose stocks are fixed and non-increasing. There is another group of living resources – the *renewable resources* – for which this is not the case. These resources have the capacity to regenerate themselves if some stock is retained. Examples of such resources are fisheries, forests, clean air and water. The capacity for regeneration has led some conservationists to argue for a solution concept known as *maximum sustainable yield*. This is the maximum yield realizable from a resource without causing any reduction in stock level.

Figure 1.2 demonstrates the economic analysis of renewable resources. In this figure the growth rate curve represents the flow of the resource that results from the retention of any given stock of the resource. This flow first increases then slows and then declines as the resource fills the available 'niche'. The concept of maximum sustainable yield is represented by the point MSY in the diagram; this is the maximum flow achievable from a fixed stock level. Of course harvesting of a living resource is not a costless activity, but its costliness is reduced by reason of the existence of greater stocks of the

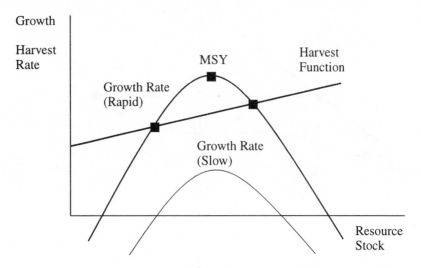

Figure 1.2   Optimal use of renewable resources

resource. Therefore a *bioeconomic equilibrium* exists where the incentives to harvest are in equilibrium with the growth capacity of the resource. In Figure 1.2 this equilibrium is represented by the points of intersection between the growth function and the harvesting function.

Will either of these outcomes (MSY or bioeconomic equilibrium) equate with the social optimum? That is what factors will determine the socially optimal stock level of a renewable resource? The answer is that the same general rule applies in the case of renewables as applies in the case of non-renewables, that is, the optimal stock is that which equates the rates of return between the natural and all other assets.

The difference between renewables and non-renewables lies in the various forms in which these returns are received. In the case of the simple depletable asset, the only return that is received is the result of 'capital gains': price increases resulting from the rate of depletion. In the case of renewable resources, however, there are a number of other characteristics of the resource that are capable of generating a return. First, the resource itself generates a flow, by virtue of its capacity for regeneration. This flow might take the form of a set of tangible goods, such as the timber from a forest or the protein from a fishery; or, it might also take the form of intangible services, such as the watershed protection and carbon sequestration of a forest.

Secondly, as indicated by the growth functions in Figure 1.1, the retention of a stock of the resource also reduces harvesting costs in the future. This is the reason that the harvesting function is upward-sloping; increased stocks imply reduced costliness in access and use. Thus a stock of a renewable resource can generate a flow of benefits either by increasing benefits or by reducing costliness. For example if a river is used for waste disposal, then it may be necessary to use alternative means to produce 'clean water' for consumption in the future (for example filtration). If the water quality were maintained at a higher level, then it would not be necessary to undertake other costly measures to produce it.

Finally, the same 'capital gains' factor applies to renewable as to depletable resources. There is no reason to deplete a resource in a fashion that causes its price to fall unnecessarily.

Therefore there are a number of different factors that contribute to the applicable 'rate of return' to be derived from a living, renewable resource as contrasted with the single relevant factor for a depletable one. Table 1.2 demonstrates the general validity of the requirement that, whatever the nature of the resource, the optimal stock level will be determined by the capacity of the resource to generate a market-competitive return (r).

Table 1.2   Factors determining optimal stock levels

Depletable:

'Capital gains'   = r ('market rate of return')

Renewable:

'Capital gains' + 'Growth' + 'Reduced costs' = r ('market rate of return')

Hence the optimal stock level for a renewable resource is probably not that which is consistent with maximum sustainable yield. If a renewable resource exists at stock levels that are at or near MSY, this implies that the last unit of the stock retained is yielding very low incremental growth (since the rate of growth is declining at this point). Therefore it is more likely that the optimal stock level will exist to the left of MSY, where the growth rate of the resource is higher.

There is one last crucial point to make here. It is even possible for the optimal stock level for a renewable resource to be zero, that is *optimal extinction*. This is the case if there exists no stock level at which the resource is able to generate a market-competitive return. For example it is often stated that the great tropical hardwoods exist in a state of virtual non-growth; that is, they have achieved the point in Figure 1.1 where the growth function intersects the horizontal axis. If these forests were thinned, it might be possible to achieve some positive rate of growth, but the hardwoods remain very slow-growing resources. They are best represented by the lower growth curve in Figure 1.1. In that case they might not be capable of achieving a return competitive with market rate, that is the rate that they would achieve if they were harvested with the returns invested elsewhere. Then this form of conversion is often what will occur.

Even in the case of renewable resources, it is not necessarily the case that the naturally endowed levels of the resources are the economically optimal stock levels. If this is the case, then it will be indicated by the resource's inability to meet the market rate of return. If the existing stocks of the renewable resource fail to generate a competitive return, then it will be optimal to convert some portion of the stock of the natural asset to some other form of asset. The movement to the new stock level under such circumstances will be efficient, even though it results from resource depletion. This is the role of natural asset conversion in the process of societal development.

2.4   Externalities in common resources: 'the tragedy of the commons'
We have examined the reasons why it is the case that the maximum sustainable yield concept is unlikely to equate with the socially optimal stock levels of a natural resource, but we have not yet examined the concept of a bioeconomic equilibrium in similar depth. Is it necessarily the case that the equilibrium that results from human exploitation of natural resources will be socially optimal? Under what circumstances will exploitation be demonstrably suboptimal?

In the previous section we examined the simple cases – where there were no externalities involved in the use of the resource. What happens to resources when externalities prevail, that is when the resource is inadequately regulated, as described in section 2? Such resources are free to be used by anyone who wishes; and, being free and of finite capacity, they are used excessively. This problem was labelled 'The Tragedy of the Commons' by Hardin (1968); it occurs frequently in resource economics, both between individuals (the 'local or community commons') and also between countries (the 'global commons' problem).

The 'tragedy of the commons' is illustrated in Figure 1.3. In this figure (a modification of Figure 1.1 above), total benefits and total costs are shown against 'effort' expended harvesting the resource (for example cutting down trees for fuel). The amount of effort expended harvesting is monotonically and inversely related to the remaining stock of trees. The total benefit curve is drawn as an inverted-U, again signifying that there exists a critical effort level, or stock of trees, beyond which the population starts to decline. The harvest at this critical level of harvesting effort – marked E_{MSY} in Figure 1.3 – equates with the maximum sustainable yield; harvests in excess of this deplete the resource stock.

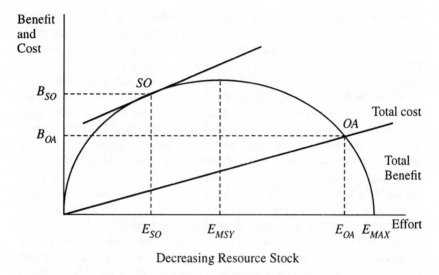

Figure 1.3   Externalities in common resources

Three points on this diagram are of interest. First, E_{MAX} is the maximum level of effort, and corresponds to zero stock of trees. Second, suppose that the entire forest were given to a single owner, who then aims to maximize 'profits' (the difference between total benefits and costs). This situation would bring about point SO (the social optimum) – the point at which the difference between benefits and costs is the largest. The effort level employed is E_{SO}, corresponding to a resource stock of R_{SO}. (This corresponds to the case examined in the previous section.) Third, suppose that no one individual possesses the property right to the forest – access is open, free and unrestricted (OA). In this, case, anyone who can make a 'profit' (obtain some net benefit) by harvesting will do so. That is, whenever total benefits are greater than total costs, someone will find it worth their while to expend effort to chop down trees. They will stop only when total costs exceed total benefits – to the right of point OA. The effort level employed is $E_{OA} > E_{SO}$, and the corresponding resource stock is $R_{OA} < R_{SO}$.

Therefore the necessary result of an inadequately regulated resource is overexploitation and inefficient depletion. This depletion constitutes a social loss because all of society would be able to benefit from better regulation of the resource. In effect the resource is being driven down to a stock level that is less than its optimal, and as a result investments in the resource would generate a return greater than the market rate. This is the social loss that results from inefficient resource exploitation.

Why don't these investments occur? The problem is that the individuals operating within an open access regime consider only their own private costs and benefits, assuming that their individual actions will not have any significant effect on the resource stock. The impact of their actions on others is ignored. This is the externality that derives from inadequate regulation.

Within the framework developed above, the result is that individuals attach a low value to the resource stock, and therefore use it excessively. They perceive the resource stock as a very poor investment asset. The single owner (or 'social planner'), on the other hand, takes into account the effects of his actions on the resource stock, that is he attaches a value to the resource closer to its actual investment value. Why is there this difference? It is because, in the multiple user context, there is uncertainty as to the identity of the individual that will capture the flow of benefits resulting from this period's investments. A natural asset may be capable of generating very high levels of benefits, but if they do so in a diffuse or non-directed fashion, they will still be perceived to be poor capital investments by individuals. This is the impact of inadequate regulation on a resource; irrespective of its individual characteristics (whether it is a high-growth or a low-growth asset), the regime will generate the perception that it is an undesirable asset for investment purposes. For this reason its stock levels are reduced below the optimal.

Natural resources and international environmental agreements   When is an international environmental agreement required for the management of natural resource exploitation? Wherever a resource or system extends beyond the limits of a single domestic regime, there will necessarily be inefficient utilization. In the context of the analysis of this section, an environmental system that spans more than a single-state will generate uncertainty as to the appropriability of the future flows from its stocks. This will limit the rate at which individual states will invest in the stocks of that resource.

Consider for example a tropical hardwood forest that generates a wide range of benefits (Table 1.3). Some of these are clearly appropriable by the society within whose boundaries the forest lies, for example the flows of timber and other commodities directly derived from the forest. Other benefits

Table 1.3   The total flow of benefits from a tropical forest: internal and external

Direct Internal Use	Indirect Internal Use	External Uses
Timber	Tourism	Biodiversity
Rubber, Rattan	Watershed	Climate

are more indirect but still largely appropriable within that single state, for example tourism and watershed benefits. However other benefits of the forest flow readily beyond its boundaries: climatic impacts, biodiversity benefits, carbon sequestration and so forth.

It is not necessary to contract in regard to the forest's provision of the first category of benefits. Since these benefits flow largely to individuals within the state in the first instance, the domestic regime alone should be adequate to regulate their supply. The second category of benefits might flow to one or two states simultaneously, for example if the watershed concerned crosses an international boundary. Then it may be necessary to supplement the domestic regulatory regime with an international agreement to internalize the benefits received by other foreign users of the watershed. Without such internalization, the owner-state will invest inadequately in the forest.

And, most clearly, in the case of global systems such as biodiversity and climate change, the regulation of the state alone will be inadequate. Since the state owning the forest receives only a small portion of these benefits, it will not invest sufficiently in recognition of their generation. Therefore an international agreement is absolutely necessary in order to correct for this systematic investment deficiency in regard to global environmental resources.

The point of this section has been to make clear when international agreements are required in response to resource depletion. It is *not* the case that all resource depletion is socially undesirable; in fact natural resource depletion is one means of asset portfolio reconstruction, which is a fundamental route to societal development. International agreements are not necessary or desirable in regard to resource conversion of this nature. However there are clear instances in which a society will underinvest in its natural resources, on account of the flow of many of the benefits of the resource outside of its own boundaries. Then an international agreement is absolutely essential in order to correct for this systematic investment bias.

3   Economics and sustainable development

This section summarizes the empirical and theoretical analysis of sustainability developed within the economics literature. In particular it explains the distinction between degradation and conversion. This is crucial to the understanding of when an environmental problem exists and at what level it exists. It is not always the case that the depletion of natural resources equates with the existence of environmental problems. Even if it is the case that such depletion is a problem, it might not be the case that the environmental problem exists within the state where the depletion is occurring. That is, the depletion of natural resources may be an act of conversion for the state undertaking the activity that endangers a system that exists only at the global level. These are the circumstances under which international intervention is necessary.

At the outset of the study known as political economy, the role of resources was at the centre of the discipline. Many of the initiators of the field – Malthus, Ricardo and Mills – placed the questions of sustainability and resource depletion at the core of their enquiries. However, by the time of the 1970s, little remained of this initial interest in the role of resources, and the analysts of the day were proclaiming the discipline free from concerns over ultimate resource scarcity (Solow, 1974a). Of course 20 years later the issue of the finiteness of the earth's resources is once again a matter of concern within the field. However the focus of the concern has shifted away from the scarcity of resources as discrete commodities (minerals, timber and so on) and towards resources as environmental systems. Section two of this module describes the evolution of the economic analysis of scarcity. Then the last few sections discuss the neoclassical framework for analysing growth and development – the so-called Solow model of growth theory. This section is synthesized with the preceding sections by means of the movement towards analysing systemic rather than discrete scarcity.

3.1   The analysis of the steady-state

The evolution of the discipline from one concerned with the ultimate finiteness of the earth to one unconcerned, and back again, is one of the themes of this survey. We will commence with the analysis of the *steady-state* developed initially by Malthus, and re-emerging now in the works of Boulding, Daly and others. The analysis of the steady-state developed the idea of the ultimately diminishing returns to production deriving from the fact of the finiteness of the earth. From this concept there was derived an aggregate production function that was declining in terms of the marginal product received from additional stocks of human labour; that is, given one clearly fixed factor (land), additional quantities of labour must at some point generate diminishing returns. Given that there is a minimum wage required for subsistence, the total number of people within the economy define a 'subsistence payroll' required for their maintenance.

The intersection of the aggregate subsistence payroll with the aggregate production function is the point beyond which production cannot expand. This is the 'steady-state' economy defined by Malthus; there is no economic growth possible beyond this point. Figure 1.4 demonstrates this steady-state analysis. Population and hence production (as a function of population) cannot expand beyond the steady-state levels specified in this diagram on account of the fixed stock of natural resources.

The steady-state analysis requires that only one assumption be fulfilled: the finiteness of at least a natural resource that is absolutely necessary for production. Malthus and those who followed him assumed that this factor would be agricultural land – the means of subsistence. However it is just as

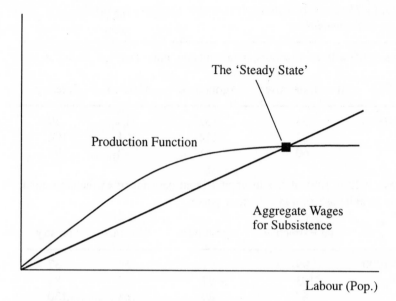

Figure 1.4   The analysis of the steady-state

possible for the factor to be a natural resource in industrial production (for example oil) or otherwise in the maintenance of humans and human societies (for example air or water). So long as the resource is necessary for production to occur and is finite in supply, the Malthusian analysis applies.

How well does the Malthusian framework describe the economy historically? A look at the empirical evidence indicates that it is not a very good fit. Table 1.4 lists a set of productivity indices from various extractive industries for a number of years between 1870 and 1957. These indices indicate that the natural resource industries, rather than demonstrating diminishing returns, were in fact generally showing increasing rates of productivity over that century. That is despite the vastly increasing scales of human activities (and human populations) and the declining stocks of natural resources, the productivity rates in the natural resource-based industries were increasing. In most cases (that is with the exception of forestry), the natural resource sectors were outpacing the non-extractive industries (as demonstrated within the latter table in Table 1.4).

Therefore the evidence that exists does not indicate that natural resources are becoming more scarce in the economic meaning of that phrase. Diminishing returns have not been established in those industries most reliant upon natural resources for their production. Instead the application of capital goods and the advance of technology has made the relative costliness of natural

*Table 1.4   The scarcity of natural resources: the case of natural
            commodities*

Indices (1929 = 100) of labour capital input per unit of extractive output

	Total Extractive	Agriculture	Minerals	Forestry
1870–1900	134	132	210	59
1919	122	114	164	106
1957	60	61	47	90

Indices (1929 = 100) of labour capital input per unit of extractive output,
relative to unit costs of non-extractive goods

	Total Extractive	Agriculture	Minerals	Forestry
1870–1900	99	97	154	37
1919	103	97	139	84
1957	87	89	68	130

Source: Barnett and Morse (1963).

resources decline over much of the past century. It was this evidence that
caused many economists to proclaim the economy 'free from the constraints
of resource scarcity' in the 1970s.

3.2   The new Malthusians: alternative approaches to sustainability
We will postpone our analysis of the sustainability of this situation to sections 4
and 5, but first we will turn to an alternative approach to finiteness and global
limits. This approach attempts to update the steady-state analysis of the classical economists. At the time of Malthus the primary source of concern was the
limitations on the quantity and quality of inputs available for production, for
example Malthus was concerned about the limits to good agricultural land.
This concern then broadened into a more general concern about the limits to a
wide range of inputs: minerals, timber, fisheries and so forth.

At present there is more concern about the limits imposed by the environmental system in terms of the outputs that it can absorb rather than the limits
it imposes by way of restrictions on the supply of inputs. The *materials
balances approach* is the basis for conceptualization of this concern about the
residuals that result from the flow of materials into production.

In Figure 1.5 the relationship between the economy and the environment is
conceptualized as a complete cycle. That is the economy is both a receiver of

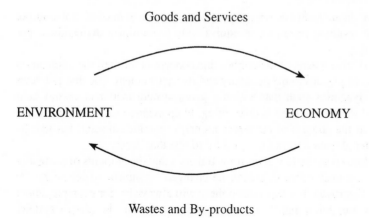

Goods and Services

ENVIRONMENT   ECONOMY

Wastes and By-products

Figure 1.5   Materials balances approach to scarcity

inputs from the environment as well as a transmitter of outputs to the environment. Similarly the environment is both a provider of inputs and a receiver of outputs. This analysis emphasizes the role of the environment as a 'sink' for wastes as well as a 'stock' for resource flows. Even if there is little concern about the environment's role in providing the latter, there remains a fundamental constraint on the growth of the economy in terms of its absorption of the former.

For example even if there is a continuous flow of materials into the industrial sector, and scarcities in certain inputs are dealt with by substitution away towards less scarce materials, there remains one fundamental source of resource scarcity: the need for the environment to absorb the wastes from these processes. In this case the 'scale' of the economy matters, because the greater the pace of activity, the greater the burden placed upon the environmental sectors capacity to absorb further residuals. In effect it is as if the arrows in Figure 1.5 were channels of limited capacity; the environment can absorb a fixed amount of residuals without harm, but no more.

Such a constraint is based on an ecological approach to the economy. There are numerous examples in the nature of *threshold effects* that result in sudden and substantial changes in the environment as a result of residual overloads. For example a lake is able to receive and absorb a certain amount of acidic material without change, but then alters substantially (for example the fish population is destroyed) when the threshold is breached.

This effect gives rise to the 'materials balances' or residuals-focused approach to the economy. It is based on Boulding's fundamental idea that we exist within a 'spaceship economy', with the earth conceived of as a closed system in space. Whatever wastes we produce, we must be able to recycle or live among them. Then one objective of economics is to maximize the output per unit of resulting residuals, or equivalently to minimize the residuals per unit of output.

An alternative means of describing this concept is through the application of the laws of physics to the economy and its environment. The first two laws of thermodynamics state that within a given system matter is always conserved, but the energy level is dissipating. In application to the economy this implies that the amount of resources on earth remains constant, but that its form is altered from a form that is useful to one that is not.

This is known as the *law of entropy*. It means that the amounts of particular forms of resources on earth cannot be changed by human societies; matter cannot be destroyed. For this reason there will always be, for example, about 8 per cent aluminum and 2 per cent manganese within the earth's system. These concentrations (and the concentrations of all other minerals) were determined at the outset of the system, and will remain constant throughout time. When iron ore is 'used' to make an automobile, there is not less iron on earth, only less 'useful' iron ore. Although concentrations remain constant, usefulness is depleted through unmanaged human usage. The automobile takes a useful concentration of iron ore and scatters it throughout the system, partly in waste disposal sites and partly in the atmosphere through oxidation (rust). The loss of useful concentrations of minerals is reflected in the continually declining 'grades' of ore being mined. For example Table 1.5 shows that mining concerns are currently working on veins of zinc that require the removal of 40 tonnes of ore for the extraction of one ton of zinc ore, whereas zinc exists at the level of only one part per 12 000 within a randomly selected part of the earth's crust. However, as human activities using zinc escalate, the

Table 1.5   The physical approach to economics: entropy

	Percentage in Random Sample of Earth's Crust	Tons of Crust for One Ton of Ore – Random	Tons of Crust – Current Mining Grades
Aluminum	8%	12	7
Titanium		188	180
Zinc		12 000	40
Copper	3%	20 000	200
Lead		77 000	50
Tin		625 000	10 000
Manganese	2%	1 000	5

amount of crust required for a ton of zinc extraction will approach the higher number.

Therefore, under any one of these approaches, it is the useful concentration of resources that is depleted by humans, and this usefulness is a one-shot acquisition. The goal of human society should, under the physical approach to economy, consist of extracting the maximum product from each unit of useful concentration of resources (energy). Under the materials balances approach, the goal is the maximum amount of product per unit of residual emissions. In either case, the point is the same, the earth's system is finite and the scale of human activities must be regulated in order to recognize our depletion of the environment. This sounds very similar to the principles enunciated by Malthus, except that the emphasis is now on the scarcity of environmental systems rather than natural resources. It is now important to return to the neoclassical analysis of sustainability, in order to see how it conflicts with the classical approach and if it is possible for the two to be made consistent. What is the best approach to the problem of global limits?

4 The theory of sustainable development: the Hartwick–Solow rule

As developed in section 3 above, it will sometimes be the case that the stocks of a natural resource will be exhausted in the course of optimal utilization. What does 'optimality' mean in this context? That is how can it be sustainable to engage in forms of production that are directed toward an outcome (absolute depletion) that renders themselves untenable?

The answers to these questions fie within a concept known as the *Hartwick–Solow rule* (Hartwick, 1977; Solow, 1974b). The Hartwick–Solow rule examines the issue of intergenerational fairness, and the questions of how to assure that current resource utilization is sustainable. It is not the case that future generations would necessarily contest all natural resource utilization, or even all natural resource exhaustion, if they were able to make their preferences known to the current generation. This is because current societal utilization of natural resources is translated into both consumption and investment; although the consumptive portion of resource use is of no benefit to future generations, the portion invested can translate into important benefits in the future.

The Hartwick–Solow rule states that sustainability (in the sense of constant levels of consumption and utility) is assured by maintaining constant levels of society's capital stocks. This means that all natural resource exhaustion must be translated into flows of income that are invested into other forms of capital (human, man-made). This is the *conversion process*: the natural capital is converted into an alternative form of capital. So long as the overall stock of capital within the society remains constant, the flow of goods and services will also remain constant. A sustainable conversion process is illustrated within Figure 1.6; here the stock of natural resources is falling towards zero over the course of time, but the stock of man-made assets is increasing in order to maintain a constant capital stock within the society.

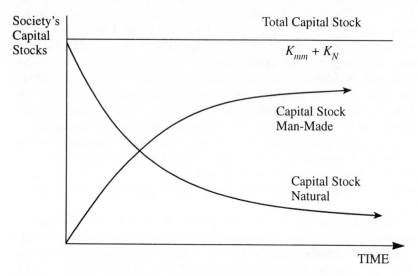

Figure 1.6   The conversion process and the Hartwick–Solow rule

Therefore, when natural resource stocks are declining, the crucial distinction between the degradation process and the conversion process is the level of societal investments in other forms of capital. If a society is selling its resources for current consumption only, then it is *mining its natural capital*, that is sacrificing its future to its present. However if another society is depleting its natural resources at the same pace but investing the proceeds, then this society is simply restructuring its capital portfolio. One society is reducing the overall level of capital on which it is relying, while the other is simply shifting assets between different capital accounts.

   For this reason it is predictable that different countries at different stages of the development process will be relying upon entirely distinguishable capital stocks. If development is assumed to be highly dependent upon portfolio balancing, then a country that is still developing will have much higher proportions of capital that is 'natural' in origin than will a country that is more developed. They will be at different points along the horizontal axis in the above Figure 1.6. If an environmental law is proposed to both that implies a halt to natural capital exploitation (or conversion), the country that is already converted might very well be wholly in favour of the law while the other might be opposed. This would not necessarily imply that the already converted country is more 'green' in its perspective, only that the costliness of an anti-conversion policy is no longer very high. This is one of the major reasons that there is a fundamental divide between the developing and the developed world regarding many of the issues of international environmental law.

5   Sustainability and substitutibility: the forward-looking nature of investments

What are the limits to the neoclassical paradigm of sustainability? That is, to what extent do limits to growth still exist now that the Solow model of growth has been accepted. One important limitation on this analysis is its assumption of substitutability between capital assets: the capacity of newly acquired capital stocks to substitute completely for all of the services provided by the original (converted) assets. The forward-looking nature of societal investments is a crucial part of the argument concerning the nature of sustainable resource utilization. That is, it is not only essential that resource utilization generates investments, it is also necessary that these investments be forward-looking in the sense that they prepare the society for impending natural resource scarcities. As indicated in Figure 1.6, Hartwick–Solow sustainability does not guarantee constant stocks of natural resources, it only generates constant stocks of societal capital. It is essential that this capital stock be evolving in a manner suited to increasing resource scarcity, otherwise it is of little use.

The final peg in the argument concerning the sustainability of economies is that natural resource exploitation should result in rising resource prices (in accordance with the Hotelling rule) and that this should cause society's investments to shift towards technologies and discoveries that economize on these scarcities. So long as society is able to think of ways to do this, the argument goes, the substitution of a man-made capital stock for a naturally created capital stock is without adverse effect on sustainability. One obvious issue that this raises is whether there are limits to the substitutibility between different forms of capital; that is, is it possible for society to rebalance its portfolio heavily towards the man-made forms of capital and away from the natural forms?

This is the case if there are human synthesizable substitutes that can perform all of the functions performed by natural resources, because then it is possible to skirt continuously around scarcity. This is accomplished by always using the least scarce resources to synthesize substitutes for the most scarce ones. This process is precisely what has occurred in the petrochemical industries. Although we have come to think of crude oil as a scarce commodity, it was only one hundred years ago that this substance was seen to be a nuisance substance, generating useless tar pits. It was the sheer prevalence of the substance that generated its many uses. It was an organic compound of little known value that could be used as a building block for many other, more scarce commodities. Thus petroleum-based synthetics have come to replace a vast array of more scarce natural resource-based commodities: rubber, steel, aluminum, sod fertility and wood. The non-scarcity of the substance generated many low-cost substitutes for scarce natural resources.

It is this 'building-block approach' to substitutibility that lies at the core of the sustainability paradigm. So long as it is possible to identify the function that a natural resource serves, and to identify the essential physico-chemical nature of a substitute, then it is very likely possible to synthesize low-cost substitutes for that natural resource.

The limits to substitutability then become equivalent to the limits of the human capacity for analysis and imagination. For example the age-old basis for the practice of medicine has been the use of the naturally generated biological interaction between plants and animals, but the question of substitutability goes to the capacity for the human mind to eliminate this step in the production of medicines. Over millions of years of evolution, plants have developed the capacity to affect animal's behaviour by evolving substances that affect them physiologically. It is the examination and utilization of these substances that has generated the practice of medicine over the ages. Part of the concern about biodiversity losses stems from the loss of plant forms which must by their nature contain novel forms of chemical interaction.

Human practices of medicine initially derived from clinical trials of plant-derived substances that were known to be biologically active. When an active chemical substance is identified, it has then usually been synthesized in a laboratory. However, over the past few decades, scientists have begun to focus more on the analysis of the physiological basis for disease, and the identification of useful chemicals commencing from an understanding of the mechanisms of the human body rather than the naturally generated chemical usefulness. If this process of 'rational pharmaceutical design' were 100 per cent effective, then it would constitute a building-block approach to the provision of medicine. The human understanding of the chemical processes within the body would substitute completely for the evolved usefulness of plant-based substances.

Therefore, for sustainability to be achievable, human understanding and innovation must be able to construct bridges over the natural resource sector, and between non-scarce building blocks (basic chemicals, genes and energy sources) and the functions required to support human societies. That is, all of the functions of natural resources and natural systems must be replaceable with these more atomistic elements (in combination with human ingenuity). This is the meaning of the required 'substitutability' for sustainability.

6 Sustainability and the steady-state: what forms of global limits exist?
It is now time to return to the issues of concern to Malthusians, old and new.
They are concerned about the overall constraints on the development process.
The analysis of this section states that, if unlimited substitutability exists,
then the only barrier to further development is that which derives from the
existence of externalities. That is, the scale of an economy (Malthus' concern)
is irrelevant, so long as the structure of the economy takes into account the
full cost of all of the resources and systems that it exploits. There would be
no limits to growth in this analysis if there are no critical forms or levels of
natural capital.

The 'externality approach' to sustainability states that even global problems such as global warming and biodiversity depletion devolve to the need
to place values on systems that will encourage substitutability. The solution
to global warming would then be independent of the scale of global economy,
but would entail only the creation of an implicit price for the carbon constraint affecting the planet's climate. Such a price would be given effect
through either carbon taxes or limited permits. Then the economies of the
world would internalize the problem by substituting away from carbon-based
production technologies.

The only means by which the pure scale of an economy might matter is
through the existence of *meta-resources*: critical forms of natural capital
which cannot be depleted below certain levels (Ehrlich, 1986). The term
'meta-resource' represents the concept of non-substitutable resources and
systems. A common example of a meta-resource is net primary product
(NPP) – the total amount of photosynthetic product available for the support
of all life forms on earth (see the discussion below). It is a fixed amount of
product determined by the relationship between the solar energy received on
earth, and the earth's evolved capacity to make use of that energy. There are
some who would argue that human society cannot exist without the maintenance of a minimum level of this product.

In the remainder of this chapter, we examine the interface between these
notions of substitutability, externality and sustainability. We want to identify
the basis upon which global limits to growth might exist.

6.1 How can growth be compatible with decreasing scarcity?
How can it be possible that resource scarcity would not be increasing, given
that many natural resources are exhaustible/non-renewable in nature (for
example petroleum)? Natural resource economists (see Stiglitz in Smith,
(ed.) *Scarcity and Growth Reconsidered*, 1979) have posited that growth can
continue unabated (in the context of resource extraction and reduction) so
long as:

- *the elasticity of substitution argument* – physical capital stocks can be developed that are always and everywhere substitutable for natural resource stocks; or
- *the technical change argument* – technical change continues to shift out the production frontier in order to allow for increased production from constant inputs.

Productivity gains are possible even with reliance on reduced stocks of exhaustible resources, so long as the reductions in their quality and quantity is compensated for by increases in a physical capital stock that is adjusted to be compatible with that increased scarcity ('substitution'), or if general technical progress allows for increased productivity from all factors ('technical progress').

6.2   Sustainability

As we have seen the natural resource economists of the 1970s endogenized the issue of capital formation, and demonstrated that (if formed in response to relative scarcities) it is possible for natural resource scarcity to be handled within the context of capital formation decision making. Whether this is possible forever remains to be seen. The critical assumptions used in the initial models were constant elasticity of substitution between various forms of capital and constant returns to scale. These assumptions may be applicable over certain ranges of the aggregate production function, but whether they will apply over parts of the production function with which we have no experience is a matter of pure guesswork.

6.3   What forms of scarcity do continue to matter?

This does not mean that scarcity is not relevant at the aggregate level, only that it exists in a very different form (than individual commodities) at that level. One form of scarcity that is clearly not taken into account concerns any of the various ecological systems on which we depend. In these cases it is not simply the case that the price mechanism is not adequately adjusted, it is also the case that the pricing mechanism may be simply inappropriate to the task.

The field of ecology concerns the exploration of the living systems within which humans and other parts of the biosphere live and interact. For example the field of ecology studies the various systems that drive the biosphere: the carbon cycle, the hydrological cycle and the nitrogen cycle. These are systems that we are just now beginning to appreciate, yet they bind together all living matter in an inseparable and continuous process. Given that we are wholly dependent upon the continuation of such ecological functions, both as individuals and as a species, how is it possible to factor such systems into our decision making? Do we necessarily commit to suboptimal choices of paths for societal growth and development if we do not do so?

A better understanding of the living world also indicates that some forms of constraints do exist on the ultimate production system, which very likely cannot be avoided by virtue of accumulation of capital stocks or through technical change. Ecologists discuss these constraints as energy-based systems. In general the earth lies in the path of the sun's energy release and receives a steady flow of energy from this source (for the time being). Life on earth is the result of the evolution of various chemical groupings (amino acids) which are able to channel this energy through themselves. All of the biosphere derives from these chemical groups, and their capacity to channel solar energy. At this more fundamental level it seems to be unlikely that human activities can alter the capacity of the biosphere to capture or utilize energy, and so it is likely that this constraint is immutable. Such a constraint links all of the existing life forms together into a single system. When human societies expand their populations or their activities, the consequences of such actions are felt throughout the biosphere by reason of the fixity of these constraints. The fundamental and fixed nature of such constraints indicates that there are no free lunches; the growth and development of human society occurs within the context of the biosphere, not within a vacuum. When societies make a development choice, this 'meta-constraint' imposes an opportunity cost to every action.

6.4   Example of a meta-constraint: NPP

For example, net photosynthetic product (NPP) is measured in petagram (Pg) of organic matter, equivalent to 10^{15} grams. Total biomass is calculated at 1244 Pg and the annual terrestrial NPP at 132.1 Pg. By considering also the potential NPP of terrestrial ecosystems (17.5), the annual NPP figure of 132.1 increases to 149.6. The total impact of humans on this global resource can be derived by summing both the direct and indirect uses. The direct uses are the destruction of organic material and land as a result of conversion to crop land and pasture land, forest clearing and burning in shifting cultivation. The indirect uses arise from the loss of potential NPP due to man's conversion of natural ecosystems into other systems whose NPP is deemed lower, such as agricultural systems, the permanent conversion of forest to pastures, desertification and conversion of natural systems to areas for human settlements. Estimating human appropriations indicates that humans consume, destroy and co-opt 38.8 per cent of terrestrial potential terrestrial productivity. In these calculations consumption of aquatic ecosystems NPP, which is anyway relatively small, is not included in order to focus on the major impact on terrestrial resources (Table 1.6).

How does a meta-constraint operate? For example, as human populations have developed, one of the fundamental changes has been the expansion of their populations (from about 10 million to 10 billion individuals over 12 000

Table 1.6   A meta-constraint? Human appropriation of net photosynthetic product

Process	Amount (Pg)
Cultivated Land	15.0
Grazing Land	11.6
Forest Land	13.6
Human Occupied Areas	0.4
Lost NPP in Agriculture	9.0
Conversion of Forests into Pastures	1.4
Desertification	4.5
Loss to Human Areas	2.6
Total Terrestrial	58.1
Percentage of terrestrial co-opted or lost	38.8

Source: Vitousek *et al.* (1986).

years). The NPP constraint indicates that this expansion of population must have a cost, and it has in the contraction and elimination of the niches of many other species. Thus our development has necessarily resulted in the reworking of the remainder of the biosphere. As this process continues through the remainder of the developing world, there are projections of massive extinctions to occur in the near future. This is the impact of human expansion in the context of a strict biological constraint (Table 1.7).

Table 1.7   Estimated rates and projections of extinctions

Rate	Projection	Basis	Source
8%	33–50%	Forest Area Loss	Lovejoy (1980)
5%	50%	Forest Area Loss	Ehrlich and Ehrlich (1981)
–	33%	Forest Area Loss	Simberloff (1986)
5%	15%	Forest Area Loss	Reid and Miller (1989)

More importantly these projections of species extinctions are very poor indicators of what is actually being lost. One of the primary factors contributing to the importance of these species is that they play a role within the overarching system of which they are part. When they are removed, these systems are debilitated, and the system may degenerate, or even collapse (Perrings, 1987;

Costanza, 1991). The regulation of human activities must take into account their aggregate impact on these systemic constraints.

6.5   Is it possible to regulate for these systemic constraints?

Why is it that these systems cannot be incorporated within human decision-making processes in some straightforward manner? For example we are able to place 'shadow values' on various other unpriced goods, such as clean water supplies; why should these other constraints be so different from the water cycle that flows through our aquifers and then through our taps? The answer to these questions follows from the analysis of the complex dynamics within living systems. In short system dynamics within these contexts are usually complex and unstable. This means that it may be inappropriate to think deterministically about many living systems, and hence it may be difficult to build appropriate regulatory systems upon the base of our usual assumptions within marginal analysis.

6.6   Example of a complex system: the carbon cycle

A look at the nature of the carbon cycle indicates the difficulty of accounting for these systemic constraints. Is it possible to regulate a process as complex and interwoven as the carbon cycle? That is will we ever know what, if any, impact we are having on the process by putting a regulatory system into place? (See Cline, 1992.)

The carbon cycle is the interchange of carbon molecules (the stuff of which life is made) between the oceans, the atmosphere and the biosphere. Table 1.8 illustrates how this interchange has occurred in equilibrium. The atmosphere has contained approximately 750 Gt. C. (0.28 per cent), and this carbon flows through the living part of the earth (the biosphere) by virtue of the process of photosynthesis, whereby 100 Gt. C. leaves the atmosphere each year. Balancing this is a take-up of 102 Gt. C. from the biosphere through the process of decay. The net gain of 2 Gt. C. by the atmosphere is then discharged to the oceans by reason of atmospheric pressure differentials, and this carbon is ultimately deposited in the very deep oceans through a very slow (200-year-long) process of oceanic mixing. In the very long run, we all wind up on the bottom of the ocean. In the meantime anthropogenic emissions of carbon (via fossil fuels and deforestation) are amounting to increases in the order of 7 per cent per annum. We have little or no idea how such emissions will impact upon this cycle (Table 1.8).

6.7   Externalities, human limits and scarcity

The sorts of scarcity that matter are probably not those concerning nice tangible and discrete natural resource commodities such as petroleum, zinc or lead. The advocates of limits to growth probably did their cause a lot of harm

Table 1.8   The carbon cycle

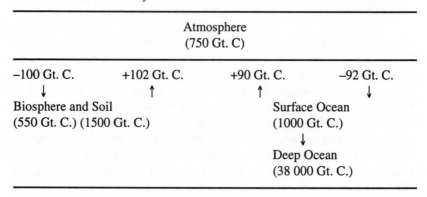

by focusing on these commodities as they have as complete and well-defined markets (current and future) as any that exist. The real scarcities that matter are those which are not so amenable to subdivision and commoditization. These systems necessarily lie outside of any one particular market, but instead intersect with and relate to a large number of different markets. The capacity to create institutions (market or non-) that will adequately address these forms of scarcity is not necessarily within the powers of our species.

6.8   Global environmental problems and global scarcities
Global environmental problems arise out of the meaningful form which global scarcities take, that is the failure of markets at all levels to take into account systemic scarcities. The source of these problems have both a physical and a social nature. They have the physical characteristics of resources (such as the carbon cycle, the ozone layer or other ecological resources) that are systems which offer a flow of services to all peoples. They also have the social characteristic of being difficult to regulate at any level other than the systemic. These are resources which do not fit neatly into either: (a) the 'commodity' category required for effective regulation by private markets; or (b) the 'national resource' category required for effective regulation by national governments. It is the failure of certain types of global resources (systemic ones) to fit within either of these already existing regulatory frameworks that makes their continuing exploitation problematic.

7   Conclusion: IEAs and global environmental problems
The international environmental agreements (IEAs) emanating from the United Nations Conference on Environment and Development are primarily concerned with issues of economic sustainability. The climate change convention concerns the regulation of state activities that generate additional carbon

dioxide emissions. The biodiversity convention concerns those state activities that endanger species.

These are two good examples of human activity that are probably compatible with sustainability requirements at national level, but threatening to environmental systems at global level. The climate change convention regulates, in large part, the emissions of carbon into the atmosphere resulting from fossil fuel combustion. There is nothing to indicate that the depletion of fossil fuels in individual countries is occurring in an unsustainable fashion; that is, there is no evidence that states are reducing aggregate stocks of societal capital in the course of their depletion of these natural resources. The problem lies in the aggregate impact of such exploitation on a global level, that is the impact of emissions on the global climate. Therefore it is necessary to intervene within national decision making regarding fossil fuel consumption to regulate for this global system.

Similarly the deforestation that is occurring now, and that has occurred in the past, is not necessarily unsustainable at national level. These conversions of land uses simply transfer lands from forestry into agricultural and pastoral lands. Individual states make these decisions largely on account of the determination that the national portfolio will generate enhanced benefits from such restructuring. However, at the global level, the loss of a balanced portfolio of naturally endowed lands and species is resulting in concerns over the long-term stability of the increasingly homogeneous biological system.

Therefore sustainability is an issue that exists at both national and global levels. The need for international intervention exists primarily where there is a difference in the requirements for sustainability at the two levels, that is where nationally sustainable policies do not aggregate to become globally sustainable ones. In such circumstances international contracting is required in order to correct for the disjunction between local and global optimum. This implies the necessity of providing for the development of international institutions that enable and in fact induce individual countries to elect alternative development paths for themselves that will support global sustainability.

2 Planning for future generations: global environmental problems and long-term impacts

1 Global development and future generations

Global development concerns current generations to the extent that it is approaching severe limits or constraints in the present or near future, but it concerns future generations because it is constantly presenting greater limits and constraints on their available futures. Our choice of development paths will determine the number of development paths from which future generations are able to choose. In the past this was not so strict a constraint, because the impacts that previous generations had were almost always on a local or regional scale. Today we have the technological ability to revise and revamp many of the world's systems and environments in a single generation. In fact we have already demonstrated this capacity in the context of such modern revolutions as have occurred in agriculture, the chemical industry and fossil fuels. One hundred years ago there were few uses perceived for the fossil fuels, and now we are consuming millions of barrels each day. Sixty years ago there was little use of synthetic chemicals; today much of the world's groundwater and atmosphere is contaminated by them. Fifty years ago the world's biosphere consisted of an incredibly wide variety of plants and animals, which have been displaced by the same small set of high-yielding varieties used in modern agriculture.

The impacts that we have on a global scale are the result of economies that have broadened and integrated, and all of this has been in the cause of social development. However we must now recognize that global development comes increasingly with the narrowing of global options. Future generations no longer receive, as we did, both the benefits of past development and the options to choose a very different course. We are increasingly presenting future generations with a diminishing set of options. They must accept the high level of development, together with the responsibility for sustaining it within an increasingly constrained world.

Do future generations really want this increasingly constrained world? Would they prefer to have a greater number of options at a reduced level of development? How is it possible to take these possibilities into consideration in current development, and why does this reflect on the importance of IEAs? These are the questions that we address in this chapter.

2 Adding up impacts on future generations: discounting and the case of global warming

The choice between alternative development paths requires that a choice is made at a given point in time, but how do we weight different impacts that will occur at different points in time? Problems such as global warming are of interest because continuation down the current development path probably has no real serious repercussions on any time scale that is relevant under normal methods of discounting. Does this mean that global warming should not factor into our choice of development paths? Should we simply proceed down the fossil fuel- based development path acting as if what is accumulating two hundred years in the future does not matter? Let us consider these questions initially within the context of a case study on global warming.

2.1 What is the global warming problem?

In scientific terms the problem of global warming concerns the prospect for an increase in mean global temperatures, or other climate changes (such as changes in precipitation and storm frequency), on account of the human-generated changes in the constituency of the global atmosphere.

Table 2.1 Summary of greenhouse gases

Atmospheric Concentration	CO_2	CH_4	CFC11	CFC12	NOX
Pre-industrial (ppb)	280 (ppm)	0.79 (ppm)	0	0	288
Present	354	1.72	280 (ppt)	484 (ppt)	310
Rate of Change (0.25%)	0.5%	0.9%	4.0%	4.0%	
Emissions (Tg.)	10^4	300	6	0.3	0.1
Lifetime (Years)	200	10	65	130	150

Table 2.1 documents the changes in the atmosphere that have occurred over the course of the industrial age. The table demonstrates why much of the focus of the current policy debate is on CO_2, since its emissions are a factor 100 times the level of the other greenhouse gases.

2.2   Why do carbon emissions matter and where do they come from?
Taking the latter part of the question first. To a large extent the problem of global warming concerns the regulation of the global development process, with greenhouse gases being one of the major by-products of standard development paths. Carbon emissions derive primarily from two principal sources: land use changes (deforestation and agriculture) 25 per cent and fossil fuel emissions (coal, oil and gas) 75 per cent. CFCs have been developed and used primarily as refrigerants and solvents; the other greenhouse gases derive primarily from our reliance upon fossil fuels and changing land uses.

Carbon emissions matter because the earth has adapted to different levels of emissions. That is the atmosphere, biosphere and the climate are three systems interconnected by reason of the carbon cycle, and this cycle (and these systems) has evolved over four billion years to an equilibrium that was not adjusted to a world with fossil fuel exploitation or agriculture. Ten thousand years ago human societies commenced massive land use changes to alter the biosphere; two hundred years ago human societies commenced accumulating a physical capital stock that was dependent upon fossil fuel throughputs. These two changes resulted in substantial changes in the amount of carbon being input into the already existing carbon cycle.

2.3   How does atmospheric carbon generate a 'greenhouse effect'?
The sun's shortwave radiation passes through certain gases in the atmosphere but is then trapped by those same gases when it is then re-radiated from the earth in longwave form. These gases which are transparent to shortwave radiation but opaque to longwave are known as the greenhouse gases. They have evolved to given percentages in the atmosphere, and together they retain enough energy to maintain the prevailing temperature on the earth's surface.

Incoming solar (SW) energy: 240 Wm^{-2} (drives mean surface temperature from −273C to −18C)
Reflected GHG (LW) energy: 180 wm^{-2} (drives mean surface temperature from −18C to 15C)

2.4   What is the extent of the human impacts on the carbon cycle?
At present:

Fossil fuel emissions	5.4 Gt. C. per annum
Deforestation	1.6 Gt.
Total emissions	7.0 Gt.
less:	
Increased ocean uptake	2.0 Gt.
Unknown uptake	1.6 Gt.
Increased accumulation	3.4 Gt. C. per annum

2.5   What impact do these emissions have on the greenhouse effect?

A formula first developed by the Swedish scientist Arrhenius more than one hundred years ago is still used to estimate the impact of carbon emissions on mean global temperatures.

$$\text{Change } T = B \, \lambda \, \text{Change } R$$

where: T is the mean global temperature; B is the positive feedback effect of increasing temperatures (estimated to lie between 1.1 and 3.4); λ is the change in temperature for a change in radiation retention (estimated at 0.3C/w); R is the increase in retained radiation for an increase in atmospheric carbon (estimated as 6.3 In C/C_0). This formula implies a change in mean global temperatures in the range of 1–3.5 C for a doubling in atmospheric carbon.

2.6   Performing the cost benefit analysis of global warming policy

The first question to ask is what possible impacts there might be from such changes in the global temperatures. The initial attempts to undertake this assessment focused on two forms of impacts: (1) loss of agricultural output on account of precipitation decline in traditional agricultural regions; and (2) loss of low-lying lands near the seaboards on account of the rise in sea levels. The next impact considered is often the increased use of energy for refrigeration/air-conditioning on account of temperature changes. The initial studies undertaken to assess these, and other impacts of global warming, are recounted below.

2.7   What are the benefits to be achieved from the abatement of carbon emissions?

Almost all of the studies examine the problem of global warming as to what the costs are of a doubling of carbon concentrations in the atmosphere versus the costliness of policies to prevent that accumulation. A series of studies has demonstrated that, for the US economy, the costs of a doubling of carbon concentrations is possibly equivalent to an annual loss of 1 per cent of GDP (Table 2.2).

The range of cost estimates run only from 1.0 to 1.3 of US output, a surprising amount of agreement concerning the potential damages to a large economy such as the USA. Studies of other OECD (Organization for Economic Co-operation and Development) countries have reached similar conclusions. (Even these assessments are probably overestimates, because they do not allow for possible beneficial adaptations. Subsequent work by Nordhaus has indicated that, with agricultural adaptation, there is a likely benefit rather than cost to US agriculture from global warming.) Studies of

Table 2.2   Estimates of impact of global warming on the USA (in billions of dollars US per annum)

Study	Nordhaus	Cline	Fankhauser
Damages			
Heavily Affected Sectors			
Agriculture	1.0	15.2	7.4
Coasts	10.7	2.5	2.3
Energy	0.5	9.0	0.0
Other Sectors	38.1		
Wetlands/Species Lost		7.1	14.8
Health and Amenity		8.4	30.3
Other		11.2	12.1
Total	50.3	53.4	66.9
(% GDP)	1.0	1.1	1.3

Source: Nordhaus (1991: p. 16).

developing countries find that the costliness is nearer to 1.5 per cent of GDP, with substantial variation between countries. The most disproportionate impacts are felt by certain low-lying island states for which sea level rise is an overwhelming consideration (for example GDP loss in Maldives (34 per cent); Kiribati (18 per cent); Tovalu (14 per cent). So the most important lesson to be derived from these studies is that, despite the initial projections of low level damages on average, there remains the prospect of substantial variation between countries.

Even damages of 1.5 per cent of global product amount to staggering amounts of money. This indicates that policies for the abatement of carbon emissions should be considered now, but then the question that is raised concerns the costs that these policies would impose on society.

2.8   What are the costs associated with policies to abate carbon emissions?
A number of different energy models have undertaken the task of ascertaining the costliness to economies of charging energy taxes that will cause carbon emissions to be abated significantly in the long run. All of these studies have been phrased in terms of the costs that would be incurred by reason of policies that reduce carbon emissions by proportions ranging from 30 per cent to 75 per cent of the level that would occur under 'business as usual' over the next 100 years. The estimates from these studies range from a

low of 1 per cent to a high of 4.5 per cent of GDP for abatement of 50 per cent (Figure 2.1).

It seems fair to say that a cost of at least 1 per cent of global GDP is believed to be necessary in order to pursue policies that will result in economic restructuring that will result in carbon emission abatement of 50 per cent (again, in the long run).

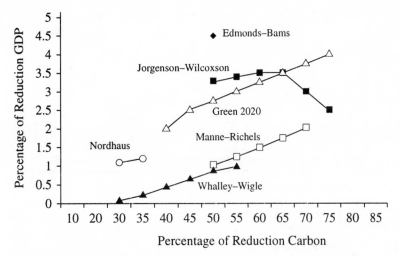

Source: Cline (1991).

Figure 2.1   Estimates of costs of carbon abatement

2.9   What is the conclusion of the standard cost benefit analysis?

Nordhaus concludes that the economically optimal path to follow involves a small abatement in carbon emissions (about 17 per cent) associated with an optimal tax rate of approximately $10 per tonne of carbon emissions. This compares with a tax rate of $100–$250 that is necessary to stabilize emissions (the goal established in Rio and adopted by the EU) or $200–$700 that is required to stabilize climatic effects (Figure 2.2).

This sort of conclusion derives from the fact that the costs of climate change are estimated to be an average of 1.5 per cent of world GDP while there is some clear capacity to abate carbon emissions at little or no cost. In such a cost–benefit scenario the imposition of a minor tax (of 17 per cent) causes substitution to occur where it can be done at little or no cost.

But is this policy taking into consideration the potential sixfold increase in the carbon dioxide concentration in the atmosphere that will occur in 200

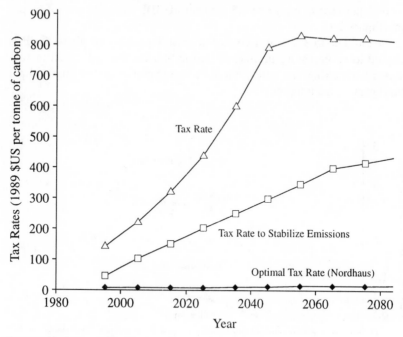

Source: Nordhaus (1991).

Figure 2.2   Climate change policy

years if fossil fuel-based development is pursued wholeheartedly for the next 50? Of course not – the standard cost–benefit analysis uses a positive discount rate that renders costs incurred beyond 100 years or so virtually meaningless, almost irrespective of their magnitude. How can these choices of a long-term development path be considered in the context of current decision making?

2.10   Is it possible to incorporate long-term impacts into current choices of development paths?

There are three primary problems with the cost–benefit analysis that is being undertaken in the evaluation of carbon policies:

1.   the problem of truncating the analysis at the doubling of carbon levels
2.   the problem of the relevant form for long-term discounting; and
3.   the problem of uncertain and catastrophic impacts versus gradual change.

2.11   The truncation of the enquiry

One hundred years ago the scientist Arrhenius cast the enquiry into global warming as a problem of the doubling of atmospheric carbon concentration levels, and there we stay. However it is apparent now that the use of fossil fuels and the expansion of land use changes has far surpassed what had been expected a century ago, and that the future holds promise of even far greater impacts on the atmosphere. At present it is believed that inexpensively accessed ($30/tonne) coal reserves amount to 4–15000 gigatonnes of carbon (Gt. C.) and moderately priced ($85/tonne) coal reserves equal 5–18000 Gt. It is believed that each tonne of coal contributes approximately 0.7 tonnes of atmospheric carbon input, and about 58 per cent of such anthropogenic inputs remain in the atmosphere. In short if the currently available coal reserves are consumed during the development process over the next few centuries, then somewhere between 3500 and 7000 Gt. C. could wind up in the atmosphere in the long run as compared to the 750 Gt. C. currently resident there now. This implies that by the year 2200 the concentration of carbon dioxide in the atmosphere would increase to a maximum estimated 0.00175 atmospheres from the current 0.00025 atmospheres – an increase of six times the current concentration of carbon dioxide (Cline, 1992)!

The current preoccupation with a doubling of carbon dioxide is a matter of mental misdirection. The real problem concerns the fact that inexpensive (at current prices) fossil fuels are available to increase the concentration of carbon dioxide sixfold over the next two centuries. As we have already seen, the carbon cycle has the capacity to adjust itself to different levels of flows, but not on time-scales of less that 200 years. If current fossil fuel-based development continues to be pursued by the developing countries in the same manner as it was pursued in the developed, then there is no way to avoid the prospect of vastly increased levels of carbon dioxide in the atmosphere. The real problem of global warming concerns these vast increases in stock levels that will only occur in two centuries' time.

2.12   The problem of long-term discounting

If the problem of global warming has so little to do with the doubling of carbon levels, then why do the analysts persist in analysing this problem? For the most part the first problem is a part of this second one – inadequate time horizons. In effect the analysts are implicitly incorporating a discount rate into their determination of the relevant policy horizon to analyse. When using any positive rate of discount a time horizon of more that 100 years makes no sense, and yet the problem of global warming involves periods far in excess of one century. Given known rates of accumulation and the direction of development, the problem is more one of the impacts that the choices we are making now will have on generations living 200 years or more in the future.

To a large extent the problem of global warming is a problem of discounting alone. This is because the emission of carbon and its climatic impact are hugely non-contemporaneous. The above formula for climatic impact of carbon emissions registers only the equilibrium impact; on account of oceanic inertia, the movement between equilibria requires approximately 50 years. This disjunction between the receipt of benefits and the incurrence of their costs means that almost any positive rate of discount will have the effect of justifying high levels of carbon externalities. So long as discounting is utilized, the standard cost–benefit analysis will adjudge the future costliness to be of little concern simply because it lies so far in the future. Nordhaus' own sensitivity analysis illustrates this effect (see Table 2.3).

Table 2.3   *Externality cost of emissions as function of discount rate (externality cost in dollars per tonne of carbon)*

Damages from CO_2 Doubling (% of Global GDP)	Social Rate of Pure Time Preference (difference between real interest rate on goods and worldwide growth rate in production)		
	0	1	4
0.25	$13.3	$3.17	$0.57
1.00	53.3	12.7	2.27
2.00	106.7	25.4	4.53

Source: Nordhaus (1991).

Compare these to Nordhaus' suggested optimal tax rate of about $10 per tonne C. Obviously the optimal tax rate is crucially dependent upon the assumptions used about weight to be given to large-scale damages that may only occur in the very distant future. How can we weight these damages appropriately when decisions taken today will clearly have impacts far off in the future?

2.13   What manner of discounting is appropriate to a long-term policy horizon such as this?

Nordhaus is using the standard approach to discounting in which the social rate of time preference is seen to be composed of two parts: pure time preference and preference attributable to expected declining marginal utility from increasing consumption.

$$SRTP = r_p + r_c$$

The first component of time preference is a residual rate that is attributable to all other concerns other than the anticipated path of consumption; for example, this term includes uncertainty about continued existence or concerns over future preferences and so on. It is a discount rate that is applied on account of all of the assortment of events that might occur between two points in time. It is often criticized as being 'myopic', and many philosophers believe that it should be given no weight whatsoever (Broome, 1992). (This is the discount rate that Nordhaus is varying in Table 2.3 above).

The second component of time preference is the consumption-based term. If the economy is growing then one facet of time will be increased levels of consumption and hence declining marginal utility. Discounting is then applied to equate points in time in terms of the impact of a marginal increase in consumption. r_c is simply equivalent to the expected growth of consumption (g) times the elasticity of utility with respect to consumption (e_c); for purposes of informing intuition (given log-linear utility functions with elasticity equal to one), the rate of consumption-based time preference will equal the expected rate of growth in consumption.

For purposes of long horizon planning, the pure time preference figure should probably be set to zero. This is because most of the concerns flowing into pure time preference (existence and so on) are individually rather than societally based. When aggregated to the societal level, there is a much reduced level of concern about continued existence or shifting preferences; hence the first term of the social rate of time preference goes to zero.

With respect to the consumption-based discount rate, it is apparent that different levels of consumption at different points in time must be taken into account. Over the past century the US economy has averaged growth of 1.7 per cent per annum. The global economy has averaged closer to 2 per cent over the past four decades (Cline, 1992: p. 251). These sorts of growth rate would appear to justify significantly non-zero discount rates.

Once again, however, it is essential to recall the time horizon over which policy is being made in this instance. Global warming policies have no impact whatsoever in less than 50 years, and the relevant time horizon is clearly no less than 200 years. In 200 years' time the carbon received in the surfacial oceans begins to mix significantly with the deep oceans, and increased uptake into that sink is possible; however it is clear that the relevant time horizon for this policy plan can be no less than two centuries and possibly as great as three or four centuries. Actions we take today will clearly affect the costs incurred by others for at least that period.

In the final analysis, the choice of the applicable long-term discount rate hinges upon the belief in the feasibility of sustaining an economy outside of a steady-state over the relevant time horizon. Growth theorists have long argued that the growth in the economy was dependent upon either the continued accumulation of capital stocks or the expansion of the technical frontier (Solow 1962; Thirlwall, 1982). This sort of capital accumulation remains possible within the developing world in the medium term, but it is not at all apparent that capital stocks can continue to expand without limit over any and all time-scales. Since global warming concerns this very long-time horizon, a discount rate (or set of discount rates) should be applied that incorporate the likelihood that growth and consumption will not continue unabated at current rates. Given these considerations, Cline argues for a discount rate of 1 per cent or less, while others argue for a 0 per cent discount rate.

3   The importance of uncertainty: applied to global warming

Another serious shortcoming of the standard cost–benefit analysis applied to global warming (that focuses almost exclusively on the impacts of CO_2 doubling) is that this elides the range of possible impacts from much greater levels of carbon accumulation. It is clear that the impact of a carbon doubling is very likely insubstantial (and very likely positive in as many parts of the world as it is detrimental in others); however the implications of a tenfold increase in carbon levels are unknown and unknowable. The problem with truncating the analysis at a doubling of CO_2 is that it limits the range of impacts to only the known, and probably the least important possible impacts. The climate system is similar to many other ecosystems, and it is likely to display large and discontinuous shifts when it is sufficiently dislocated (Daly *et al.*, 1992).

Chichilnisky and Heal (1993) discuss global warming as an example of a multilayered uncertainty. At one layer of uncertainty, the individual agent does not know where within a distribution of possibilities it will lie; at a higher level of uncertainty, the pool of agents do not know which of a set of possible distributions will actually apply. They assert that standard insurance contract pools are able to resolve the former uncertainty problem, but not the latter. This is because the insured risks need to be small, independent and similar: they need to be similar enough to be part of a known distribution that applies to all but distinct enough to be uncorrelated at the time of occurrence. This is of course just the opposite of the case of the unknown impacts of global warming, in which case all persons will bear the costliness of climate change simultaneously if it occurs. For this form of uncertainty futures markets are required, in which climate pessimists are able to trade state-contingent contracts with climate optimists for compensation in the event of large climate shifts (a 'catastrophic risk' futures market is currently operating on the Chicago Board of Trade.) Both forward-looking futures contracts and current insurance-pooling contracts are required to address the uncertainty inherent in a global environmental problem such as climate change. A simple cost–benefit analysis over the next 50 years is eliding all of these important uncertainties, even though alternative institutions do not exist to internalize these costs.

4   How to choose the correct development path: weighting the future

It is important to recognize that the optimal regulation of the global warming externality (via a carbon tax, say) does not imply a unique choice of development path, and that these alternative development paths might result in very different impacts from global warming. The internalization of the global warming externality requires only the application of a tax that sums up the expected damages from the accumulation of greenhouse gas stocks. The global impacts of the development process will depend upon far more than simply the choice of an externality tax. For example equally or more important to determining the aggregate impacts of the development process on various global environmental resources will are: (a) the levels of investment by earlier generations; (b) the extent of conversion of natural resources by earlier generations; and (c) the forms of capital in which investment occurs (Swanson, 1995: part A).

4.1   Levels of investment

In the context of global warming, Howarth and Norgaard (1995) demonstrate that the internalization of the global warming externality (via an energy tax) is not sufficient to determine more than the broad outlines of what the consequences of this tax would be for future generations. More important to determining the welfare of future generations is how much current generations are discounting their own immediate future welfare, and the impact of such discounting upon investment levels. When they discount intergenerational welfare heavily (0.45), the result is that there are no significant levels of investment for the future. When they discount welfare lightly (0.90), the result is that there is heavier investment in capital that provides a much brighter future in general, even allowing for the routing of additional investment into GHG mitigation. The important point here is that the welfare discount rate is linked to but distinct from the prevailing interest rate (marginal return on capital) in that substantial welfare discount rates can lead to high interest rates because welfare discounting causes investment capital shortages that generate the higher interest rates. The failure to care about the future is affecting the development path here primarily because of reduced investment rates that result from this lack of care.

4.2   The 'green golden rule' for investment

Howarth and Norgaard argue for the importance of investment in determining environmental outcomes. How should the level of investment be determined? The golden rule of economic growth provided by Meade–Phelps–Robinson stated that investment should take the form necessary to establish the growth path that gives the highest indefinitely maintainable level of consumption per head. This is one means of defining 'sustainability': the maintenance of a non-declining level of consumption. However the golden rule did not incorporate the role of natural resources as both production goods (generating a flow of consumption through their use) and also as consumption goods (generating a flow of direct utility). This is the method by which the 'stock related values' of natural capital may be brought within the analysis (see Krautkraemer in Swanson, 1995).

How is it possible to incorporate the concept of 'indefinite maintenance of consumption' into the societal objective? Chichilnisky argues for an alternative to the standard utilitarian objective function that allows 'time dictatorship': the domination of either the present or the future in the societal objective. The utilitarian objective function is a simple summation of all utilities across time, with a price (the discount rate) charged for utility that arrives in the future rather than in the present. The alternative objective function looks something as follows:

Weighting the future:

$$\theta \int_0^\infty U(C_t, A_t) e^{-\delta} dt + (1 - \theta) \lim_{T \to \infty} \inf_{t \geq T} U(C_t, A_t)$$

In this societal objective function, the distant future is given an explicit weight to include with the standard discounted flow represented by the utilitarian objective function. The lim *inft* of an infinite sequence of numbers is the largest number such that only a finite number of elements in the sequence are less than that number. It provides a means for defining the weight to be given to the 'last generation' in the line. It also provides a means for avoiding the unpalatable result derived from looking at Rawlsian (maximin) sorts of objective functions, which rank all development paths by reference to their lowest ever consumption value. The problem with maximin objective functions was that they often implied the total absence of investment along the path, in order to avoid low consumption outcomes in early periods. By contrast the objective function ranks all development paths by reference to their aggregate utility (rather than their lowest) but also gives weight to their end-point. In regard to long-term planning it is essential to incorporate both: a method that will encourage the maximization of period on period utilities and also a method that will allow some weight to be provided to the future (Beltratti *et al.*, 1995).

4.3 Development paths and global warming

The problem of global warming is not a problem equivalent to making a marginal choice given where society stands on a given path. This is the only question that standard cost–benefit analysis addresses, and it is not the correct question in the context of this sort of problem. It is instead a problem of choosing between some very different paths across time. This will require consideration of the very general questions of capital accumulation/consumption/investment across time, not just externality internalization.

In addition this problem also concerns the issue of whether the globe is able to sustain development when it is pursued in like manner by one after another nations – in this case, the issue is whether fossil fuel-based development can be pursued in like manner by all nations successively. That is, can the development path be a *uniform* choice across all nations? Perhaps the globe can sustain a lot more development, if it is not of precisely the same form. Then the issue is not just one of investment scale, but the uniformity of the investments themselves. It is to this subject that we turn in the next chapter.

5 Choosing between development paths: giving effect to future generations' preferences

One facet of global environmental problems is the importance of giving some weight to the preferences of future generations. Clearly one important way in which to do this is by means of adjustment of the discount rate; a rate that is too 'high' will make the preferences of distant generations largely irrelevant. Another important consideration is the problem of estimating the preferences of future generations from own current preferences. It is not possible to query these people who will live far off in the future in very different societies from our own. How can we be sure how they will feel about the choices we are making? Is it reasonable to assume that they will feel the same about the alternatives they will be presented with, as we do from our current position.

The point is that analysts tend to make the discount rate do a lot of work in equating effects across long-term time horizons. We tend to assume that every point in time is equivalent, but for the two effects that we mentioned previously: pure time preference and increasing consumption. The passage of time may include many other processes other than these two and, if it does, then these other time-embedded processes must also be included within the analysis of the choice between development paths.

John Krutilla was the first economist to attempt to describe some of the various processes embedded within time and the development process. He believed that these processes should be included systematically within the discount rate, just as with increasing consumption and impatience. This discounting-based approach to future generations' preferences has not been developed. However, economists have developed other means of including extraneous preferences within their frameworks of analysis. This section explains these approaches.

5.1   Development and the valuation of natural assets

It has been seen that development may be conceptualized as the process by which natural assets are converted to human synthesized ones. In this case many natural resources will be lost simply as a by-product of the process of development. If these development choices are made consciously, then when will natural resource conversion constitute an environmental problem? One way to conceptualize any environmental problem is as the failure to give adequate weight to one of two alternative development paths. For example if the problem is cast as the decision whether or not to develop, then the non-development option may be given too little weight systematically if its environmental attributes are undervalued by the current decision maker and the goods acquired through conversion overvalued. If the decision maker is taking development decisions with regard to the conversion of natural assets, then many of these decisions may be 'irreversible', meaning that the decision is being taken on behalf of future as well as current generations.

5.2   How is that one development path might be 'overvalued' relative to another? What is the meaning of 'irreversibility'?

5.2.1   The Krutilla's hypothesis about the direction of development   Krutilla hypothesized that development decisions with irreversible implications for future generations must be evaluated with respect to parameters different than those prevailing at a single point in time (that is the present). Irreversibility implies that a decision being made at one point in time will be applicable at all future points in time, and so there must be some weight given to predictable changes. Specifically Krutilla hypothesized that the passage of time would generate three predictable changes in prevailing parameters affecting decisions regarding the conversion of natural environments. They are:

5.2.2   Krutilla's hypothesis concerning development and societal preferences

1. Continued growth from conversion and technical progress: increasing incomes by reason of development (reshaped capital stock) and general technical progress; and
2. Relatively increasing demand for natural capital-sourced goods and services: positive income effect on demand for natural capital-based goods and services, but relatively diminishing marginal utility for all other

consumer goods and services (derived from non-natural capital stocks) on account of satiation.

5.3 What are the implications of these intergenerational differences for current development?

Krutilla argued that the consideration of an irreversible development decision must take these factors into account; otherwise, the development will proceed by reference only to currently existing preferences (and other parameters) and destroy precisely that which will be demanded in future. Consider the standard cost–benefit criterion for determining whether a development project should go ahead (as opposed to 'preserving' the natural capital).

Net present value of development:

$$NPV \equiv \int_0^\infty e^{-rt}(b_t^d - b_t^p)dt$$

$$\text{where}: b_t^d \equiv \text{benefits development}$$
$$b_t^p \equiv \text{benefits preservation}$$

The meaning of the Krutilla hypothesis is that, although current period benefits are able to be estimated for the two development options, there is no reason to extrapolate these values linearly into the future. We can hypothesize various reasonable options as to how these current values might alter across time. For example general technological progress is likely to make preferences for general consumption goods more easily accomplished in future. Similarly increasing incomes are also likely to expand the demand for natural environments. This means that the discount rates that should be applied to different flows of goods and services should be derived differently. In effect a single discount rate applied to all flows of utility implies that all societal development processes have the same implications for all stocks of capital. Since this is clearly not the case (for example much of societal development has been based on the conversion of natural capital), then it makes little sense to abide rigorously by this assumption. Krutilla assumed that, throughout the development process, the ease of acquiring utility from consumer goods and services would be increasing by reason of general technical progress, while it would be declining for natural resources-based utility by reason of irreversible conversions.

$$b_t^d \equiv b_0^d \ e^{-\tau t}$$

$$b_t^p \equiv b_0^p \ e^{\alpha t}$$

where : b_0^d = the current period value of development

b_0^d = the current period value of preservation

τ = the rate of technological progress

α = the rate of expanding demand for nature

5.4   Correcting current choices on account of future changes

The result of the Krutilla approach to development valuation is that two different discount rates would need to be applied, one reflecting the diminishing demand for consumption goods and services and another representing the expanding demand for 'natural' goods and services.

$$NPV \equiv \int_0^\infty b_0^d e^{-(r+\tau)t} dt - \int_0^\infty b_0^p e^{-(r-\alpha)t} dt$$

The evaluation of the choice between 'development' and 'non-development' paths requires that future generations' preferences be consulted (on account of irreversibilities), and this will require alterations in the current generation's calculus regarding the two paths. This may seem to be an *ad hoc* approach to the evaluation of project benefits, but Krutilla's point is that it is just as *ad hoc* to use equivalent discount rates, *if it turns out that his suppositions are correct regarding the direction of the various time-embedded processes*. Time implies development, and development implies: (1) rearranged societal portfolios (and hence conversion of natural into other forms of capital); and (2) increased incomes as a result and hence the expansion of societal demands for natural environments. Reduced supplies with increasing demands implies a different trend in the value of these goods and services than for others. Krutilla's analysis captures the fundamental importance of this intergenerational conflict in evaluating development.

5.5   Example: 'the optimal scale of development'

Consider the example of a hydroelectric dam that is proposed for a given unconverted river valley. As the scale of the dam is increased, more of the valley will be flooded, hence converting a natural asset into a physical one. The benefits of the dam will be measured in terms of the electricity it is able to generate, which will of course rise with the scale of the dam. Electricity is useful for the efficient production of virtually all manners of general consumable goods and services. On the other hand this general increase in the level of wealth in the society will not be able to purchase one of the goods that is most clearly linked to income growth, that is natural environments, as these will already have been irreversibly converted. Even if the dam were removed, the naturalness of the river valley may never be retrieved.

What is the optimal scale (*S*) of this hydroelectric project?

$$\text{Let} \quad b_t(S) = b_0^d(S)e^{-\tau t} + b_0^p(S)e^{\alpha t}$$

$$b_t^*(S):\frac{\partial b_t}{\partial S} = 0$$

$$\text{Then} \quad b_t^*(S):\frac{\partial b_0^d}{\partial S} = -\left(\frac{\partial b_0^p}{\partial S}\right)e^{(\tau+\alpha)t}$$

$$\therefore \quad \text{For} \quad t \to \infty, \quad S \to 0$$

These equations state the simple truth that Krutilla's assumptions imply – that the optimal approach by society to development would involve the construction of a very large dam today and its disassembly slowly over the future (as time goes on and on, the scale of the dam goes down and down). The problem with this approach is that the natural resources that the society wishes to retrieve may no longer be there when the dam is removed. If future societies would like to have some of the nature that we are able to experience today, these things may not be there when the industries are shut down and the dams are removed; instead a very different place may exist.

6 An alternative approach: current values for future preferences
The Krutilla–Fisher model gave one possible approach to bringing non-development values into the equation, that is hypothesizing about possible conflicts between present and future generation's positions and preferences. This approach to valuing non-development options will always seem *ad hoc*, simply because it will be difficult to justify one set of assumptions about the movement of future preferences over another. The alternative is to create 'non-use values' within the current generation's choice framework, asking this generation to express a valuation for various categories of value that arise out of non-development. That is this approach focuses on the current generation's attempt to express preferences for meeting future generations' preferences.

6.1 Krutilla's concept of total economic value
Krutilla hypothesized that current generations do indeed hold valuations for the holding of 'stocks' of natural resources, even when there is little or no direct/individual interest in experiencing a 'flow' from that stock. These stock-related values must then be rationalized by reference to others who the individual is hoping to benefit from that stock's flows. These are the 'non-use'

values of stocks of undeveloped natural resources. The various categories of value utilized in the determination of *total economic value* are listed in Table 2.4.

Table 2.4   Categories of value (Krutilla)

Total Economic Value =			
Direct Use +	Indirect Use +	Option Values +	'Existence Value'
Production	Systemic Functions	Future Uses	Intrinsic Values
Consumption		Irreversibility	Surrogate Values
		(Informational)	

Note that all of these values relate to a particular decision-making framework, usually whether to conserve or convert some particular natural resource or habitat. 'Direct use' values are those which are comparable to those obtained from non-environmental goods and services; these flow from individualized benefits from consumption and production in the non-converted environment. 'Indirect use' value relates to individually received benefits derived from systems remaining intact by reason of non-conversion, for example the maintenance of the benefits of a watershed. These first two categories concern flows of services received by the current generation from the natural asset. The latter two components relate more to stock-related (future generations' flow) values. 'Option values' relate to the dynamic nature of such decision making. 'Option value' itself is the value to an individual of an option to acquire the good or service at some point in the future at a specified price; that is, it is a current value received from fixing a current price, and not a stock-related concept. 'Quasi-option value' is an informational value described first by Arrow and Fisher. It is the value of retaining a given range of options while information is still arriving that may render one of those options important in future decision making. It is the value of flexibility. 'Existence value' is the residual category of value, corresponding to a very wide range of motivations for which individuals might value a stock of the resource.

6.2   The non-use values (assessing preferences of absentees?)
With respect to the assessment of the preferences of those who are not present at the time of the decision making, it is the non-use values that are of interest. Non-use does not necessarily mean that the resource will never be used – it implies that the current decision makers are placing it aside for possible future use (or, at least, for availability in its current condition for

future decision makers). The value of 'leaving something aside' may be assessed in at least two fundamentally different ways:

1. determining the value of 'leaving all options open' for future decision makers (quasi-option value)
2. giving weight to future consumers and decision makers preferences by implicit assessment of them by current decision makers (possible motivation for existence values).

Consider first the idea of quasi-option value. It is the difference in the value between making a decision under uncertainty, or waiting for the uncertainty to resolve itself before making that decision.

6.3   'Quasi-option value'

$$\text{Quasi-option value} \;=\; U^{\theta}(d_{t1}) - U(d_{t1})$$

$$\text{where} \quad U(d_{t1}) \;=\; \underset{\underset{d_{t1}}{\text{Max}}}{U_{t1(d_{t1})}} \;+\; \underset{\underset{d_{t2}}{\text{Max}}}{E[U_{t2}(d_{t1},d_{t2};\theta)]}$$

$$U^{\theta}(d_{t1}) \;=\; \underset{\underset{d_{t1}}{\text{Max}}}{U_{t1}(d_{t1})} \;+\; E\left[\underset{\underset{d_{t2}}{\text{Max}}}{U_{t2}(d_{t1},d_{t2};\theta)} \right]$$

In this depiction of quasi-option value, the difference in value lies in the difference in the two approaches in decision making. In the one case decisions are made under the assumption that relevant information will be used in the next period's decision concerning development. In the other it is anticipated that no further important information will be used in that period than is available now (that is the expected value now is the best guess as to the development decision next period). To the extent that future relevant information is expected to arrive, the value of retaining greater flexibility (postponing irreversible decisions) will be enhanced.

6.4   'Existence values'
The other important non-use value is the concept of existence value. These values have been given credibility simply because there are individuals who demonstrate a willingness to pay for the provision of a resource, even though it is clear that they themselves will receive none of the use of that resource.

There are a wide range of possible motivations for giving stock-related values other than the retention of flexibility for future generations. The following list contains a number of plausible reasons why a person might give a positive value to the 'existence' of a particular species. Note that many of these motivations are in fact just one person's attempt to give weight to another (absentee's) potential preferences. Hence some of the broader current valuations of conservation options at least provide the flexibility for the inclusion of current assessments of future generation's preferences.

6.5   Some motivations for positive existence values – vicarious valuations?

- *Bequest motive* – the importance of providing the species for the use and enjoyment of future generations of human societies.
- *Vicarious enjoyment motive* – the importance of knowing that other individuals than yourself are currently enjoying the species.
- *Animal benefactor motive* – the importance of providing an enjoyable style of life or existence for individuals of a given species.

The important thing about all of these motivations is that they are all 'vicarious valuations', that is they are attempts by individuals to give value to the enjoyment of the resource that will be acquired by others. People clearly are willing to pay for resources that will be enjoyed by others, including future generations and even the resources (often animals) themselves.

One possibility is that current generations are implicitly addressing the problem of providing for a natural world in the future, by means of including the utility that will flow to others from this within their own preferences. That is, unlike the maintenance of a supply of automobiles or televisions, the current generation of individuals does care that the future generations have supplies of natural resources and environments, and they probably do give concrete values to this possibility. Although this is not a very accurate method for ascertaining future generations' own preferences for the supply of those resources, in the light of irreversibilities there is probably no better approach available for giving effect to this potential value.

7   Conclusion: global environmental problems, future generations and IEAs

The cumulative impact of development is often felt more by societies that will exist in the future than by ones that exist at present. Overexploited environmental systems will sometimes not recover for hundreds of years, and other times the impacts are partially or wholly irreversible. In these instances it is important that development choices be made taking into consideration the external effects on the future, as much or more so than the external effects in the present.

The problem is that each individual country has little reason to act unilaterally to attempt to preserve a particular option for the future. If one country takes such action, it will have little if any impact in a world where others continue with business as usual. For this reason it is essential that countries act jointly to preserve future paths for future generations. This is why IEAs are essential for the solution of these sorts of problem.

This chapter has developed a very practical approach to the problems of future generations. It has simply demonstrated the problems associated with the attempts to incorporate the preferences of future generations within current decision making, via either discounting or valuation. The more general and complicated problem concerns the choice of development pathways for global development that allow important futures to be preserved for their consideration. In the past this was probably not so important. Past generations had substantial impacts on the globe and on societies' relationships to it, but they did not have the technical capacity to overhaul completely the biological and environmental systems that existed. We not only have that capacity; to a large extent, we have already exercised it over the past half-century. The biological world has been remade over much of the face of the earth (through agriculture), and the environmental systems have been substantially altered by this and other revolutions. (These sorts of capacity are the subject of Chapter 3).

Given these pervasive powers to reshape the world in which we live, the preservation of options for future generations is more important that it was previously, otherwise, we will present these societies with few options other than to deal with the very limited world within the very substantial limits with which we present them. One of the objectives implicit within the conventions developed within the United Nations Conference on Environment and Development (UNCED) is to address these problems of unmanaged development on the global scale.

3   Global development and global externalities: a case study of the need to regulate biodiversity's decline

1   Global development and global biodiversity

Global environmental problems are usually situations that cannot be resolved through uncontrolled development, as this is precisely its source. Many other environmental problems do generate their own solutions with adequate national growth and development. For example sanitary water and adequate air quality tend to be in disproportionately greater demand as living standards increase, and hence adequate income growth often affords the prospect of improving previously degraded air and water quality. For this reason the most cost-effective prescription for many environmental problems brought on by industrialization and development in many of the poor countries may often be simply 'to grow out of them' (Beckerman, 1994).

This is not the case in the context of the environmental problem of biodiversity, for two reasons. First, in biodiversity we have an example of a resource which is generally discriminated against within the process of development, simply because development is usually practised in a very uniform fashion, for example the clearing of land and the establishment of agriculture. As will be discussed in further detail below, development is often seen to be synonymous with the conversion of diverse natural resources to a common roster of uniform national resources: cattle ranching, specialized agriculture and the many other forms of activities that are common across most of the world. Therefore the standard practice of development uniformly discriminates against diversity.

The other reason that it is impossible to allow time and development to work a solution to the biodiversity problem is that it is unlikely that there will be any of these resources remaining at the point in time at which they are adequately demanded. The problem here is one of foreseeable demands in combination with irreversible supplies. As development proceeds it is likely that the demand for diversity will increase (as it does for other environmental resources), but it is the conversion of biodiversity that often lies at the base of the development process as it is currently practised. Since existing biological diversity is a non-retrievable resource ('only God [4.5 billion years] can create a tree'), the engine of development is often consuming the very resources for which it will generate demand in the near future.

The regulation of biodiversity requires the regulation of the development process as it is currently practised. In particular it will be necessary to create global incentive schemes that will induce individual developing countries to pursue development in a manner very different from those states before them. It is a very risky strategy to commit to a unique path of development, different from that undertaken by those who have gone before you, and it is unlikely that any given nation would do so in any substantial manner in the absence of sizeable international inducements, and this will require the establishment of international institutions for that purpose. The problem in the past has been that international institutions themselves have developed in the wake of the first countries' development, usually responsive to and supportive of the choices which they have made. If a diversity of development paths are to be pursued, based upon a diversity of resources, then it will be necessary for a diversity of international institutions to exist in order to support these alternatives. It is the object of this chapter and Chapter 4 to demonstrate generally how the biodiversity convention should be conceived in order to fulfil this role.

2   The development process and the biosphere

Conversion of natural environments has long been part and parcel of the development process. Societies which we know as 'developed' are those which have previously built their economies upon a productive set of assets; societies which we know as 'developing' are those which are still in the process of assembling their asset base. Hence economic development in human societies derives in part from the substitution of more productive assets for the less productive. When this process of substitution is applied to natural resources, it is usually known as the *conversion process*, as in the case of the conversion of forests into ranchlands.

Natural resources may be conceived of as simply *natural assets*: assets whose initial form was determined by nature rather than society (Solow, 1974a). The natural form of any asset is necessarily competitive with other forms in which humans might hold these same assets. Humans can, for example, remove forests for factories or fields. If development is defined as the process by which a given set of assets is selected by society, then development must necessarily imply the decline of natural asset balances, simply because nature initially selected 100 per cent of the assets on which society depended. As humans become more actively engaged in the selection of the form that assets will take, this necessarily implies that the proportion of naturally chosen asset forms must fall.

Conversion in the process of development lies at the root of the endangerment of most biological resources. For example the decline of many traditional plant and animal varieties occurs when the lands on which they are grown are converted to a specialized modern variety. The loss of many other diverse resources also has its source in the development process, albeit less directly. For example a tropical forest replete with many diverse resources may be lost on account of logging activities. In this case the natural asset (the forest) is being converted in a less direct fashion through the liquidation of the standing resources. That is the natural resource is converted to another asset form indirectly through sale with the proceeds then potentially invested in other forms of assets (such as education), resulting in the conversion of the natural asset (to another asset such as 'human capital').

Development is a process which has long been antithetical to natural resource conservation. This is because it has been based upon the idea of conversion of assets to preferred forms – from forests to factories, from heathlands to health services, from wetlands to water sports. In the past the natural form of the asset was not seen as providing any special recommendation for its retention; if a market-preferred alternative was available, it was pursued. More recently local and national land-use planning legislation in the developed countries has allowed for a broader set of values, other than those which are simply market-based, to be taken into consideration in regard to local resources. These institutions have come far too late for many of the diverse resources that existed in the developed world, and the institutions still do not exist in many of the countries in which they would have the greatest impact on biodiversity. One of the basic objectives of the biodiversity convention should be seen to be the development of the necessary institutions for the incorporation of the values of biodiversity within the land-use decision-making processes of those nations which still host vast amounts of the resource. That is one fundamental object is to develop institutions that generate incentives for land-use management in countries where development has not yet itself generated that institution (since these are many of the same countries which have not yet depleted their biodiversity through development).

3   The impact of development at the global level

Economic development is of course a constructive force in nearly every context in which it occurs. Development has been seen to provide not only the basic needs of many societies, but it is now also seen to provide many of the other requirements, such as environmental services, health services and even individual rights. However the diffusion of the development process on a global basis is also one of the primary forces contributing to diversity losses. The initial, local conversions of natural resources had little impact on the global portfolio of assets, but the aggregation of thousands and millions of these discrete conversions has generated a phenomenon of worldwide importance.

In effect the global conversion process may be conceived of as the diffusion of the idea of asset conversion across the globe, from country to country. Some countries commenced the conversion of their habitats thousands of years ago; for example the forests of Britain were largely removed during the course of the Iron Age. Other countries still retain the vast forests that have been there since time immemorial. The global biodiversity problem comes to our attention now because these processes of conversion are working their way towards the last refugia on earth. The majority of the world's remaining species reside in a small number of the world's states. These are the same states that have been the last to have substantial parts of their territories remaining unconverted (Table 3.1).

Table 3.1 Countries with greatest 'species richness'

Mammals	Birds	Reptiles
Indonesia (515)	Colombia (1721)	Mexico (717)
Mexico (449)	Peru (1701)	Australia (686)
Brazil (428)	Brazil (1622)	Indonesia (600)
Zaire (409)	Indonesia (1519)	India (383)
China (394)	Ecuador (1447)	Colombia (383)
Peru (361)	Venezuela (1275)	Ecuador (345)
Colombia (359)	Bolivia (1250)	Peru (297)
India (350)	India (1200)	Malaysia (294)
Uganda (311)	Malaysia (1200)	Thailand (282)
Tanzania (310)	China (1195)	Papua New Guinea (282)

Source: McNeely *et al.*, 1990.

Asset conversion that has occurred for a millenia on a local and regional scale has now aggregated to become a force at the global level. At base this restructuring of the global portfolio of biological assets is driven by the desire for human development gains obtained from the conversion of assets to more productive forms. However, as this basic strategy for human development reaches the final refugia of many of the world's species, it is projected that a cataclysmic 'mass extinction' of species may result (Lovejoy, 1980; Ehrlich and Ehrlich, 1981). Development practises which had little negative impact when practised on a small and local basis have now aggregated to bring about massive changes on a global basis.

Therefore at the very base of the biodiversity problem is the capability of humans to change the nature of the biosphere from its natural to a human-preferred form. The gains from conversion have been causing the restructuring of the biosphere on a regional basis for several millenia. Now, with the diffusion of this strategy to the final terrestrial frontiers, conversion of the biosphere seems set to occur on a global basis.

3.1   The nature of the global conversion process

Reconstruction of the portfolio of biological assets on a global basis is a powerful force, capable of reshaping the whole of the earth's biosphere. However it is not in itself sufficient to explain the potential for a mass extinction. For this, an explanation must be found that will generate not only an expected reshaping of the global portfolio of natural assets, but also a narrowing of that portfolio.

Conversion as an economic force explains only why it is the case that the natural slate of biological resources might be replaced by another on any given parcel of land, depending upon relative productivities. It does not explain why a small number of species would replace millions across the whole of the earth. That is this force implies conversion but not necessarily homogenization. In order to explain the global losses of biodiversity, that is *a narrowing of the global portfolio*, it is necessary to identify the nature of the force that would generate this homogenization of the global biosphere.

This indicates that the depletion of diversity is not a natural phenomenon; rather, it is a socio-economic one. There are good reasons to believe that prevailing methods of production are biased against the maintenance of a wide range of diversity. The idea of agriculture, that originated about 10 000 years ago in the Near East, was centred on the idea of creating species-specific technologies. This implied the inclusion of two new important factors of production in the production of biological goods: species-specific capital goods and species-specific learning.

In terms of biological resources, the capital goods applied in production are the chemicals, machinery and other tools of agriculture. These capital goods usually do not enhance the photosynthetic productivity of the biosphere; rather, they increase its productivity by means of the mass production of large quantities of a homogeneous output from much reduced inputs from other factors, for example labour.

The productivity gains in agriculture go hand in hand with diversity losses; in fact, they are often derived from the reductions in diversity. For example farm machinery is developed to work in fields that are planted uniformly in a single crop. Chemicals are fine-tuned to eliminate all competitors of a single species. The fields themselves are 'cleared' for the introduction of the machinery and chemicals of the production process. These capital goods are effective precisely because of the homogeneous environment within which they operate, and they create incentives for conversion by reason of their effectiveness.

At present this process of conversion is working its way across the developing world, having completed its journey through the developed world. The frontier is discernible by reference to the relative rates of conversion and capital good accumulation. For example the number of tractors in Africa increased by 29 per cent over the past 10 years; they increased by 82 per cent in South America; and by 128 per cent in Asia. During the same period the number of tractors decreased by 4 per cent in North America (World Resources Institute, 1990). It is the extension of this previously successful strategy for development to the four corners of the earth that is at the base of the concerns about what is presently happening to the biosphere.

It is not difficult to ascertain the approximate location of the technological frontier in this context. For example data on worldwide land-use trends document the rates at which conversions of lands to uses in specialized agricultural production have been occurring. Between 1960 and 1980 the developing world in aggregate increased its land area dedicated to standard specialized crops by 37 per cent, while the developed world experienced a small decrease in the same (Repetto and Gillis, 1988). Therefore deforestation and land-use changes continue to occur on large scales in those countries with natural resources remaining to convert; it cannot do otherwise. For example the amount of 'wilderness' (that is 20 square kilometres of unaltered landscape) on the European continent is now virtually zero, versus a global average of approximately 30 per cent (World Resources Institute, 1990). These states of the 'North' are the 'already converted' states; it is only a small selection of the states of the 'South' that retain a significant amount of diverse resources.

At present the forces for specialized conversions have moved to the boundaries of the last handful of states with substantial amounts of unconverted territory: Brazil (and the other Amazonian states), Zaire, Indonesia and a few others. These states are in a rapid phase of development and conversion, following in the paths of all those states that have gone before. One very large part of the biodiversity problem is the extension of this same development strategy to each and every country on earth, no matter how different their initial conditions are. This sameness, extended to countries initially so different, is one of the major reasons that the world is being depleted of diversity.

4   The biodiversity problem in agriculture: convergence on specialized varieties of species

The same process is at work within agriculture as is at work against nature. Natural resources continue to be replaced by the sameness that exists within agriculture as it is extended across the globe. Equally the differences that have always existed within traditionally practised agriculture are also being replaced by the sameness of modern intensive agricultural practices. This has created another facet to the biodiversity problem that is sourced in the same fundamental causes – the problem of genetic erosion in agricultural species. In order to understand the forces driving biodiversity's depletion and their relationship to development, it is instructive to enquire as to how biodiversity depletion has occurred within agriculture as well as within nature.

Within nature the problem of biodiversity depletion has been explained as the workings of the force of specialization within the natural world. Human societies have selected a small set of species and relied upon these for their sustenance, replacing diversity with the cultivated and domesticated varieties as part of the process of development. Through specialization societies have been able to achieve productivity gains by combining certain species with specially developed tools and methods of production. The question remains: why only a couple of dozen distinct species, and why only those which were chosen initially? The answers to these questions give further insights into the general nature of the biodiversity problem, and especially to the nature of the problem within agriculture.

The answer comes from considering the agricultural production process as it has developed across time. Besides the tools and chemicals used in agriculture, the other important factor that has been important in the evolution of modern agricultural production methods has been species-specific learning. With more experience with a particular species, it was possible to become even more efficient in its production (by reason of increased understanding of its biological nature, as well as intervention to determine the same). This information became another crucial factor for agricultural production, but it existed only in one form – embedded in the received forms of the domesticated and cultivated varieties.

As previously mentioned agriculture originated approximately 10 000 years ago in the Near East. It consisted of a set of ideas, a set of tools and a set of selected species. At that time and in that locale, each of these selections was locally optimal. However the set of ideas–technology–species were transported out of that region as a single unit, as the continuing investments in this combination caused the ideas and tools to become embedded in the chosen species. For example when the species of sheep and goats were domesticated in the Near East, a lot was learned in the process. It was of course possible that other peoples in other places might take note of the practice of domestication, and apply it to the species indigenous to their parts of the world; however this would require that much of the knowledge associated with sheep and goats be relearned in the context of other species. In most cases it would likely be easier to simply adopt the already domesticated species, and the existing learning with it.

In short a bias was introduced within the decision-making process, by reason of the non-rival nature of the information embedded in the specialized species (that would be costly to produce for any diverse species). This is the essential difference between the specialized (domesticated) species and the diverse (wildlife) species. For one group an information set is publicly available as an input into their production; for the other it is necessary to construct that same information. The global conversion process has consisted of the extension of these chosen species' ranges. As a consequence much of the face of the earth has been reshaped in order to suit these few species and the tools used in their production. It is the diffusion of this 'bundle' of ideas–tools– species that is at the base of the biodiversity problem.

Therefore it is not simply the globalization of the strategy of asset conversion that is determining the global portfolio of species, it is also the special way in which conversion occurs under agriculture. It is the perceived gain from the substitution of the specialized biological resources for the diverse that is generating an ever more narrow portfolio. It is this force, now acting globally, that is shaping the incentives for investment, and hence extinction.

This is a form of *dynamic externality* in operation with regard to decision making; that is earlier choices regarding conversions are having an impact on the way that later ones are being made. In the context of the biosphere, this bias is creating a 'natural monopoly' for a small number of species. The biosphere is converging upon this small, select group of specialized species as the sole providers of living resources to human societies.

This is seen in the fact that an increasingly narrow roster of species meets all of the needs of humankind. Of the thousands of plant species which are deemed edible and adequate substitutes for human consumption, there are now only 20 which produce the vast majority of the world's food. In fact the four big carbohydrate crops (wheat, maize, rice and potatoes) feed more people than the next 26 crops together (Witt, 1985). The same applies with regard to protein sources. The *Production Yearbook* of the Food and Agricultural Organization lists only a handful of domesticated species (sheep, goats, cattle, pigs and so on) which supply nearly all of the terrestrial-sourced protein for the vast majority of humans. The number of domesticated cattle on the globe (currently over 1.2 billion or one for every four humans) continues to increase, while the numbers of almost all other species continue in decline.

The same process of specialization is evident with regard to variety within a species. Not only are human societies becoming more reliant upon a narrower range of species, they are also becoming reliant upon specific varieties of these species. Specialization works beyond the species level of genetic convergence to produce a technically calibrated uniform biological asset, something which is capable of working well with the specific tools of agriculture: tractors, harvesters and so on. For this reason the problem of biodiversity concerns the conservation of greater varieties of specialized species as much as it concerns the conservation of any varieties of non-specialized species.

The global diffusion of specialized species within agriculture is demonstrated in Tables 3.2 and 3.3 below. It presents a snapshot portrait of the conversion of various countries to modern high-yield varieties in agriculture. Table 3.2 provides a static portrait of the progress of this technological change in the period 1978–81. It shows that some developing countries had already embraced this strategy of specialization (for example Philippines with 78 per cent of their rice production converted) while others were only just initiating the process (for example Thailand with only 9 per cent of the same).

Table 3.2   Area devoted to modern rice varieties (11 Asian countries, 1978–81)

Country	Year	1000 ha	% of Rice Area
Bangladesh	1981	2325	22
India	1980	18 495	47
Nepal	1981	326	26
Pakistan	1978	1015	50
Sri Lanka	1980	612	71
Burma	1980	1502	29
Indonesia	1980	5416	60
Malaysia W	1977	316	44
Philippines	1980	2710	78
Thailand	1979	800	9
South Korea	1981	321	26

Source: Anderson and Hazell (1985).

Table 3.3 shows the progress of this process within individual states. In those states that initiated modern agricultural specialization (for example the USA), food production is now almost entirely specialized (the majority of food production involving only a few varieties of a small number of species). In the states adopting the strategy more recently, this 'scoping in' process has reduced the number of varieties in production from thousands to a few in a small amount of time (Table 3.2).

Hence the biodiversity problem is a problem with its source in the ever increasing specialization taking place within the biological production sector. All societies are embracing the strategy of supplying their needs from a mere handful of species, and increasingly it is the same small group of species and

Table 3.3 Examples of genetic uniformity in selected crops

Crop	Country	Number of Varieties
Rice	Sri Lanka	from 2000 varieties in 1959 to 5 major varieties today 75% of varieties descended from one maternal parent
Rice	India	from 30 000 varieties to 75% of production from less than 10 varieties
Rice	Bangladesh	62% of varieties descended from one maternal parent
Rice	Indonesia	74% of varieties descended from one maternal parent
Wheat	USA	50% of crop in nine varieties
Potato	USA	75% of crop in four varieties
Cotton	USA	50% of crop in three varieties
Soybean	USA	50% of crop in six varieties

Source: World Conservation Monitoring Centre (1992).

varieties that is supplying every society. This means that the biodiversity problem has two interrelated but very different facets: the problem of ensuring an adequate supply of genetic diversity for the supply of specialized industries such as agriculture and medicine and the problem of ensuring an adequate supply of unconverted habitats for the supply of genetic diversity.

The two problems are interrelated in that unconverted habitats are one source of supplies of the genetic diversity required by specialized industries. The two are also distinct because industrially important genetic diversity can be supplied through means other than non-conversion, for example the retention of genetic diversity in 'banks', and because non-converted habitats can generate many other values than those emanating from the specialized industries, for example the values from visits or known existence. However, in the first instance, it is important to focus on the need for diversity to sustain the specialized methods of production in order to establish an overall constraint on the process of conversion. Once again this approach is adopted in order to place a 'floor' under the minimum required amount of biodiversity. There can be no argument (even from the most rabid pro-growth perspective) for the continued pursuit of the gains from specialization by sole reliance upon a strategy that places those same gains at risk. Biodiversity provides many different values to human society, however its most fundamental value is in the support of the specialized production system which is its greatest threat.

5   The 'uneven' nature of global conversion: human development and diversity depiction

Before we proceed to the discussion of the value of biodiversity, it is important to recognize the benefits received from specialized development to human societies. These conversions from diverse to specialized resources have generated substantial worldwide productivity gains. World cereal production grew at an average annual rate of 2.7 per cent between 1960 and 1983 (Anderson and Hazell, 1989). For example the substitution of specialized rice varieties for diverse is estimated to have increased yields by 1.0 tonne/hectare on irrigated lands, and by 0.75 tonne/hectare on non-irrigated lands. Although the conversion of lands from diverse to specialized production methods must reduce global diversity, it is apparent that these losses are compensated for, and driven by, development gains.

The economic relationship between conversion and development is demonstrated in part by the state of human development in the 'diversity rich' states. Almost without exception, these are some of the poorest nations on earth in terms of human wealth. They range between 1 and 7 per cent of the OECD average per capita income. Although non-human species are faring relatively well in these countries, the human species is doing comparatively poorly (Table 3.4).

Table 3.4   GNP per capita in the species-rich states

Country	1988 GNP p.c.	Country	1988 GNP p.c.
Tanzania	$160	Papua, NG	$810
Zaire	$170	Thailand	$1000
Uganda	$280	Bolivia	$1099
Ecuador	$284	Colombia	$1139
China/India	$340	Peru	$1300
OECD Average	$17 400		

Source: World Bank (1990).

From this perspective the decline of diversity has been closely linked with the human development process. The conversion of biological resources has taken the form of substituting the specialized species for the diverse causing diversity to decline. This has generated a gain for that human society, a gain that could be allocated to either increased wealth or fitness. Thus conversion to the specialized species has been a strategy for generating human development gains.

To date much of the gain achieved from this strategy has been expended on the expansion of the human niche. For the human species a revolution in niche expansion has occurred over the last 10 000 years. Scientists estimate that the introduction of the ideas of agriculture at that time coincided with a 'take off' in the level of the human population. Since that time the human population has expanded from approximately 10 million to approaching 10 billion individuals.

Despite the scale of the human population it remains the method of appropriation that is the gravest threat to diversity. This has been demonstrated in various ecological studies. The ultimate scarce resource, biologically speaking, is known as net primary product (NPP). This is the total biomass generated by the process of photosynthesis on this planet. It is also the total amount of usable solar energy available for the sustenance of all life forms on earth. The expansion of the human niche has resulted in the exclusion of most other species from a substantial part of NPP. Ecological studies show that the human species now appropriates about 40 per cent of terrestrial NPP (Vitousek *et al.*, 1986).

Most importantly, however, the same study argues that the vast majority (90 per cent) of all human niche appropriation occurs 'indirectly', that is for reasons other than direct use. The vast majority of NPP appropriated by the human species is not used but rather lost to other species, by reason of clearing and burning lands in particular. The biodiversity problem is as much a problem of diversity-unfriendly methods of production as it is human niche expansion. Still these gains are usually routed initially to the expansion of the human niche, and this is indicated by the growth in the human populations on the conversion frontier (Table 3.5).

Therefore development (human development) is a process that has been driven in part by the process of conversion. This has resulted in a remarkable

Table 3.5   Population growth in the species-rich states (percentage per annum, 1980–90)

Tanzania	3.1	Papua, NG	2.5
Zaire	3.2	Thailand	1.8
Uganda	2.5	Bolivia	2.5
Ecuador	2.4	Colombia	2.0
China	1.4	Peru	2.3
India	2.1		
OECD Average	0.6		

Source: World Bank (1992).

asymmetry in the world. The states with high 'material wealth' have low 'diversity wealth', and vice versa. The problem of biodiversity stems primarily from the attempts of the remaining, unconverted states to follow this same development path. At present the margin of the global conversion process rests at the threshold of the last refugia for diverse biological resources. If development continues in the future in these states as it has in the past in all others, then there will be much less global biodiversity to be concerned about in the very near future.

6   Regulating the global conversion process

To a large extent the problem of biodiversity depletion may be attributed to the absence of an international institution dedicated to its conservation. That is the global biodiversity problem may be conceived of as the set of difficulties that derive from the fact that the conversion process has been regulated on a globally decentralized basis. Historically each state has been able to make its own conversion decisions regarding its own lands and resources without regard for the consequences for other societies. This creates an important regulatory problem because the cost – in terms of the value of lost services – of each successive conversion is not the same. The global stocks of biological diversity generate a flow of services to all societies on earth. As we shall see in this chapter, all of us rely upon the stocks of diversity for the maintenance of our various support systems: agriculture, medicine and ecosystems. The first subtractions from global stocks did little to hinder the flow of these services, but the final subtractions from these stocks will render these flows non-existent. As the last refugia for diverse species dwindle, the cost of each successive conversion (in terms of diverse resource services lost to all societies on earth) escalates rapidly. The absence of any mechanism to bring these costs into the decision-making framework of the converting state is a big part of the biodiversity problem.

Although it may be threatening the very existence of a continuing flow of services from global stocks of biological diversity, the depletion of these stocks may nevertheless be to the clear benefit of the individual or society that is undertaking it. This is the nature of the regulatory problem of biodiversity losses – it is a conflict between what is in the interests of the development of the individual country and what is necessary for the protection of a production system relied upon by the global community. The individual country simply wishes to undertake the conversion process, as have all states that have preceded it in this development process, while the global community wishes to internalize the global costliness of the final conversions to these last, unconverted states.

Therefore the global policy problem of biodiversity losses involves the management of the global conversion process so as to reach the correct end-point, taking into consideration the 'global externalities' that individual societies do not. That is it is necessary to ascertain a global stopping rule that will determine when the marginal conversion by an individual country is not globally beneficial, and then alter the decision-making framework of that state so that the conversion will not occur.

The development process drives society to convert more and more of its land area to specialized uses over time. Each such conversion confers a gain upon human society – the value of converting between assets – and thus continues to drive the conversion (and development) process. The pertinent question then becomes: what forces might halt the conversion process prior to total conversion? What countervailing force is there to offset the perceived value deriving from specialized conversions?

It is the value of diversity itself that should provide the stopping point in the global conversion process. That is, with successive conversions, the quantities of lands in specialized production will be increasing while the quantities in diverse resources decline. At some point in this process the relative values of the two uses might switch, so that the use of the land in diverse resources is preferred. It is the value of biological *diversity* that should arrest the conversion process at its optimal point. The stock of global diversity provides important inputs into the processes of biological production, and it is this value (and not the individual values of the biological materials themselves) that is the essential force to be given effect within the biodiversity regulatory process.

Without intervention it is very unlikely that this force will be of any effect. As indicated the main source of benefits from diverse resources lies in their 'stock-related values'. In other words these are benefits that accrue to the world at large, rather than to the state hosting them. Such diffuse values will not in general be taken into consideration in state decision making regarding conversion. If diverse biological resources are systematically undervalued, then they will be too readily converted to their specialized substitutes. This will result in the retention of a quantity of diverse resource stocks that is less than optimal.

Figure 3.1 demonstrates how the non-appropriability of these stock-related values will lead to the mistargeting of the conversion process. That is this is a figure illustrating the misdirection of the conversion process over the very long run, as conversions erode the remaining diverse resource stocks, on the relative values of lands in specialized and diverse biological resources. This diagram demonstrates that the quantities of lands dedicated to the production of specialized resources in the very long run (allowing all factors to adjust) will be determined by:

- *domestic supply of conversions* (S) – this downward-sloping curve represents the *internalized* marginal cost of converting to specialized

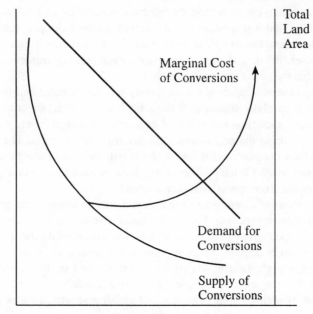

Figure 3.1   Optimal policy regarding conversions

resources. This curve is perceived to be downward-sloping because of
the increasing returns to scale available to capital-intensive methods of
production. Each state that decides to convert its resources incurs
decreasing costliness because of the fixed costs incurred by its prede-
cessors.

- *demand for conversions* (D) – this is the perceived benefit to the
  marginal state from the conversion of its resources (that is reshaping its
  portfolio from diversity to specialization). This benefit is declining
  because there is consumer resistance to the acceptance of specialized
  substitutes for some naturally diverse resources. It is also declining
  because the by-products of conversion, that is human niche expansion
  and development, probably yield positive benefits (with consequent
  population growth, urbanization and industrialization) but at a declining rate as these characteristics become less scarce with additional
  conversions. In short the downward-sloping demand curve takes into
  account both the declining value of specialized resource flows and the
  increasing appropriated values of diverse resource flows.

- *global marginal cost of conversion* (MC) – one of the important marginal costs of the conversion of lands from diverse resources to

specialized is the opportunity cost of foregone diverse resource stocks. These costs are included in MC, but not in S, because these represent the full costs rather than the domestically appropriable costs of conversions.

Even accounting for the global values of biodiversity, a large part of diversity would be converted into specialized resources; however there would necessarily be a stopping point in this process as the value of diversity began to bite. Figure 3.1 indicates where the stopping point would occur in the unregulated global conversion process. This is the point where the marginal piece of land remains unconverted because the benefits of conversion are no greater than the actual benefits flowing from its retention in its natural state.

The divergence of the S and the MC curves in Figure 3.1 provides the explanation for the mistargeting of the global conversion process. In this scenario the supply curve for specialized lands is misperceived, because of the failure to internalise the full costliness of increasing the land area dedicated to specialized production. The global externalities flowing from reduced stocks of diversity are not being considered in the supply cost of marginal lands, and as these are increasing with each successive conversion (and especially when the final stocks are endangered), the supply curves deviate from one another more substantially with each conversion. The individual or state making the conversion decision considers only this costliness (within a 'decentralized' regulatory framework), and thus an excessive quantity of specialized lands (Q_d) results under a domestic decision making regime. It is possible, even probable, that Q_d would fall at the point of total conversion, in the absence of institutions that render some of these global values appropriable.

The global problem of biodiversity is the result of this decentralized approach to the global conversion process. Each state has converted its lands to specialized resource production without consideration of the stock-related costliness of these decisions. Early conversions were able to be undertaken at low global costliness (because S and MC did not diverge significantly when substantial quantities of other stocks remained). However, as the final stages of the conversion process are undertaken, this divergence becomes increasingly severe and ultimately unbounded. The global problem of biodiversity involves the creation of an international regulatory mechanism which will bring this divergence within the decision-making framework of the remaining, unconverted states.

7 The need for international environmental agreements
This chapter has demonstrated how the developmental process has generated several different facets of a global environmental problem: declining levels of

the resource, asymmetric holdings of the resource and asymmetric wealth in the nations involved. In the case of the resource we call biological diversity, the pursuit of development in the same manner in one state after another has resulted in a world increasingly devoid of biological diversity. There also appears to be a coincidence between those countries which developed first (and hence have least biological diversity) and those with highest levels of material wealth. These asymmetries contribute to the problem, because they contribute to the level of difficulty involved in solving it.

Most importantly it is clear that the continuation of the unregulated development process cannot by itself resolve this problem. This problem, and others, are in fact the result of the pursuit of development on a decentralized, state-by-state, basis. When this is the case there are certain resources which every state relies upon but which is unavailable in sufficient quantities to support the same sort of development in each and every country. Then the decentralized development process, when pursued to its logical conclusion, will result in far too much pressure on a few important resources.

This is the case in the context of biological diversity. If every country on earth completely converts its biological resources to the same small set of species, then there will be insufficient variety remaining on earth to support that level of development. It is also the case for the atmosphere. If each and every country pursues fossil fuel-based development to the same extent as those countries of the West, then the stress on the natural climatic and atmospheric systems will just be too great, and environmental conditions may change dramatically.

This means that the global development process, when pursued on a decentralized basis, sometimes provides adequate global resource stocks for the first countries to develop, but that these resources are then too heavily utilized to provide the same support for all later countries to develop to the same extent. In effect the first developing countries have had the benefit of free use of the global commons while there were sufficient resources available, but increasing pressure requires some sort of a rationing mechanism.

This is the reason that there is a need for international environmental agreements – they provide the mechanism for rationing global resources between states competing for their use in their development. This is also the reason that it is very difficult to agree on the shape of these new institutions – they will determine explicitly the shares of individual countries to necessary global resources and they will determine implicitly the shares of individual countries to global development and global product.

4 Relations between nations: the reasons that different states view the same problem so differently

1 Uneven development and disparate perspectives

One of the largest hurdles to the development of effective international environmental law is the range of perspectives on a given problem. Although the resources to be regulated are 'common' to all of the states concerned, each state views the resource uniquely. Then each comes to the negotiating table with its own well-defined perspective on the management of the resource (based in this individual viewpoint), and finds that every other state is similarly armed with a very different perspective. These differences drive much of the disagreement about the joint management of common resources.

Similarly the same problem emerges when joint management is based upon a uniform standard. That is, even if the parties are able to agree upon a regime of resource management, the proposal of a management regime based upon uniform treatment of the parties is unlikely to receive much support. This is because the parties each view their own contribution to the management regime differently – in accordance with their own views on what they should contribute and how much they previously were contributing to the management of the resource.

All of this results from the fact that resource management is a function of development status. Many studies have shown that investment in public goods rises with the level of accumulation of private goods, and in fact that individuals tend to demand relatively more public goods when their stock of private goods are already very high. This makes sense: there are many substitutes for consumer goods and services but very few for the services of the environment (air, water and aesthetics). Hence we see at national levels that countries with substantial quantities of basic consumer goods tend to increase their demands for environmental ones.

At international level this same phenomenon exists, albeit at a diminished rate on account of the fact that the provision of the public good is embedded within the IEA process. Nevertheless different countries (dependent upon their development status) will view their individual interest in the efficient management of a common resource differently. Individual countries will even invest in the management of a common resource differently, even when other countries sharing the same resource refuse to do so.

These differences between national perspectives are implicit within the fact of uneven development.

This chapter develops these differences more carefully. It does so initially in the specific context of the debate concerning the trade in toxic wastes. It queries: why would the developing world view toxic materials so differently from developed ones, that they would be willing to accept the garbage of the developed world? Then the second part of the chapter develops these questions much more generally, in a discussion of the relationship between development status and environmental management. The chapter concludes with a case study on the relationship between development status and the management of one global public good: the ozone layer that protects us all from harmful ultraviolet rays.

2   The trade and environment debate

The debate over the environmental effects of international trade is an instructive example of the profoundly different perspectives countries can have on the same environmental impact. The trade in toxic wastes is one example of this difference in perspectives. Why would one country value the environmental impacts of poisonous wastes so differently from another, that one would pay the costs of shipping it halfway across the world for its disposal? One possibility is that there is an information failure, that is the country accepting the wastes does not realize the full extent of the harm it might cause. This was the reason for the adoption of the principle of 'prior informed consent' (PIC) in the Basle Convention on International Trade in Hazardous Wastes. The 'Basle Convention' required that the exporting country fully inform the importing country on any health or environmental hazards posed by a waste shipment, as well as the disposal methods required by the exporting state. Then the importing state was allowed to make an informed decision on whether or not to allow the importation of that particular shipment, which required explicit issuance of a permit. This PIC procedure was developed in order to avoid the informational problems that might drive the waste trade.

Even despite the procedures within the Basle Convention, the outcry against the hazardous waste trade between developed and developing countries continued, and it was gradually prohibited. Initially, this prohibition took the form of an agreement of African states to disallow the importation of hazardous wastes (the 'Bamako accord'), then the European Union acted to disallow the exportation of hazardous wastes (based upon the 'proximity principle'), and finally the Basle Convention was amended to disallow the trade in the most hazardous wastes between developed and developing countries. So now, even after the creation of a procedure to address the informational problems in the trade, the trade in hazardous wastes between developing and developed countries has been banned.

This raises the questions concerning whether it should exist, or why it should not. Is there any rationale under which a developing country might view the impacts of hazardous waste shipment differently than would a developed country? Let us now consider the differences in development-driven perspectives that drive the trade in hazardous wastes.

2.1   The crux of the issue – differences between developing and developed countries

This infamous internal World Bank memorandum serves as a useful introduction to the differences between developed and developing countries, which systematically generate different perspectives on the same environmental problems:

> Just between you and me, shouldn't the World Bank be encouraging more migration of the dirty industries to the LDC's? I can think of three reasons:
>
> (1) A given amount of health-impairing pollution should be done in the country with the lowest cost, which will be the country with the lowest wages. ... I think the economic logic behind dumping a load of toxic waste in the lowest-wage country is impeccable and we should face up to that.
> (2) The costs of pollution are likely to be non-linear as the initial increments of pollution probably have very low cost. I've always thought that under-populated countries in Africa are vastly under-polluted.
> (3) The demand for a clean environment for aesthetic and health reasons is likely to have very high income-elasticity.... Clearly trade in goods that embody aesthetic pollution concerns could be welfare-enhancing. While production is mobile the consumption of pretty air is a non-tradeable. (World Bank Memorandum, 1992)

Giving this World Bank economist credit for logic, if not diplomacy, the thrust of the argument seems to be that the trade between developed and developing countries is driven by real differences between countries at different development levels:

- differences in economic structure
- differences in environmental structure
- differences in preference structures.

The memo seems to be arguing that: given that these differences are real, and that they are what is indeed driving the environment-consuming trade, then surely these trades must be welfare-enhancing? That is, all of international trade theory is based on the idea that real differences between traders create opportunities for gains from trade, and these differences appear to be as 'real' as any other. Why should not trade be geared to take these differences into account?

2.2   The environmentalists' response

The environmentalists respond by pointing out the pernicious nature of much of the environment-intensive trade. For example many point to the trade in toxic wastes as an example of the sorts of trade that derive from this reasoning. They do not see the obviousness of the point that dumping toxicity in low-wage states is a good thing. Implicitly environmentalists are arguing that there is a minimally safe environment to which all persons should be entitled, and that the regulations in some (northern) countries should not be enforced in a manner that shifts, rather than reduces, the toxic risks that these societies are generating. They see the role of environmental regulation as risk-reduction, not risk-shifting, and the toxic waste trade as an example of an industry exploiting a loophole.

Table 4.1   Major hazardous waste importing and exporting countries (1989)

Country	Production	Export	Import
USA	265 m.t.	45 t.t.	203 t.t
Belgium	915 t.t	914 t.t.	0 t.t.
FRG	5 m.t.	1695 t.t.	1.5 t.t.
Hungary	1 m.t.		15 t.t.
Guinea	0		15 t.t.
Nigeria	0		4 t.t.
Zimbabwe	0		6.9 t.t.

The trade in toxic wastes is a good illustration of the points from both sides of the debate (Table 4.1). The World Bank economists might argue that the flow of toxic materials from north to south is an indicator of the remaining relative endowments of environmental resources (for absorbing the incremental toxicity), or the economic values of the harms that might be caused (by marginally increased rates of illness, say). They would say the exports from the USA to, say, Nigeria is evidence of American preoccupation with health risks that would be considered minimal in a country with a much lower life expectancy. The environmentalists might argue that the force driving the trade is the intent to avoid the regulation of these industries within the northern countries (by shifting the wastes to the unregulated southern countries). Imports by countries such as Guinea and Nigeria from the developed world merely represent the exploitation of the loophole represented by a national boundary – the waste trade constitutes the dumping of garbage over the boundary line. Then bans on trade simply give effect to otherwise avoidable national laws.

Which side to this debate is correct? Is international trade in the context of material differences – economic, environmental, preferential – necessarily exploitative of the environment? Or is it simply another example of the gains attainable through trade between heterogeneous parties?

3 A review of trade theory (with environment as a factor)

In order to understand how countries' differences drive international trade, it is necessary to consider trade theory and the manner in which it bases trade on the differences between countries.

Consider a country with an open economy that has a choice of two goods to produce with its resource: Good A (an environment-intensive product) and Good B (a non-intensive user of the environment in its production). This means that the first good requires a substantial amount of environmental services to produce while the latter does not; consider for example the difference between the chemical industry and the software industry.

Now we get to the crux of the issue regarding the role of regulation in the location of environmentally unfriendly industries. The essential difference between environmental resources (E) and other resources such as capital and labour (K, L) is that the supply price of E is determined wholly by the government of that state (initially, we will assume a price of zero). That is, if the government does not regulate the resource, then it is freely available to all users, but any form of regulation (standards, taxes, bans) imposes an explicit or implicit 'shadow price' on the use of the resource.

Two types of product:

$$A = F\,(K,L,E)$$
$$B = F\,(K,L)$$

Figure 4.1 demonstrates the situation where this country has a comparative advantage in the production of the environment-intensive good, and hence it produces and exports this good to other countries in return for imports of the other good B. This comparative advantage is illustrated by the fact that the productive possibilities of this country are relatively biased towards the production of A, relative to its consumption preferences. This means that the 'world terms of trade' line in Figure 4.1 (the straight line in that figure) makes it possible to convert units of A into B at the rate indicated by the slope of that line. This country is able to move from its production frontier onto a social welfare contour that lies outside of its production possibilities, simply by converting its production of A into the other good at world terms of trade.

This is how comparative advantage works. A country that is endowed with resources or skills that make it relatively more able at producing a good will

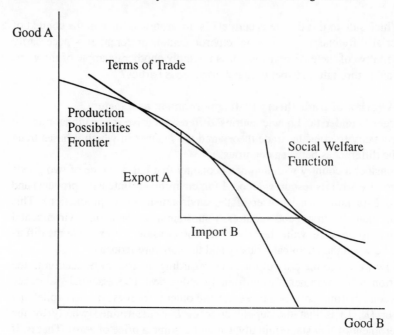

Figure 4.1   Production and trade

focus on its production, and then convert it to other more desirable goods by means of international trade. For this reason we would expect each country to focus on the areas of industry in which it is comparatively well-endowed, while trading to reach completely different points of consumption.

3.1   The impact of environmental regulation

We assumed initially that this country was well-endowed in environmental quality, and so it allowed free access to the resource. This low price of the environmental resource led to its comparative advantage in the production of the environmentally intensive good *A*. At the same time, however, the quality of the environment must be deteriorating on account of the failure to regulate access to the resource. What happens if this country decides to increase the supply price of the environmental resource away from zero?

In effect the country will be causing the production possibilities frontier to shift along the *A* (environment-intensive production) axis. This means that the country is no longer able to produce the same amount of *A* at prevailing international terms of trade. Figure 4.2 demonstrates that the primary impact of environmental regulation is to direct production toward the good that is less environment-intensive, while reducing the production of the environment-intensive good. Although the country continues to export *A*, it does now

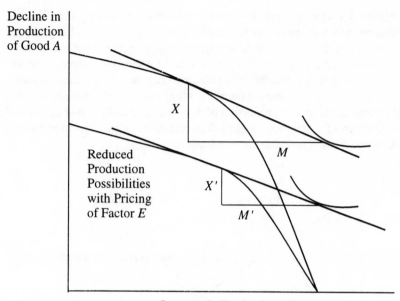

Figure 4.2   Impact of increased regulation of environment

in quantities of X' rather than X – a dramatic reduction on account of the increased restrictions on the use of the environment in the production of A.

Therefore the impact of introducing regulation of the environment is to alter the mix of production techniques that are used throughout the state's economy. Previously the low implicit 'price' (zero) charged for the use of the environment translated into a preponderance of industries that made use of those resources. The introduction of regulation means that the cost of using these resources is increased dramatically, and the entire industrial structure of the country is potentially altered.

3.1.1   How does this regulatory change impact upon other countries?   When a country unilaterally introduces restrictions on the use of its environmental resources, this will cause its production to shift towards less environmentally intensive products, such as good B above. This shift towards the production of B does not necessarily imply a corresponding relative increase in the consumption of B in this country. It is still able to trade with other countries in order to maintain its consumption of A at previous levels. If other countries maintain their regulatory regimes with regard to environmental resources at the pre-existing levels, then there may be a much smaller reduction in the amount of A consumed than there will be a shift in the producer of that quantity.

Figure 4.3 demonstrates the relative amounts supplied by the domestic producers and foreign producers, both before and after the change in the regulatory regime. It is assumed that the increased regulation of the environmental resource E does not affect the demand for the environment intensive good *A*, but that this regulation is reflected only in the increased domestic supply price of *A*. Because the domestic supply price of *A* increases with the regulation, the domestic production of *A* falls dramatically, while the overall consumption of *A* falls only slightly. The remainder of the consumption of *A* must come from other countries' production.

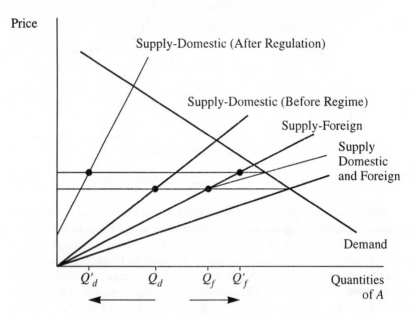

Figure 4.3   Change in supplier given environmental regulation

Therefore the unilateral introduction of environmental regulation is often seen to have the same impact as environmental trade: the shifting of the costs of certain methods of production from the domestic regime to another state. Examples cited of this manner of environmental shifting include:

- *toxic waste trade*: the USA has adopted regulations for the disposal of hazardous wastes that imply costliness in the region of $2000 per tonne of hazardous wastes disposed. Rather than incur these costs, many firms have shipped (legally and illegally) their wastes overseas. For example the government of Guinea Bissau entered into five-year contracts for the receipt of such wastes from the USA for a sum of

$600 million. The entire waste trade was estimated to be equal to 600 t.t. in 1989.

- *relocation of 'dirty production' by multinationals*: equivalently, many corporations are now engaging in multinational production, with the placement of particular stages of production in those jurisdictions which price its residuals at the lowest level. An example would be the Mexican maquiladora programme which existed prior to NAFTA and allowed US corporations to establish plants in border zones of Mexico and then import and re-export goods without duties or taxation. The result was the relocation of many but not all of the stages of the production in many US industries (such as electronics) (Johnstone, 1996).

3.1.2 What is the evidence for the existence of this phenomenon? Oddly, and despite the predictions inherent within the theory of international trade, numerous attempts to document the impact of environmental regulations on the US economy and in particular on its trade deficit have been unsuccessful. That is, there is little empirical evidence to support the supposition that US (unilateral) environmental regulation has had a pronounced impact on its trade position. An example from the literature is shown in Table 4.2.

Table 4.2   Estimated impact of pollution abatement expenditures on US trade (millions of 1977 US dollars)

	1973	1977	1982
Impact on:			
US Exports	–133.5	–258.8	–426.3
US Imports	–1247.9	–2133.5	–3978.9

Source: Robison (1988).

Why do these studies find so little relation between the US environmental regulation programme, and the deterioration of the US trade balance (when there have been so many tangible results such as the maquiladora programme and the toxic wastes trade)?

The two possible explanations are:

1. *spurious correlations* – the relocation of dirty industries and shipment of waste residuals may simply be parts of a more general process of enhanced global trading which have been occurring, in order to capitalize

on other generous factor endowments (for example labour) or on account of technological change in shipping and reduced transactions costliness

2. *poor accounting procedures* – most of these studies are undertaken by reference to the US statistics on pollution abatement expenditures, a self-administered survey by US business firms. It is very difficult to separate out abatement expenditures from expenditures for other purposes (for example, is an expenditure that enhances general factor productivity an abatement expenditure?) and it is difficult to vest too much credibility in these 'volunteered' statistics that are maintained for no reason other than to provide to the government.

Very likely the problems associated with (2) above obviate much of the meaningfulness of these studies. Nevertheless it must be noted that there is little solid econometric-based evidence to date that environmental regulations are having substantial impacts on the patterns of world trade. In order to find evidence of impacts, it is instead necessary to undertake the study of the environmental regulation's impact on a cast study basis.

3.1.3   If it does exist, is it something to be concerned about?   If there is trade that is induced by reason of differences in environmental regulation, is this a matter for social concern? This brings us full circle to the arguments of the World Bank economists and their environmentalist detractors. The World Bank economists would need to argue that the differences in environmental regulatory regimes are themselves derived from real differences between the countries, and hence reflective of the differential endowments between countries. Environmentalists need to argue that the differences generating this trade are endogenous (not fundamental), and that inequality is fundamental.

Real factor-based differences
Some examples of real differences between countries that may generate different approaches to natural resource scarcity are:

- *tastes* – different societies have very different aesthetic senses in regard to nature and natural resources, and so they may place very different values on those same resources
- *factor endowments* – different societies have very different factor endowments (human, physical capital, natural capital), and hence place different scarcity values on the flows from these various assets; and
- *income levels* – different societies have very different levels of income and hence differing capacities to command the goods and services that income provides, resulting in differing levels of consumer satisfaction from the marginal consumer good (*A* or *B*) relative to *E*.

In order to support the case for environment-neutral trade, economists would have to argue that the differences between environmental regulations observed across the globe derive exclusively from societal differences in real trade-inducing differences between countries. These differences between countries then generate differential views on the optimal social menu of production within that country. (Country *j* in Figure 4.4 has differential endowments that cause it to view the production of good *B* [the non-intensive good] more favourably than does country i.) So, despite the fact that the production process causes precisely the same harm in country *j* as in *i*, it is valued differently in each in accordance with each country's relative endowments of real factors (preferences, factors, incomes). This is precisely what the World Bank memo was arguing.

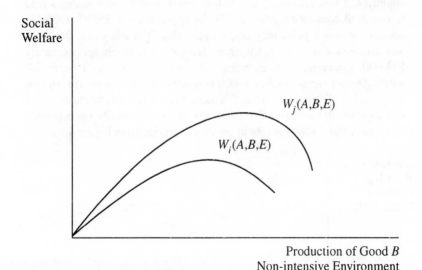

Figure 4.4   Differences between countries

3.2   Trade, minimum standards and the environment

The appropriate response from the environmentalist is probably along the lines that none of the items listed above is fundamental in the sense of a causative factor, other than income, and that the problem of vastly different income levels should not be addressed through the mechanisms of environment-based trade. How is it that income is the most fundamental of the above factors?

1.   *Tastes* – a strong income effect corresponding to environmental resource consumption has been well-documented, both within and across countries.

This means that preferences become more biased towards environmental resources as income increases. This has been demonstrated in various contexts: natural environments, existence of species, cleanliness of water and air. In a cross-section study involving eighty countries Lucas *et al.* (1992) found that there was an inverse-U relationship between GDP per capita and total toxic emissions relative to GDP, with the pollution-intensity of economies increasing until a certain point, beyond which emissions fall. This relationship is also borne out by time-series studies which indicate that the relative toxic intensity of economies in individual countries tends to rise over a portion of the development path before falling. Grossman and Krueger (1992) reach similar results in their analysis of concentrations of SO_2, dark matter and particulates relative to income levels in different countries. It was concluded that SO_2 and dark matter concentrations tend to rise until countries reached a GDP of approximately $5000 (1985 US dollars), at which point they began decreasing. The study also indicated that concentrations rise again once income levels reach approximately $14 000. Conversely concentrations of suspended particles tend to fall until GDP per capita reaches $9000 at which point they stabilize. Hence, across many different cultures, this same phenomenon is witnessed, and this supports the assertion that tastes are dependent heavily upon income levels in regard to environmental goods and services (see Figure 4.5).

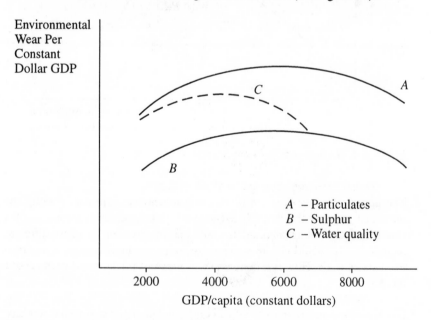

Figure 4.5   Income and environmental usage

2. *Factor endowments* – similarly there is little reason to believe that governments' lax approaches to environmental resources are representative of relative factor abundance rather than general capital scarcity. The same evidence cited above indicates that governments will allocate funds to the internalization of externalities when funds become available (holding factor endowments constant). Once again it is wealth that determines the capacity for internalization, rather than relative scarcities. Different property right structures exist in poorer countries on account of wealth differentials rather than resource endowments (Chichilnisky, 1994).

If the primary difference between countries that is driving the trade in environment-intensive goods is income levels, then it would seem that there would be some argument to be made for placing some sort of a 'floor' beneath the sorts of good and service that might be exported on account of this differential. Similar reasoning is used to rationalize the prohibition against the trade in children or internal organs. It does not seem to be all that remarkable to require that some minimum standards of civilization and decency to continue on across international boundaries (*Ecological Economics*, January 1994).

3.3   The state of play: WTO and Basle

The development of international minimum standards in fields of environment, labour and so on has been the subject of discussion in several fora, but the issue has come to rest at the door of the newly created World Trade Organization. This is because this forum is specifically devised to resolve disputes between nations on the issues' differences in domestic regulation. Thus far the position of this institution and its predecessor, the General Agreement on Tariffs and Trade (GATT), has been that domestic regulatory differences are matters for national determination. For example the Mexican Tuna decision by the GATT expressly prohibited the unilateral imposition of minimum standards by one nation as against another (there, by the USA against Mexico in regard to dolphin-friendly tuna fishing), calling instead for the development of such standards on a multilateral basis (Esty, 1994).

Therefore it is apparent that the development of minimum standards on a multilateral basis is a need that derives from uneven development. One of the primary roles of international environmental agreements must be seen to be to create this foundation of agreement on which international trade may continue.

Conclusion

This chapter has been intended as a demonstration of the fundamental reasons for the difficulties that are faced in international environmental negotiations. This chapter has shown that the way that different countries manage environmental resources is dependent upon their development level; that is, it is dependent upon the extent to which the people of that country are willing to trade-off environmental quality against further consumer goods. For this reason it is a sad fact that there can be no such thing as an objective basis for an environmental standard. Perceptions on acceptable environmental quality are too highly dependent upon the development status of the particular party – and development status is too unevenly distributed – for objectivity to play a determining role in this sphere. Acceptable environmental standards must remain a matter of national perspective until such time as all peoples on earth attain something approaching the same development status.

For these reasons the negotiation of international environmental agreements is concerned fundamentally with the issues of development, and ultimately with the questions of global distribution. Countries in the past have made use of global and international resources in the course of their development, and other countries wish to do so in the future. The only difference is that in the past there was little aggregate pressure upon these resources, while in the future there is the prospect of substantial overexploitation. Nevertheless, the poor countries of the present would view the exploitation of these resources as their development right, just as did the poor countries of the past (that are now the rich countries of the present). The currently rich countries however view this trade-off very differently – they would prefer to preserve the remaining global environmental resources at the expense of continued development. The problem underlying negotiations lies in this fundamental difference in perspectives on the same resources.

At the risk of oversimplifying these issues considerably, it is possible to view the set of global environmental systems (atmospheric, biospheric etc) as the one fundamental constraint on global development. In that case the set of international environmental agreements concerning these systems represent an attempt by the global community to manage these resources – by agreeing a distribution of these resources across all of the peoples of the earth. If these systems truly do represent a constraint on global development, then such an agreed distribution is absolutely essential and it is also representative of agreed shares of aggregate global production. It is no wonder that the negotiations over these resources are so problematic.

PART II

DEVELOPING INTERNATIONAL ENVIRONMENTAL LAW

Timothy Swanson

5 The foundations of international environmental law: recognition, negotiation and evolution

1 The elements of international environmental agreements

International environmental law consists of a set of agreements between sovereign states. These international environmental agreements (IEAs) are a necessary part of the modern world. They are a consequence of the division of the world into numerous autonomous political units. Since some effects of human activities extend beyond the boundaries of a single political unit ('transnational effects'), it is necessary to engage in forms of regulation that also span these boundaries. We cannot live in a world with hundreds of imaginary, political boundaries without consequential costliness; one of the costs of these boundaries is the need to manage the resources which span them.

The primary reason that such management is necessary is on account of the fact that environmental resources stubbornly refuse to confine themselves within these political boundaries. Resources such as the ozone layer and the gene pool impact upon us all in more or less the same way, irrespective of which country we inhabit; they are termed *global public goods* because they have the capacity to affect us all. It is not the case however that only resources with universal effects are the subjects of international environmental agreements. Resources are seldom respectors of the boundaries we have drawn, and this has significant implications for the doctrine of national sovereignty and the role of international environmental agreements. Rivers flow from one country into another. The atmosphere and water supply are usually continuous phenomenon, never halting at an international boundary line. The lines of geopolitics seldom confine the systems of nature.

This is not meant to imply that all domestic resource management is necessarily inefficient. The doctrine of national sovereignty implies, in part, that each country is responsible for the management of its own natural resources. This makes sense from an economic perspective. It is analogous to the role that private property rights play at local level. The theory of property rights tells us that the role of a property right is to place investment decisions with those individuals who are the best investors in that particular asset (Hart and Moore, 1990). An owner of a resource should be the person who understands the resource best, and understands how best to invest in its productive capacity. This implies, for instance, that it will often be better to devolve property rights to those individuals who are living with the resources concerned, and thus have the best information on how to use them (Swanson and Barbier, 1991). National sovereignty is the embodiment of the principle of the importance of locally determined investment decisions. Under this doctrine local resource management decisions are believed to be determined best by local decision makers.

The fundamental issue that remains is: how can national sovereignty be made compatible with international resources? This is the role of the international environmental agreement. The IEA allows domestic decision makers to coordinate their resource management decisions across national boundaries. This is an essential task given the existence of boundaries (that is national sovereignty) and transboundary effects (that is environmental resources). The IEA brings together the representatives of the various local regimes in order to negotiate methods for managing the impacts that necessarily flow across their boundaries.

Why are these problems gathering attention only now, when national boundaries have been in place for hundreds of years? The initial response to this question might be that international agreements concerning transboundary resource flows have been negotiated for more than 100 years. This book charts the history of the development of the international law concerning transboundary impacts, and much of this is indeed of recent vintage. However it is not only environmental resources that flow easily across national boundaries and international law initially developed around some of these other diffusive resources. This volume includes a discussion of the Paris Patent Union of 1886 which concerned the regulation of industrial information. Information flows are very difficult resources to manage on account of their capacity for diffusiveness; new inventions and ideas are readily observable and then replicated in other countries and manufactured without licence. Very early on national governments recognized the importance of coordinating efforts in the management of this elusive resource. Without some sort of international agreement on the subject it would have been impossible to have substantial investments in science, information and communication. To some extent the current form taken by the developed world has been dependent upon these early efforts to coordinate in order to enable investments in humans, science and information.

This should now be seen to be the role of IEAs as well. The creation of an effective IEA creates a potential future in that it establishes a possible development path. It makes possible a set of investment decisions and choices that would not be possible in its absence. That is, just as the Paris Patent Union made it possible to develop a part of the world built on investments in 'human capital' (science, ideas, information and communication), other international agreements should make it possible for other parts of the world to develop their own capital bases in manners optimal from a global perspective. Most importantly the emphasis of this concept is upon the role of an IEA in the encouragement of development, not as a constraint upon development. It should make possible development choices down certain paths, but not prohibit others. This book places IEAs within this context: the role of international agreements as regulators of global development and development pathways. It is essential, for globally optimal development, that the international externalities of development be internalized through a set of agreements between the states involved.

1.1 Why now? The need for IEAs

There are two further reasons why human activities increasingly are found to have transboundary effects: the expansion of human technologies and the extension of human knowledge. First, the increased scale of human technologies ensures that its effects are no longer primarily local. An example of this would be the effect of some agro-chemicals which persist within the hydrological system or the food chain so that they are ultimately found hundreds or even thousands of miles from their original point of application.

Second, the expansion of human knowledge concerning the natural world has allowed us to appreciate the nature of various systems that previously were not known to exist. We now appreciate the impact that even very localized activities (such as burning an ovenful of coal) have on regional (for example 'acid rain') and global (for example 'greenhouse effect') systems. Table 5.1 lists a few examples of the sorts of technology and system which

Table 5.1   Technologies and systems requiring IEAs for their efficient regulation

Technologies	Systems
	Regional:
Nuclear	Rivers
Chemical	Fisheries
Energy	Atmosphere
	Global:
	Ozone
	Carbon
	Biodiversity

generate the need for IEAs. These technologies share the characteristic of potentially significant off-site impacts; they are human activities with a significant potential for impacts across a wide expanse of territory.

In contrast, the systems cited are transnational by the mere fact of their existence. They are systems that do not stop at one nation's borders. Irrespective of the human technology utilized, these systems require international cooperation for successful regulation.

These technologies and systems require international cooperation in one important sense: even if the existing domestic regulatory regime is first-best from the viewpoint of the national interest, they may be suboptimal from an international perspective. Then it is possible for an international contract to correct for this suboptimality. This is the function of an IEA. Recent examples include the Montreal Protocol to regulate substances that deplete the ozone layer and the conventions on biodiversity and global warming adopted at the United Nations Conference on Environment and Development. Such contracts are an absolutely essential part of an efficient system for the regulation of the resources or technologies that they concern. Our increasing understanding of our expanding impacts gives rise to an increasing need for the coordination of our management of these resources across international boundaries.

1.2   Negotiating IEAs: the difficulty of solutions to international environmental problems

From the economic perspective there are at least three important elements to the development of an effective solution concept for the problem of transboundary resources. First, there is the need to estimate optimal aggregate resource use in the context of a given resource or system. That is what is the optimal amount of usage given the total number of users with access to the resource. Second, there is the need to allocate the optimal aggregate resource usage between the competing demands of individual states, and to reach agreement on these rates of usage. Third, there is the need for the development of a credible monitoring and enforcement mechanism regarding these agreed rates of use.

Given the nature of international law and of the developmental process, the accomplishment of these tasks becomes far more complicated than their mere statement would indicate. International environmental law is unique in that there does not already exist any form of external enforcement mechanism for any newly created law: the new regulation itself must contain the means of monitoring and enforcement. This means that the law must induce its own acceptance. Unlike domestic laws there is no in-built mechanism for subjugating the minority to the majority's will. The law must itself induce its acceptance and provide the mechanism for its enforcement. For this reason the perceived benefits and costliness of the provision – from each and every nation's individual perspective – is crucial to its activation.

Equally importantly there is little reason to expect that there will be any sort of symmetry between nation's perspectives on a given problem. This is because every nation differs from another in at least one aspect, that is its development status. Some nations are fully industrialized, with high incomes and high population densities. Others have some of these characteristics, but not others. The approach to and perspective on environmental problems, even global ones such as climate change and biodiversity decline, will vary hugely between countries depending on these sorts of characteristic. For this reason the obvious symmetric sort of solution to any environmental problem (that is equal tax rates, total bans and so on) does not work, because equality in terms of policy does not translate into equality in terms of impact. Different perspectives on a problem require different impacts to flow from a solution.

International environmental problems are difficult to resolve because of these two problems: the requirement of unanimity and the existence of asymmetry. The negotiator of an IEA must have a clear understanding of both the objectives appropriate to such agreements (see Table 5.2) and also the contexts within which such negotiations occur (the international law of the environment and the principles of development). It is a matter of the predictable asymmetry of various countries' perspectives on these problems resulting from their different standings within the development process.

Table 5.2   The elements of an IEA

---

1. Efficiency: ascertain optimal aggregate resource use
2. Distribution: allocate individual resource use
3. Implementation: create monitoring and enforcement mechanisms

---

1.3   The need for and negotiation of a biodiversity convention – an example
The movement for an international agreement for the regulation of biological diversity provides a good example. In this instance many thousands and millions of individual activities occurring in many dozens of states are contributing to the depletion of a resource that only exists at the global level. That is the concern emanates from a large number of individual 'local' activities: the filling of wetlands, the clearing of forests, the burning of pastures and so on. Each of these activities might be optimal from the local perspective, in the sense that the conversion of the land use probably generates greater benefits to the individuals actually undertaking the conversion. However, when each of these individual activities accumulates to the national, regional and global levels, large-scale land-use changes are implied which threaten to alter a

substantial portion of the prevailing biological system. Such large-scale change may have very significant impacts on the future capacity of human societies to produce agricultural and/or pharmaceutical goods and services. At the global level it makes sense to regulate these millions of individual activities that are often optimal from the local perspective.

Table 5.3 demonstrates the global impact of local activities when the resource is global. It sets forth the projections of prevailing extinction rates and ultimate species' losses from current human activities. These projections of 15–50 per cent of all species lost provided the impetus for the adoption of the biodiversity convention.

Table 5.3   Biodiversity case study: rates and projections of extinctions

Rate	Projection	Basis	Source
8%	33–50%	Forest Loss	Lovejoy
5%	50%	Forest Loss	Ehrlich
–	33%	Forest Loss	Simberloff
9%	25%	Forest Loss	Raven
5%	15%	Forest Loss	WRI

However, as Table 5.3 shows, the basis for each of these projections has been the rate of deforestation currently occurring throughout many of the tropical countries. In most of these countries these activities are being undertaken by many thousands of individuals, for the purpose of establishing pasture or agricultural lands, and for the most part these activities are occurring in order to better the prospects of the individual frontier dwellers. It is the regulation of the activities of these many thousands of individuals for the preservation of the global resource that lies at the core of the international contract concerning biological diversity.

Therefore the first point that must be emphasized in the economic analysis of international environmental agreements is the extent to which they regulate domestic activities. That is IEAs do not concern solely those national activities whose impacts fall wholly upon international resources; they are addressed fundamentally to the regulation of all national activities that have any impact upon global interests. They do so for legitimate reasons based in efficient resource usage; however they have unavoidably profound effects on sovereignty over domestic resources. The first objective of this module is to train the negotiator to appreciate the specific nature of an international environmental problem, and the precise extent to which intervention within domestic affairs is required in order to address it.

The second point that must be emphasized in the economic analysis of IEAs is the importance of bargaining in their resolution. It is important to realize that there is the prospect of both 'winners' and 'losers' in any contracting situation, and especially in one involving resources. The goal of an IEA is to realize a joint gain by more efficiently utilizing a common resource, and the *bargaining problem* is the economist's term for the problem of determining how to distribute this gain between the parties as a part of the process of agreement. Sometimes it can be very difficult, and costly, to ascertain the basis on which the costs and benefits of an IEA should be apportioned.

Again biodiversity provides a useful case study to illustrate this point. As mentioned above the biodiversity problem refers to the prospect for a mass extinction of 15–50 per cent of all existing species over the next century. Even if it is agreed that this is an event that the global society should attempt to avoid, the apportionment of the costs and benefits of such regulation remains a difficult issue.

If the costs of species preservation were left to fall to the individual states hosting them, the impact of the convention would be very asymmetric. A universal requirement to 'preserve species' may sound neutral in its statement; however its impact would vary widely between states. Those states with large numbers of species and habitats containing endangered species would bear most of the burden of such a contract, while those states with few species and habitats to protect would receive an equal proportion of the benefits of the agreement while bearing little of the costliness. It is estimated that only about a half-dozen of the world's states contain approximately half of the earth's species (the so-called mega-diversity states). Table 5.4 illustrates the unevenness in the distribution of species, by listing the top 10 states in terms of diversity for two different animal groups.

This non-uniformity in countries' initial positions makes the construction of fair and efficient IEAs problematic. It is important to recognize that non-uniformity is generally the case. Asymmetries between states arise for many reasons (such as location and climate), but one of the most fundamental differences between societies is their development status. A society's level of development has an impact on almost every facet of environment, economy and society within that country.

For example, note that all of the nations on the 'top 10' lists in Table 5.4 below are developing countries, with per capita incomes ranging from 1 to 5 per cent of the developed country average. This is because species diversity is closely linked to natural habitat conservation, and most developed countries converted most of their natural habitat long ago. For this reason there is a systematic correspondence between diversity retention and development status. It is often the case that development and the global environment

Table 5.4   The in-built asymmetry between species and material richness

Mammals		Birds	
Species	Country ($GNP p.c.)	Species	Country ($GNP p.c.)
515	Indonesia (570)	1721	Columbia (1260)
449	Mexico (2490)	1701	Peru (1160)
428	Brazil (2680)	1622	Brazil (2680)
409	Zaire (220)	1519	Indonesia (220)
394	China (370)	1447	Ecuador (980)
361	Peru (1160)	1275	Venezuela (2560)
359	Colombia (1260)	1250	Bolivia (630)
350	India (350)	1200	India (350)
311	Uganda (220)	1200	Malaysia (2320)
310	Tanzania (110)	1195	China (370)

are interrelated concepts, as in the case of biodiversity. This once again contributes to the complexity of negotiations for solutions to international environmental problems.

How can the problem of biodiversity's decline be resolved? There is a wide range of possible implementation mechanisms, each with its own distributional consequences. For example one possibility might be a tax on tropical timber sales, assessed by the major consumer states (USA, EU and Japan). Such a tax might reduce the rate of deforestation (or it might not) but it certainly would have important distributional impacts: the producer states (such as countries in Latin America, southeast Asia and central Africa) would have their revenues from this resource reduced while the consumer states would now receive a new flow of tax revenues from this source. An alternative might be to agree uniform proportions of land area that must be placed into reserve or protected area status. Such a proposal has the initial appeal of uniformity, but uniform restrictions have very different effects on countries depending upon their development status. For example over the past 30 years the proportion of land within the developing world that has been brought into agricultural use has been rapidly increasing while over the same period in the developed world, the area dedicated to agriculture is actually in decline. The processes of development are working in very different directions in different parts of the world, and these differences imply the need for non-uniformity in treatment.

The example of the biodiversity convention indicates the way in which the logically separate requirements of an IEA (efficiency, distribution and implementation) all come intertwined in one complicated bundle imbedded within a framework of environmental, developmental and institutional processes. It is not possible to discuss any one of these elements of a convention without ramifications for the others, and it is not sensible to discuss these requirements outside of their environmental, developmental or institutional context.

1.4 Negotiations after negotiations: the evolution of an IEA

International environmental law is as much a process as it is a method of problem solving. The process commences with meetings of country representatives for the discussion of draft text for the proposed convention. The initial text is often quite simple, even a page or two, and often drafted by an international organization (such as the United Nations Environment Programme or the International Union for the Conservation of Nature) in consultation with various country representatives. This initial text then serves as the focus for a series of meetings, usually conducted under the umbrella of some international organization. For example the United Nations Environment Programme served as the host for the meetings that led up to the United Nations Conference on Environment and Development in 1992. These meetings may occur periodically over a number of years, and at each meeting proposed changes and amendments generate discussions over both the objective of the IEA and its method of implementation. The overarching objective is to achieve agreement on a text that is then to be put forward for signature at a conference on the issue. Meetings occurred for several years with regard to draft texts for the Biodiversity Convention and the Framework Convention on Climate Change prior to the meeting in 1992 where the texts were put forward for signature.

The fact that the goal of these meetings is to achieve a substantial level of agreement on a single text often results in the dilution of the terms and obligations within the proposed treaty. The irony of the situation is that the solution of the problem requires agreement, but agreement seems to require that the problem go unsolved. As we have already discussed above the problems of efficiency, distribution and implementation are all intertwined in this context, and it is difficult to unravel the problem into its separate parts. Even though there are substantial incentives to reach agreement in order to solve the problem, the need to resolve simultaneously the problems of distribution and implementation often stymies real progress. Who should get what share of the common resource? Who should limit their uses or emissions? These sorts of issue make it very difficult to resolve with finality the solution to an international environmental problem – in such a manner as will attract substantial if not unanimous acceptance of the agreement.

For these reasons the conclusion of negotiations over an agreed text often results in an agreement to reach agreement through the mechanism of a series of future meetings or 'conferences of the parties': the outcome of the negotiations is simply an agreement to continue negotiations. These sorts of text are usually referred to as *framework conventions*. They are conventions that set out the nature of the problem and the willingness to solve it, but not a solution concept itself. Then the framework convention is made available for signature, and nations which sign and ratify the convention are *parties* to the ongoing negotiations over the solution concept for the global environmental problem.

It is often in the context of the regular meetings of the *conference of the parties* that real progress is made towards a solution. These conferences result in either agreed *resolutions* by the parties at the conference, or the agreement of new textual amendments to the convention known as *protocols*. These additional texts constitute mechanisms through which the parties continue to make steps toward the actual solution of the underlying environmental problems: they are the mechanisms for the evolution of a true international environmental agreement.

This process is itself full of pitfalls. Although the additional time allows for ongoing negotiations, it also generates its own set of perverse incentives. Since the process becomes one that takes place across time, it becomes possible for individual countries to benefit from the order in which acceptance occurs. The first countries to accept and implement a regime of restrictions on the use of a common resource simply free up more of the resource for those countries which have yet to do so. This is the problem of free riders, or hold-outs or rent-seekers. Within this framework of incentives the reaching of agreement becomes even more difficult because individual countries perceive the benefit from refusing to do so. The agreement to regulate a valuable resource becomes stymied through countries' jockeying for positions in the order of acceptance, rather than the pursuit of acceptance.

1.5   Summary: recognition, negotiation and evolution

In this first section of this book we have attempted to draw the biography of an international environmental agreement, tracing it out from the forces that drive its development through the stages of negotiation and then its final evolution within the context of ongoing conferences. As the reader can see, international environmental law is very much an ongoing process – an organic rather than a mechanistic one – and this process is as much a part of the substance of the area as is the text of the treaties themselves.

In the remainder of this volume we will attempt to draw a clearer picture of this process, in the context of a series of discussions of principles and case studies. The purpose is to describe and analyse this relatively unique field of human interaction and institution building, rather than a definitive statement of the laws in these areas. We present an introduction to the economics of international environmental agreements, and in the remainder of this part of the volume we provide case studies illustrating the concepts of need, negotiation and evolution. Finally there is a discussion of the actual legal structure that is resulting from this process.

2   The making of an international environmental agreement: efficiency, distribution and implementation

This section identifies the basic logical nature of an international environmental agreement. It consists of an agreement by at least two different countries to work together in the management of some particular system or resource, but it is also a mechanism which is capable of doing this. That is it must be both an undertaking to cooperate, and a means of doing so. International law must do both for it to be effective. This section sets forth the basic nature of each: the solution to environmental problems and the distribution of the benefits and burdens of doing so.

2.1   The problem of externality

Today the concern of most economists is much less focused upon the prevalence of *externalized costs or externalities* in production. An externality represents the failure of a producer to take into account the full social cost of its use of some factor or factors in production. An externality arises when the decisions of some economic agents (individuals, firms, governments) – whether in production, in consumption, or in exchange – affect other economic agents, and are not included in the priced system of commodities, that is they are not compensated. An alternative way of expressing this problem is to say that economic agents consider only their private marginal costs when making decisions; they do not consider the total, or social, (marginal) costs of their actions. For example a polluter might only consider its own cost of burning coal (the price of the coal), not the costs inflicted upon its neighbours (loss of visibility, acidic rainfall and difficult breathing conditions). The former are 'internalized costs' while the latter are 'externalities'. It is the gap between private and social marginal costs that gives rise to the problem of externality (see Figure 5.1).

Externalities result in market 'failure': a distortion in the market's allocation of resources. This market failure translates into resource degradation by reason of the excessive exploitation of the unpriced factor; that is, Q-private is greater that Q-social in Figure 5.1. For example, in the case of the burning of coal, the unpriced factors are the air supply, for which numerous users are competing. Some individuals wish to use the air for breathing and viewing, while others are using it for the disposal of their wastes. If there was a market for the use of air, then any given user would bid for its own air supply. When resources are held in common, however, all users may simply exploit the

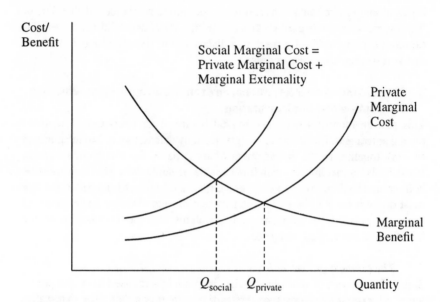

Figure 5.1   The neoclassical approach: externalities in production

resource without regard to their impacts on others. This is the concept of an externality, and it results in the overexploitation and degradation of the resource (individuals are using the resource more heavily than is socially desirable). More of the resource would be available over time if it were less heavily exploited in the present.

This means that it is in the interests of the whole of the affected society to correct for externalities. We term the persistence of externalities in the presence of societal expressions of willingness to resolve them as an 'environmental problem'. That is an environmental problem is a situation in which it is in the interest of the whole of the society to institute some solution that would limit aggregate use of the resource.

2.1.1   The contractual nature of externality   A valid question to ask at the outset of this discussion is: why do externalities persist? That is if externalities are truly 'costs to society', then why don't societies always act to eliminate them? The answer to this question is termed 'transactions costs'. In essence it can be as costly to eliminate an externality as it is to retain the externality (due to the various forms of transaction costs), and then the externality will persist. In the absence of such costliness, cooperation between members of a society can successfully eliminate all significant externalities (this is the so-called Coase theorem).

For example if two firms are situated on the same river, one using the water for the operation of its brewery and the other as a receptacle of its waste products, then an externality may exist. However it would be anticipated that (in many such cases) the two parties would be able to identify the nature of their interaction and to act jointly to coordinate their usage of the common resource (that is the river). For example the brewery might negotiate to use the river only when the other party is not (essentially partitioning 'implicit property rights' to the river between the two users). When the parties achieve such cooperation (*à la* the Coase theorem) the externality will be removed by reason of their joint action.

The discovery of persistent externalities therefore boils down to the search for situations in which the Coase theorem, as it is known, does not hold. In surprisingly many cases the theorem does hold (for example Cheung, 1973 showed that apple-orchard owners and bee-keepers incorporated the reciprocal externalities of nectar provision and pollination); in many others it does not. Baumol and Oates (1988) quote an example which illustrates both the benefits of and limitations of contracting for the removal of externalities:

> On the outskirts of Gothenburg in Sweden, an automobile plant is located next to an oil refinery. The automobile producer found that, when the refining of lower quality petroleum was under way and the wind was blowing in the direction of the automobile plant, there was a marked increase in corrosion of its metal inventory and the paint of recently produced vehicles. Negotiation between the two parties *did* take place. It was agreed to conduct the corrosive activities only when the wind was blowing in the other direction *toward the large number of nearby inhabitants who, naturally, took no part in negotiation* (emphasis in the original, p. 11).

Transaction costs arise from many sources. First, when many individuals are affected by the same externality, separate bargaining with each 'victim' would be prohibitively expensive; this costliness is reflected in the above quotation. The costliness of the externality was not removed in the process of the negotiations but only shifted towards those with no voice in the negotiations. It was their sheer numbers (and the transaction costs that they imply) that rendered this externality non-internalizable with regard to them.

Second, there is the possibility of free-riding. Suppose that a bargain between a single polluter (a factory producing smoke say) and many victims (for example householders), which involves the householders making a 'payment to the factory to reduce smoke emissions. Each individual householder has little incentive to join the collective bargain, however, but instead will hope that all other victims are sufficiently damaged by the smoke, and will therefore pay a little bit more to ensure that the bargain is made. The non-paying householder then gains the benefit of a smoke-free environment, without having to pay his share of the bargain. In the limit, no bargain at all will take place, as everybody attempts to be a free-rider; in intermediate cases, more than the efficient level of smoke production occurs.

Third, there is the problem of identification and representation. That is even if the parties wish to make an effort at cooperation, it may be costly or impossible to identify those parties to the interaction. This is often the case, for example, with respect to pollution of ambient media such as groundwater; it can be virtually impossible to trace the pollution back to its source. Finally, even if it is possible to identify the parties affected, it may still be impossible to bring them into the bargain.

Finally there is the pure costs of bargaining; the costliness of finding agreeable solutions to the 'bargaining problem'. That is, even if all parties agree on the aggregate amount of usage that occur with regard to a resource (Q-social in Figure 5.1), it is necessary to ascertain a formula by which this aggregate rate of usage may be allocated between a number of individual users. Since it will be profitable to argue for greater individual shares of the resulting product, such disagreements may defer the resolution of the under-lying environmental problem. An example would be the North East Atlantic Fisheries Commission, which has regulated stocks of herring in the North Sea over the past two decades. Each year the Commission ascertained a joint utilization rate that would maintain fish stocks, but individual members refused to undertake the harvest restrictions required to attain the optimal aggregate rate. The result was excessive utilization of the fishery, declining fish stocks and ultimately much reduced harvests. The costliness of this bargaining problem failure was experienced through the degraded resource.

Therefore from one perspective, environmental problems exist simply because the agreement to solve them has not been negotiated and implemented. This makes clear the reason why IEAs are so important for the resolution of environmental problems; to a large extent, the problems only exist because the IEAs have yet to be adopted and executed. Whenever an environmental system flows beyond the boundaries of a single state, there will be the need for an IEA to internalize the external effects of the various users of this 'common resource'; otherwise an environmental problem will necessarily exist. The role of an IEA is to fill this regulatory hole that exists by reason of the existence of environmental systems that do not fit neatly within a single state's boundaries.

2.2 Optimal policy for externalities

If the problem is one of transboundary externalities, then the solution is to internalize this externality within the decision-making framework of the polluter. The problem is that it is sometimes very costly to internalize externalities effectively. This section briefly restates the basic principles of optimal environmental policy making, but its emphasis is on the economic analysis of the international contracting necessary for the implementation of optimal environmental policies.

In the international context contracting is particularly difficult, because there is no general contract monitoring or enforcement mechanism in place. This means that the contract must be constructed to be self-enforcing. In addition, on account of the doctrine of national sovereignty, international agreements must also be voluntary; that is, they must induce the cooperation that they require. These characteristics make efficient international environmental policy very difficult to achieve.

It is very easy to state the general objective of optimal environmental policy: the internalization of all external costliness. In terms of Figure 5.1 this implies the establishment of aggregate usage level Q-social in the face of incentives to exploit the resource to the level Q-private. The private incentive to pollute (or overexploit) derives from the 'externalized cost' (represented by the vertical gap in Figure 5.1) between the 'social marginal cost' and the 'private marginal cost' of some activity. The internalization of this externality requires that each decision maker be presented with the additional cost represented by the distance between the two curves that exists at the quantity Q-social. When the decision maker is faced with this additional bill in its decision-making process, it will then select the socially optimal level of resource exploitation (rather than the private level).

Therefore, in the abstract, there is little that is complicated in the resolution of environmental problems. It is in the contracting process that difficulties arise. The previous section analysed the nature of the problems that arise in the domestic context (general transactions costs), and the remainder of the sections have made note of their implications for international contracting. In this section a detailed analysis of the problems of international contracting is undertaken.

2.3 International environmental problems: externalities across frontiers

Environmental degradation has no respect for man-made borders. In many cases an environmental problem will not confine itself conveniently to one area, but overlaps areas of jurisdiction and control. In the absence of one single authority to control and prescribe the solution to the problem, international externalities will be plagued by lack of coordination and concomitant inefficiency.

International externalities can take many forms. For example a pollutant may move across a border carried by rivers, sea currents or winds. A pollutant (for example waste materials) are often transported by humans across national frontiers, with the danger of accidental spillage. Alternatively pollution or environmental degradation in one country may simply be of concern to other countries. For example Brazilian deforestation causes concern in the

West for the preservation of tropical forests (for cultural and aesthetic reasons than the effects of the global climate). In the first instance it is fundamentally important to identify the existence and nature of the externality for which regulation is being sought.

Solutions to transfrontier problems must, in general, come from voluntary agreements (multilateral contracts). The problem is, as we shall see, that the 'game' structure for bargaining is the 'Prisoners' Dilemma'. The pursuit of self-interest is a strictly dominating strategy in the simplest game situations of this form. This means that even when there is a joint gain to be achieved from cooperation, the first-best result (from the perspective of each nation) is to pursue non-cooperative behaviour while the other countries pursue the cooperative form of action. The reasoning is straightforward; the other countries' cooperative behaviour releases more of the resource for the countries who do not cooperate. Although this conclusion changes as features of the game are flexed (for example if the countries interact in many different areas of activity and over a long period of time), it remains an underlying weakness of bargaining.

Multilateral contracts are even more likely to be jeopardized by the problems of free-riding and hold-outs. In particular the nature of the international contracting process exacerbates these problems. Countries are allowed to join an international environmental agreement in a sequential fashion, and this creates incentives to manoeuvre for a place far back in the queue. Countries who join an IEA early on implicitly transfer additional resource rents to those who join later. This is one way in which different countries are able to achieve different levels of benefits from the same IEA, but it is also a system of incentives which delay effective resource management. All of these problems will be discussed in more detail in the next chapters.

3   The distributional impact of international environmental agreements

From the perspective of a domestic environmental problem, there may be little difference between alternative approaches to the implementation of a solution to an environmental problem when each approach is constructed efficiently. However, when the society of concern is a global one, the distributive impact of different instruments is of prime importance. This is because, unlike a domestic regime, there is little provision within the international system for international income transfers. Therefore an environmental regulation regime must not only resolve a problem efficiently, but it must coincidentally distribute the gains achieved in a fashion that induces compliance with the law. Therefore distributional impacts are of concern both for enforcement and equity purposes. This section analyses how different institutional approaches (instruments) for resolving environmental problems will imply different distributions of benefits and burdens.

3.1   Hold-outs and distributional implications

As was indicated in the section above, one of the primary approaches to achieving a preferred distribution of resource rents is via refusal to cooperate in the management of the resource. Under international environmental law there are many options available to states which allow them to defer their acceptance of the strictures of a fully effective resource management regime. States may simply avoid signing the IEA (non-accession). They may sign but still except themselves from the operation of certain terms of the convention (reservations). They may sign and agree to the full force of the convention, but still render it ineffective against themselves on account of their refusal to enforce it within their jurisdiction (non-implementation).

If these forms of non-cooperative behaviour are pursued while other states are pursuing cooperative forms of behaviour (that is implementing effective restrictions on the use of the resource), then the non-cooperative state is able to transfer some or all of the value foregone by the others towards itself. This is the primary form that rent-seeking takes within this context, and it is a substantial barrier to the creation of effective international environmental law. Much of the substance of Chapters 3 and 4 addresses the problems of bargaining and hold-outs in IEAs.

3.2   Alternative instruments and alternative distributions

Another way in which member states to an IEA might influence the distribution of the rents created by effective resource management is through the choice of the instruments used in the management regime. International environmental law currently operates through the agencies of the member states. IEAs do not operate via the creation of an effective secretariat or international agency with full powers for internal monitoring and implementation; instead they operate through the administrations of the member states within each of their jurisdictions. This means that the instrument used to regulate the environmental problem must be one that is applied by the member states, and the choice of instrument determines the identities of those member states that implement the regime. This choice will often influence the distribution of rents under the resource management regime.

A good example is the problem of 'global warming'. This concerns the emission of carbon dioxide and other greenhouse gases and their affect on the global weather systems. It has now been agreed under the terms of the climate change convention that certain levels of greenhouse gas abatement will be implemented over the next five to ten years. The issue that remains is how these levels of abatement will be achieved. Under the theory developed within this chapter, the problem is one of excessive use of the atmosphere for carbon-related wastes, without consideration for the external impact that these wastes will have on the global climate system. Therefore the optimal policy is to cause emitters, to reduce aggregate emissions from Q-private (the unregulated level of carbon emissions) to Q-social (the level that will result from optimally regulating the externality).

Once it is agreed what this level abatement might be (tentatively believed to be 20 per cent below 1988 levels by some states), the issue then is the means for implementation. A tax on all carbon emissions or an allocation of emission permits can achieve the same effect. A tax would be calibrated after the estimation of the demand elasticity of carbon emissions, which would give a prediction as to how emissions would respond to taxes. If more certainty was desired, then an aggregate quota could be agreed with emissions permits distributed to the various states (according to some agreed formula). In general the two approaches are equivalent.

The distributional implications of a carbon tax are made clear in Table 5.5. Here the implications of different forms of taxes are demonstrated for different groups of countries. Although the 'worldwide' impact of the tax remains relatively constant, the impacts on different groups of states varies remarkably.

Table 5.5   Distributional implications of alternative carbon taxes

	High Income	Low Income	Oil Exporting	Worldwide
	(In Billions of $US and % GDP)			
National Production Tax	−180 (−1.7)	−151 (−4.8)	+47 (10.8)	−284 (−2.0)
National Consumption Tax	−67 (−0.6)	−121 (−3.8)	−108 (−24.9)	−269 (−2.1)
Globally Administered Tax	−253 (−2.4)	+94 (3.0)	−123 (−28.2)	−282 (−2.0)

Source: Barrett (1990).

Table 5.5 demonstrates that a national production tax (collected by the producers of carbon products such as petroleum) will benefit primarily the oil exporting states, while inflicting most of the costs of the regime on oil consumers. Conversely a consumption tax would place most of the costliness of carbon reductions on the producers (and the low-income countries). A global system that remedies the negative impact on low-income countries still places a substantial load of global costliness on the oil producers. Therefore although a carbon tax based on raising prices equivalent to 2 per cent of worldwide GDP may have the correct environmental impact, the method by which it is implemented will demonstrate the costs and benefits of this policy very differently.

This is an illustration of the general concept of 'tax incidence', that is the respective burdens borne by various individuals in the provision of a public good. This concept has been discussed intensively in the context of global public goods (that is the regulation of global resources) under the name of 'incremental costliness'. This represents the differential impact that regulatory regimes may have on different states, by reason of differing starting positions. In the case of global warming, different states respond differently to the regulation of carbon emissions by reason of their initial endowments of fossil fuels and carbon-emitting industries.

It is absolutely essential to recognize that the provision of global public goods (such as climate, biodiversity, clean seas and so on) does not imply symmetric burdens and benefits. Each state must assess the burdens and benefits from a particular agreement from its own perspective prior to entering into agreement. Since general international wealth transfer mechanisms do not exist to remedy asymmetries that are generated by efficient management regimes, it is then necessary to negotiate for these transfers within the context of the international environmental agreement. This includes the recognition that different forms of implementation (instruments) have asymmetric impacts, just as different forms of obligations do.

3.3 Standards, bans and trade conditionality

At the domestic level one of the most commonly used instruments for environmental regulation is the adoption of 'quality standards'. These are usually minimum standards that a product or process must satisfy in order to be licensed by the regulator. It is usually part of the command and control process.

There have been attempts to extend domestically enacted standards beyond the borders of the regulating state. A topical example is the US dispute with Mexico over its use of drift-nets in tuna fishing, which were banned for use by the US fishing fleet by reason of their impact on marine mammals. The USA then banned imports of Mexican tuna products for their failure to meet US environmental standards.

This case illustrates two important trends in current international environmental regulation. First, there have been some recent attempts to extend the 'standard'-based approach to the international context. Secondly, there has been a long-evolving trend towards the use of trade sanctions for the implementation of environmental standards.

The GATT panel deemed that the US actions were in violation of that treaty, because they constituted attempts to extend US regulation to processes used by parties outside US jurisdiction. The GATT panel supported the use of standards if they were developed on a multilateral basis. This decision supports the general trend toward the harmonization of environmental standards within international fora, and the development of international agreements to regulate international resources.

This is one reason why the negotiation of international environmental agreements is something that will remain on the national agenda for most states. The globalization of the economy and the increasing importance of international trade will require the harmonization of necessary social and environmental regulation. However it remains important to emphasize that harmonization does not imply uniformity. Harmonization implies only that different states coordinate their policies so as to address the externalities that arise in their interaction. For the reasons indicated throughout this document, the efficient and equitable regulation of international environmental problems will not often imply the adoption of uniform regulatory policies (because of the asymmetries in the positions of individual countries).

The second point that this GATT panel decision raises is the use of trade sanctions as an international enforcement mechanism. Trade sanctions have long been part of the US bargaining strategy in regard to environmental resources, initially with regard to marine mammals. This approach was extended to the international context under certain trade treaties, principally the Convention on International Trade in Endangered Species (CITES). This treaty has promulgated certain standards that must be met in the processing of certain species before they may enter into international trade. If these standards are not met, then the member states may not trade with them in these species.

Some commentators have raised the issue whether trade sanctions are themselves inefficient, or in violation of GATT. It is imperative to emphasize that trade responses are an essential part of the enforcement of international agreements. In the absence of a credible international enforcement mechanism, it is only the ongoing relationship between two states that provides the method for enforcement of agreements between them. So long as the standards are agreed between states (rather than foisted by one upon the other in an act of extraterritoriality), then the use of conditionality in trade is an essential part of the existing international enforcement mechanism.

4   Conclusion – economics and international agreements

The purpose of this part of the book has been to demonstrate the precise extent to which intervention is required in order to regulate international externalities and international resources. It should now be clear that there are certain circumstances in which it is absolutely necessary to engage in international environmental agreements. This will be increasingly the case in the future, with the internationalization of the economy and the consequential need to harmonize environmental regulations.

Despite the need for these agreements there are no prevailing incentives for their adoption. In point of fact all of the incentives will be for individual states to attempt to hold out in order to capture more of the gains from the agreement. Although it would benefit the whole of global society to make these agreements and to make them effective, this will not happen in most cases simply because they are so difficult to negotiate and to enforce.

Does this mean that all states should be encouraged to adopt globally uniform environmental legislation in an attempt to overcome these bargaining obstacles? This is emphatically not the case. The distribution of the gains from cooperation is equally important as the acquisition of those gains, and it is essential that each state assesses its starting position and negotiates from it. Each state is different in terms of the benefits and burdens that each regulatory regime implies for its citizenry. In addition there is no objectively observable form of exploitation that constitutes 'environmental degradation' under all circumstances; this also depends upon the initial position of the state in terms of financial and environmental resources.

Therefore, in negotiating an international environmental agreement, each state must make certain that it understands the nature of the international interest at stake (that is look for the 'externality' with respect to some 'common resource') and it must then assess its 'initial position' in regard to this international interest. Then it can enter into negotiations in order to protect its own position and to protect the international environment simultaneously.

6 Economics of international environmental agreements: an introduction

1 Common resource management: cooperative versus non-cooperative behaviour

The fundamental objective of international environmental agreements is to move from non-cooperative behaviour to cooperative behaviour in regard to the use of a common resource. The problem lies in the fact that the world has been divided up into a large number of independent governance units – the various sovereign states. The use of states makes sense as the governance units for the resources within their jurisdictions. Each state has the incentive to develop and to implement resource management regime with regard to the resources within their boundaries and which advance the interests of their peoples. In fact the division of the earth's societies into the various states for the purpose of resource management makes as much sense as the delegation of authority over resources to 'property holders' within each of these states. In both instances the rights holder has the incentive to invest in the creation of local management regimes that are effective and efficient.

The problem lies of course in the fact that, no matter where the lines are drawn between these various states, there will be some resources that lie between them. These 'common resources' are the sources of the external effects – or externalities – that render independent decision making inefficient. When a substantial amount of the effects from resource use flow outside of the boundaries of the governance unit, then a resource management regime that fails to take these into account is necessarily suboptimal. This form of independent decision making in a world with significant interdependencies is what is termed *non-cooperative behaviour*.

The objective of international environmental agreements (IEAs) is to develop mechanisms for joint decision making in regard to these common resources. It is to move from the inefficient outcomes which result from non-cooperative behaviour towards the more efficient outcomes that result from joint decision taking in regard to these resources.

The special problems of IEAs lie in the additional fact that the solution to this problem depends upon the development of management regimes across states, in a world that is accustomed to institution-building only within them. IEAs are some of the first attempts at developing not only the efficient management regimes for these resources but also the initial templates for concrete and effective international governance. It is the complexity and necessity of solving both problems at once that makes the field so interesting, and difficult.

However, at the base, the fundamental problem is always the same: the movement from resource management outcomes resulting from non-cooperative behaviour to those based on cooperation. The next layer of the problem is the development of the contracting procedure that will allow these movements to occur expeditiously and efficiently.

In this section, we shall demonstrate the economic concepts involved in the analysis of contracting to move towards cooperation. We shall concentrate on one case study to demonstrate the difficulties that arise: acid rain, an example of a regional reciprocal externality.

1.1 A case study in international contracting: acid rain

Sulphur and nitrogen oxides are emitted when fossil fuels are burned, and in some industrial processes. The oxides are oxidized in the atmosphere and from there are carried long distances. They may be absorbed in the dry state by surface water, land or crops (dry deposition), or washed out of the atmosphere by rainfall (wet deposition). Both forms of deposition are acidic, and both are referred to as 'acid rain'.

The nature and extent of damage caused by acid rain is still a subject of some debate. There seem to be three effects. First, acidic deposition reduces the pH of lakes and rivers, with effects on aquatic life. Second, these depositions cause direct damage to leaf surfaces of crops and trees. Third, the increased acidity of rainfall causes greater solubility of soil ions; consequently, forest soil is both stripped of nutrients, and left with toxic ions – aluminium in particular – which, through run-off, can affect rivers, lakes, and eventually human drinking water.

Both North America and Europe are afflicted with the problem of acid rain. In the former, acid compounds located in the atmosphere of the northeastern United States and eastern Canada have (it is claimed) increased because of emissions in central and southern United States. In the latter, emissions in the central belt and east of Europe have caused soils to acidify in Scandinavia in particular. In both cases, forest damage may be a result, although the evidence is, as yet, inconclusive.

Acidification of soil and rivers in both continents is, less controversially, a result of acid rain depositions – although the damage that this causes is not clear (we mention the effects above; but the extent to which this acidification causes economic and/or environmental damage is still unclear). Three conclusions can be reached, however: acid rain is undesirable; acid rain is no respecter of international boundaries; therefore international agreement is necessary to combat the problem of acid rain.

Let us concentrate on the problem of acid rain in Europe. First, consider the case where two countries both emit sulphur and nitrogen oxides in equal amounts, and both impose an acid rain externality on each other to the same extent. The set-up of this problem is familiar – it is, once again, the Prisoners' Dilemma. The 'payoffs' to the game are shown in Table 6.1, in the usual game matrix in which the pay-off to Player A is the first of each pair and the pay-off to Player B is the second. The pay-off matrix demonstrates how the pay-off to each of the countries is dependent upon the interaction between each country's choice of strategies (either reduce or maintain emissions).

Table 6.1   The Prisoner's Dilemma in the context of acid rain

		Country B	
		Reduce Emissions	Maintain Emissions
Country A	Reduce Emissions	0,0	–10,5
	Maintain Emissions	5,–10	–5,–5

The reasoning behind the pay-offs is as follows. If both countries maintain emissions at the current level (the status quo), then both suffer from the acid rain externality, and their pay-offs are correspondingly low ((–5,–5) in the game matrix); this represents the 'social loss' from the lack of environmental management. If both reduce emissions, then both are made better off (by the same extent), since the externalities are removed, and their pay-offs become (0,0). If however, one country reneges on the bargain, and maintains emissions while the other reduces, then the reneging country does even better – it keeps the private benefits of the status quo (for example, higher levels of industrial production, or lower expenditure on emission-abating technology), while not incurring the cost of the externality imposed by the other country. The exact converse is true for the 'honest' country – it both loses its private benefit, and bears the externality cost. The pay-offs are therefore (5,–10) respectively.

This is the standard Prisoners' Dilemma story. In the language of game theory, {reduce emissions, reduce emissions}, with a pay-off of (0,0), is the Pareto (socially) efficient outcome. However {maintain emissions} is a strictly dominating strategy for both players; and so, {maintain emissions, maintain emissions}, with its pay-off (–5,–5) is the (Nash) equilibrium of the game. This means that the incentives (in the absence of some enforcement mechanism) are for the continued existence of the environmental problem.

Are there no solutions to this problem? How are agreements ever reached (for we do indeed see agreements made)? No sophisticated argument is needed to see that in the international context a solution is difficult to achieve. This is because there is no pre-existing institution to dictate the efficient solution, and provide for a distribution of its benefits. In order to achieve the efficient solution, the two countries must solve two problems at once: the resource management one and the creation of the institution that will do so.

In the absence of a management institution, we are left in the world of contract between the two parties in the above matrix (Table 6.1). The two countries could enter into a contract that dictates the efficient solution of the problem (reduce, reduce) and provides for the distribution of its benefits; however, in the international context we are still left without an underlying institution for the enforcement of that contract. If one party reneges after contracting, there is no international police force that is able to enforce compliance. Any agreement must therefore be voluntary; but the incentives within the Prisoners' Dilemma context indicate that voluntary agreements will always be broken. Hence, we are left in the same situation: the parties must create both a solution and a management institution to implement it.

One solution to this problem is to think of the field of international relations as providing the framework within which commitments will be made and enforced. For example, assume that the above game will be played many times – in fact, an infinite number of times. To see why a finite horizon does not solve the problem, consider what happens when both countries know that it is the last time that the game will be played. Both will have the incentive to renege on any agreement, and the outcome is the Nash equilibrium (–5,–5). Following the argument backwards, in the penultimate period, both will know that both will renege in the next (last) period, so both will renege in the penultimate period. By this backward induction argument, we can see that the finite game 'unravels', and the Prisoners' Dilemma maintains its grip. In an infinitely repeated game, however, there is no last period, and so the game cannot unravel. In short, this means that the Prisoners' Dilemma loses some of its grip when the players (countries) realize that they must continue to deal with one another throughout the indefinite future.

What is the nature of the relationship that will make the Prisoners' Dilemma soluble? Obviously people are mortal, so 'infinity' does not mean 'infinitely-lived'. Instead it means that the players are uncertain about the actual duration of play; they have an ongoing relationship with no fixed date for termination. One way in which to introduce this uncertainty within the above 'game' is for the players to discount the future; this captures the fact that the countries (in our example) know that the 'game' cannot go on forever, but that neither knows for certain when it will stop. It is then possible to show that the cooperative (socially efficient) outcome may be achieved (provided the discount rate is not too high).

The single-play conclusion is contradicted, therefore, and on the basis of this simple, symmetric example, we would expect voluntary agreements for the solution of environmental problems to be attainable. Yet this extreme seems as unrealistic as the first conclusion of perpetual reneging – the middle ground of reality falls somewhere in-between. What we recognize as ongoing diplomatic relations between states are the relationships that actually exist in order to address joint concerns, such as international environmental problems.

At this point, we relax the assumption of symmetry – what happens when the players are different? Alternatively, what is the effect of non-symmetric pay-offs in the game matrix of Table 6.1? This injection of reality makes the problem much more difficult.

Evidently pay-offs can be constructed so that the conclusions of the game are unchanged, that is in the single-play case, reneging is the dominant strategy. The question is, however, how does one player *know* that the conclusions are unchanged – how does the country know the values attached by the other to continued and reduced emissions? Bargaining in the presence of this information asymmetry (each country knows the value it attaches to reduced acid rain, and the cost of abatement, but these values are unknown to the other) is considerably more complicated. Again countries may be able to learn over time approximate costs and benefits to other countries. Often, however, asymmetric information will destroy the ability to bargain – in the extreme one country may think that the other country has no desire to bargain at all (that is it is acting only in pursuit of 'free-riding rents') and that there is no mutually beneficial set of actions to agree upon. The further examination of the acid rain case study makes clear the difficulties that arise in the context of asymmetric and uncertain bargaining positions.

1.2   The Prisoners' Dilemma and European acid rain

Now consider the possibility of asymmetry when *many* countries participate in the game. This is the case for European acid rain – sulphur and nitrogen oxides are produced in varying amounts by all countries. Some countries, however, are more 'downwind' than others. For example the UK is very much 'upwind' in Europe, and therefore receives little acid rain; Sweden, on the other hand, is 'downwind', and suffers from a large amount of acid rain. Abstracting from informational problems, so that all countries know the costs and benefits to each of reductions in acid rain, will a cooperative outcome (voluntary agreement to reduce sulphur emissions) ever be reached? Maler (1991) calculates the net benefits to individual European countries from the full cooperative solution as in Table 6.2.

Table 6.2   The full cooperative solution to the acid rain problem in Europe

Country	Percentage Reduction in Sulphur Dioxide	Net Benefits (Millions of Deutschmarks)
Bulgaria	43	–7
Czechoslovakia	75	152
Finland	14	–2
France	10	879
German Democratic Republic	80	11
Germany, Federal Republic of	86	328
Italy	33	–83
The Netherlands	62	565
Poland	27	599
Soviet Union	2	1505
Spain	14	–29
Sweden	4	606
United Kingdom	81	–336
All Europe	39	6290

The full cooperative solution would require a Europe-wide reduction in sulphur emissions of around 40 per cent, but notice that the load is spread very unevenly among the countries, as are the benefits. The UK in particular, since it receives little acid rain from other countries, but donates much to others, would be required to cut emissions by over 80 per cent at a net (dis)benefit of DM –336m. It seems unlikely, therefore, that (all other things being equal) the UK would participate in this voluntary agreement.

In fact five countries – Bulgaria, Spain, Italy, Finland and the UK – have strict incentives to *free-ride*, that is enjoy the benefits of the cooperative reduction in emissions by other countries, while continuing to produce sulphur oxides themselves (see Table 6.3).

This conclusion is a little stronger than the earlier Prisoners' Dilemma result – there cooperation was desirable for both players, but not voluntarily sustainable (in the short term); here, for some countries at least, not even cooperation is beneficial. The solution, although simple in words, is difficult in practice. There must be *transfers* from those who benefit to those who lose under the cooperative outcome. For the UK this transfer must be somewhere in excess of DM300m. In the jargon the full cooperative outcome must be a potential Pareto efficient equilibrium – another way of saying that the gains to the 'winners' must exceed the loss to the 'losers', so that the former can

Table 6.3   The incentives to non-cooperation in the acid rain context

Country	Emission reduction (%)	Net Benefit (Millions of Deutschmarks)
Cooperating Countries		
Czechoslovakia	75	125
German Democratic Republic	80	−47
Germany, Federal Republic of	86	78
Poland	27	544
Soviet Union		1372
Sweden	3	478
Total for cooperators	37	4933
Defecting Countries (Non-participants in Solution)		
Italy		150
United Kingdom		87
Total		247
Total for Europe	28	5180

Source: Maler in Helm (1991).

compensate the latter and still be better off than under the non-cooperative outcome. Exactly how this transfer is arranged is another matter. Indeed whether this transfer is morally acceptable may be a problem – in this case it is to advocate that the *victim* pays (rather than the morally more palatable measure of polluter-pays).

Transfers may solve the problem of the attractiveness of cooperation to all parties; how is free-riding to be overcome? As before one may argue that extending the time horizon to infinity (or, equivalently, introducing uncertainty as to duration), or allowing for reputation-building (for whatever motive) may allow the cooperative outcome to be achieved. As before the caveat that this is not the only attainable outcome, and that not all of these are in any way efficient, must be applied.

Two difficulties remain, however. We have distinguished (implicitly) above between free-riding for opportunistic reasons (when players have symmetric pay-offs, reneging is the dominant strategy), and free-riding due to heterogeneity (for example cooperation is clearly undesirable for the UK in the acid rain game). We have claimed that the answer to the former is to extend the time horizon, and to the latter, transfers and side-payments. Opportunistic free-riding is encouraged, however, by the sequential accept-ance mode of bargaining adopted in international matters. In this case the behaviour is known as hold-out (see Swanson, in Helm (1991) for more detail). The standard approach to international lawmaking allows a lengthy time period – several years in some cases – during which countries may accept a treaty's proposals. Once a sufficient number of countries have ratified the convention, it comes into effect. Even after this date, non-participating countries can choose to accede to its laws, and become part of the convention.

This sequential acceptance feature allows the costs of bargaining to con-tinue long after the convention comes into effect. As Table 6.3 shows, by holding-out – not obeying the text of the convention while others voluntarily do – a country can redistribute bargaining rents, appropriating a larger share for itself. It will do this for as long as the window of opportunity afforded by the terms of the convention remains open. In addition the incentives for non-acceptance increase when the context is altered from few parties to many – holding-out becomes more valuable with each successive acceptance.

The second problem arises due to information asymmetry. An individual hold-out may be due to opportunistic behaviour (in which case threats and arm-twisting must ensue), or to heterogeneity (in which case, side-payments are required). Ascertaining which is the case may not be an easy matter. Indeed there may be no logical distinction between the two, if current hetero-geneity is a result of past opportunism. 'Compensable burden' and 'free-rider rent' may not be distinguishable, and some arbitrary judgement must be taken to identify the point in time at which previously reasonable non-acceptance becomes an act of opportunism.

To summarize, the 'acid rain game' has shown the complexities of bargain-ing when (1) countries do not consider the costs that their actions impose on other, neighbouring countries that is a transfrontier externality exists; and (2) when no recognized (or obeyed) international body exists to establish prop-erty rights and enforce contracts. Bilateral bargaining *may* produce a cooperative outcome if the players (countries) are uncertain about the dura-tion of the 'game' (which seems a reasonable assumption), *and* if they are certain about the other player's values – a less convincing assumption.

Multilateral bargaining is more likely to be problematic. The sequential acceptance process of international lawmaking encourages free-riding prob-lems; and informational asymmetries not only make bargaining values hard to estimate, they also allow opportunistic free-riding to masquerade as reas-onable non-acceptance. The process of multilateral bargaining is, therefore, prone to inherently high costs. It is likely that full cooperation to abate degradation will not be achieved on account of the incentives to hold out and to free-ride on the commitments of others.

1.2.1   Contracting costliness and IEAs   IEAs are very difficult to create. Many states are necessary parties for an effective agreement (and all states are necessary parties in the context of global environmental problems), yet there are rents that may be demanded by each and every state as the price for not 'holding-out'. This is the reason that there is tremendous pressure placed on non-signatories to embrace various IEAs; they are of little impact without the agreement of every state. It is important to cooperate in these matters (without demanding 'free-rider rents'), otherwise no international environmental problem is capable of solution. This is the reason that the vast majority of states are suspicious of calls for 'compensation' in return for accession to IEAs.

Nevertheless it is clearly the case that there are asymmetries between states in terms of the international benefits they are rendering and the national costliness they are incurring. Many of these asymmetries arise for the simple reason of their respective stages of development. These asymmetries cannot be ignored, but must instead form the basis for arriving at fair and efficient agreements. The important point is to phase the bargaining position in terms of these differences, rather than general claims to compensation for signature.

2   Free-riding on others' cooperative behaviour
In the previous section we saw that heterogeneity in the impacts on various parties render it difficult to achieve agreement on the basis of uniform standards. The equal treatment of unequals does not usually equate with a sense of fairness. This is one of the fundamental reasons that states do not readily agree to an IEA: the perception that their individual positions regarding the resource are not being treated fairly. The solution to this problem is the creation of a system of side-payments that recognizes the unequal burdens of individual states. For example the Global Environmental Facility (GEF) has been created in a joint venture between the World Bank, the United Nations Environment Programme and the United Nations Development Programme in an attempt to provide side-payments to those states who are burdened disproportionately by reason of their commitments under the Montreal Protocol and the Biodiversity Convention. States from the developing world are allowed to claim for compensation from the GEF for projects undertaken to implement their obligations under these IEAs if the benefits from these projects flow disproportionately to the global community, rather than the state itself.

These sorts of side-payment are necessary to induce heterogeneous states to join into a concrete and effective IEA. The problem is that there are also other reasons that states would require side-payments, even in the absence of heterogeneity. This problem derives from the fact that, by definition, the common resources involved are *public goods*: resources that have the characteristic that they generate a flow of services to a large number of states, possibly the entire globe. This implies that one country's provision of these public goods rebounds to the benefits to others as much as to themselves, and this implies that other countries are able to free-ride on other countries' provision of such.

When the resource is a public good, there will be an optimal number of states involved in an IEA. The argument is that acceptance of an IEA depends upon the marginal benefit of the IEA to the marginal state. So long as the marginal benefits from additional supplies of the public good are declining (from the perspective of that state) and marginal costs remain constant (again, from that perspective), then we know that there will be an optimal number of member countries within the IEA. This is because the abatement undertaken by any given country will redound to the benefit of all, and hence the marginal benefits from individual abatement must be lower if others are already undertaking abatement. For this reason any given country will not consider it individually rational to join an IEA that has more than an optimal number of members within it.

Consider an example from Barrett (1994) and the case where individual benefits (B_i) are a function of aggregate abatement (Q) but individual costs of abatement (C_i) are only a function of individual abatement. Let N be the total number of states (potential signatories to the IEA) and Q (or q) the amount of abatement, aggregate and individual.

$$B_i(Q) = b(aQ - Q^2/2)N \qquad (6.1)$$

$$C_i(q_i) = c\ q_i^2/2 \qquad (6.2)$$

$$\pi_i = B_i - C_i \qquad (6.3)$$

Figure 6.1 demonstrates the difference between the non-cooperative (or open access) equilibrium and the cooperative equilibrium with regard to the joint resource. It is clear that there is a gain to cooperation to be achieved from moving towards the joint management of the resource (that is the cooperative equilibrium). But will an IEA be able to muster the necessary signatories in order to achieve this equilibrium?

Barrett's analysis leads to the conclusion that the number of parties to an IEA will depend upon the relative slopes of the curves corresponding to marginal benefits (of joint abatement) and marginal costs (of individual abatement). That is the number of parties to the IEA will be equal to the number

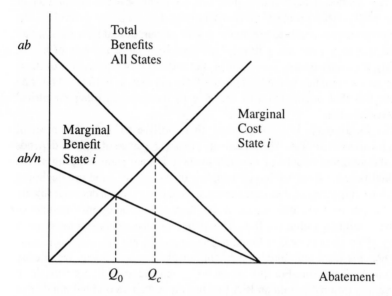

*Figure 6.1   Cooperative (Q_c) versus non-cooperative (Q_0) equilibrium –
multilateral agreements on abatement of emissions*

where the marginal country's benefits from accession are greater than or
equal to its marginal costliness. In effect each country considering joining the
IEA is not considering the sum of the MB (as should be the case in the supply
of a public good), but only its own marginal benefit; it is this collective action
failure that renders the IEA membership suboptimal. Table 6.3 demonstrates
the proportion of potential members (α) that will enter into the IEA (where a
= 100, b = 1, c = 0.25, N = 10), when comparing the benefits (π) to signatories (s) and non-signatories (n). The table demonstrates the amount of
abatement that will be undertaken by both sets of states, and the aggregate
amount of abatement (Q) and benefits ($\prod$) incurred by the entirety of the
states.

Note two things about this simulation. First, the aggregate benefits to the
entire group of states continue to increase with each additional state joining
the IEA (as indicated by the final column). Secondly, and despite this gain
from universal cooperation, a group of non-cooperators consisting of fewer
than 60 per cent of the total number of states will always receive benefits
greater than those cooperating in the IEA. This means that, if for any reason
the IEA achieves some number of accessions exceeding 40 per cent, there
will be no other state that will see any return from agreeing to the IEA. By
this point the cooperating states have undertaken sufficient unilateral restraint

Table 6.4   *Example of the benefits to various sized groups of signatories and non-signatories*

α	qs	qn	πs	πn	Q	Π
0.0	–	8.0	–	472.0	80.0	4720.0
0.1	1.9	8.5	476.8	468.1	78.7	4690.0
0.2	4.2	8.7	474.0	466.6	78.2	4681.2
0.3	6.7	8.4	472.3	468.9	78.9	4699.4
0.4	8.9	7.6	472.2	474.9	81.1	4738.1
0.5	10.5	6.3	473.7	482.5	84.2	4781.2
0.6	11.3	4.9	476.4	489.4	87.7	4816.0
0.7	11.5	3.6	479.5	494.3	91.0	4839.8
0.8	11.1	2.5	482.7	497.3	93.8	4855.9
0.9	10.5	1.6	485.4	498.8	95.9	4867.8
1.0	9.8	–	487.8	–	97.6	4878.0

Source: Barrett (1994).

so as to cause the others to perceive sufficient private benefits from the IEA. They gain by acquiring the public good without having to undertake any private expense to achieve it – the classic free-rider problem.

It is important to note that the example above assumed that each and every state was identical in its perceived costs and benefits from the IEA; there is no heterogeneity involved in the problem. It is also important to note that the joint first-best outcome would be to move from the non-cooperative situation to one of unanimous agreement. The failure of unanimous agreement is resulting from the fact that the individual states each perceive the benefit from free-riding on the others' cooperation as an option. This belief in the ability to distort the distribution of benefits from joint management by reason of non-cooperation is one of the primary barriers to cooperation in the commons.

It is also important to note that the process of sequential accession is fundamental to the achievement of this internal equilibrium. In an 'all or nothing' situation the entire group of states would commence at the point of non-cooperation ($\alpha = 0$) and they would only be able to move from this position by means of universal cooperation ($\alpha = 1$). It is the availability of intermediate options that create the opportunity for states to manœuvre for a position between these two points.

3   Economic theory of bargaining – distribution as the barrier to cooperation

Clearly one of the most fundamental hurdles to the development of effective IEAs is this belief in the ability to distort distributions through non-cooperation. This is known as rent-seeking in some economic literature, and it is known as free-riding in others; however in its most fundamental guise, this is the essence of the *bargaining problem*: the inability to acquire the gains from cooperation until such time as their distribution has been agreed.

The economic theory of bargaining discusses the possible outcomes from negotiations over the gains from cooperation. The best-known concept for discussing this problem is the Nash cooperative bargaining solution. See Harsanyi (1989) for a discussion of several solution concepts. In Nash cooperative bargaining theory, the terminology revolves around the *conflict pay-offs* (c) and the *cooperation pay-offs* (u*). The problem is to define the range of possible pay-offs and the likely outcome of cooperative bargaining.

In Figure 6.2 the set *F* represents the range of feasible outcomes of the choices the two states can make, while the point *C* represents the outcome of conflict; this would accord with our non-cooperative (Nash) equilibrium in a resource management situation. It is the best that each state could achieve independently, and without regard for the effects that it each might have on the other.

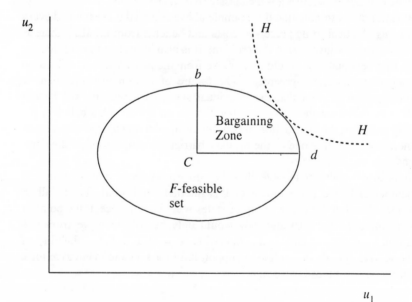

Figure 6.2   Nash cooperative bargaining theory

This conflict point defines the range of cooperation. The parties will consider making their choices jointly, if each believes that it can achieve a result better than it could acting independently. This zone of potential cooperation is the *bargaining zone* to the northeast of the conflict point. The upper right-hand boundary of F is the set of Pareto optimal solutions to the bargaining game. b is termed player 1's concession limit and d is player 2's concession limit. Anything within the area bounded by this Pareto frontier is a feasible point for the bargaining process, and anything on this frontier is the best that can be achieved jointly.

The *cooperation point* or agreement point for this bargaining game was defined by Nash as that point ($u*$) that maximizes the joint product net of the non-cooperative outcome in the bargaining game. That is the cooperation point maximizes the product $(u_1 - c_1) (u_2 - c_2)$. This is represented in Figure 6.2 by the rectangular hyperbola HH and its tangency to the bargaining frontier. This point of tangency defines the solution to the Nash cooperative bargaining game.

In essence, the *Nash 'bargaining solution'* allocates the gains from cooperation by reference to the best that the parties can achieve jointly by reference to their individual positions that would exist under non-cooperation. Hence the baseline for ascertaining where the bargaining zone commences is the point (or path) of non-cooperation.

This result is fundamentally important. It provides that the framework for the distribution of cooperative gains must be ascertained by reference to the best that each country can do acting independently. This is so because this is the framework that each individual country will be using when evaluating its decision concerning whether to cooperate or not. This means that all distribution rules are irrelevant which are based upon criteria that fail to recognize this framework. Individual countries will reject even very sensible rules of distribution, if they fail to recognize the path that the country could achieve unilaterally.

The dynamic equivalent to the conflict point is a *baseline*. A *baseline analysis* is based upon the extrapolation of the path that the countries concerned were following unilaterally. This is the path of non-cooperative behaviour, and it is the baseline against which any cooperative behaviour should be measured. The measurement and allocation of the costs and benefits from cooperative management of a resource must be assessed with reference to such a baseline.

4 The range of possible distributions: domestic and international contrasted

Despite the fact that the Nash 'bargaining solution' seems to indicate a single point of agreement for the distribution of the rents from cooperation, this is not the case in general. The entire area 'northeast' of the conflict point is available as potential outcomes to the negotiations between the states, and there is no mechanism which will cause each state to recognize a single solution (as Nash assumed that some objective joint welfare function – such as *HH* – would do). In fact the states will have very different perspectives on what form this joint welfare function should take, and without it there is no means by which to distinguish any one point within the bargaining zone from another.

The states must agree on some distribution rule that will determine which of these points results. In an efficient management regime, the distribution rule will place the two parties on the bargaining frontier; however, it is usually the case that some if not all of the gains from cooperation will be dissipated in the bargaining process. Essentially the bargaining frontier will continue to collapse towards the conflict point as the parties fail to agree on an enforceable rule for the management and distribution of the resource's rents.

What is the potential range of distributions under discussion between the states? We know that the conflict point provides the lower bound for any given state's demands, but what will provide the upper bound? Will it always go to the entire rents from the resource (the concession point above)? One way in which to attempt to place an upper bound on the rents that a given state can command is to consider that state as if it were an uncooperative agent of the others, and determine the incentive scheme required to cause it to move towards the cooperative outcome.

In game theoretic terms this change in framework is known as a *Stackelberg* form of game. When a public good is provided in this manner, the bargaining process is abstracted from and the sole issue is what is required in the way of a side-payment (or other incentive mechanism) to cause the state to move towards the provision of the public good. In effect this analysis assumes away the issues of rent distribution, and instead focuses on the 'compensation' required by the state for the movement away from its non-cooperative position.

Cervigni (1998) in fact argues that this level of compensation establishes the maximum payment that should be required for the provision of the public good. He terms the minimum payment necessary to maintain a participating country at the same level of welfare (that is the same as it was prior to the acceptance of the IEA) as the 'net incremental cost'. He defines the payment required to induce the participating country to elect to undertake the restraints implied by the IEA as the 'gross incremental cost'. He argues that the actual outcome should lie somewhere within this range.

This terminology derives from the workings of the Global Environmental Facility. This is a fund that has been established, and twice replenished, in order to compensate states for meeting some of their commitments under the biodiversity convention, the Montreal Protocol and various international waters' regimes. The GEF has received about two billion US dollars to date in order to fund such undertakings.

The question that Cervigni is addressing is a slightly different one than the IEA literature addresses. He is examining the issue of how much compensation a state should receive *given that it has already undertaken efforts to meet its obligations under the convention*. In the literature of microeconomics, the question of compensation has been covered meticulously where the object is to reinstate the individual to a pre-existing level of welfare after a new constraint has been imposed. The concepts of *compensating variation* and *equivalent variation* ascertain what sort of lump sum is required to compensate an individual for the change in prices that such a constraint implies.

The problem with this analysis is, of course, that the individual state under international environmental law need not accept mere compensation for the provision of the public good; it may demand resource rents as well. The difference is between the costs incurred by the individual country, and the benefits it confers to all other countries. In a domestic context the most sensible criterion for the private provision of a public good is 'fair compensation', but in the international context this criterion has yet to be established. The additional costliness of the provision of international public goods when the criterion for compensation has not yet been established is another one of the primary barriers to the implementation of IEAs.

The nearest counterpart to international manœuvring that occurs within the domestic sphere is with respect to surrogate markets, that is the development of marketable permits and such to control the use of a resource. In this context the firms in the domestic industry are often seen to pursue strategies that are directed towards rent appropriation rather than efficient allocation. For example firms will often attempt to hoard permits in order to generate market power, and capture a large share of the resource rents (Atkinson and Tietenberg, 1986; Misiolek and Elder, 1989; see generally Tietenberg, 1984). The firms in a small industry that are related to one another through a common resource are in a very similar situation to the states on earth interacting through international resources. Although there is a fundamental gain to be had through cooperation, an underlying competition for resource rents often places this at risk in both situations.

The most important difference between the two is that there is a government that is able to dictate the distributional rule that must be used in the domestic context, while at the same time must be negotiated in the international one. In effect this means that the common resource problem is removed from the natural environment and into the international negotiations. States are now able to pursue rents in the context of international conferences and various other negotiating techniques. The critical difference in the international context is precisely that the rent-seeking problem cannot be contained by a state-ordained criterion for compensation.

5   Example: distribution of the gains from managing climate change

A better approach to placing boundaries around the range of possible distributions is to consider all of the various cooperative bargaining rules that might be applied relative to the baseline that a country would pursue otherwise. These are all variants on the Nash Bargaining Solution, but with the provision of differing weights for the various determinants of the distribution of the rents from cooperation. The various weights that might be applied to the distribution of rents are infinite; in the international context, for example, these weights might be based upon state characteristics such as population, income, physical location, natural endowments or any combination of the above (see the discussion in Chapter 3). When some set of weights are agreed, then the shape of the distribution rule (the rectangular hyperbola HH in Figure 6.2) would be determined and a unique point on the bargaining frontier would be indicated.

Therefore the most useful approach to the investigation of possible solutions to the bargaining process is one that considers a wide range of possible solutions to the bargaining game. These solutions will all consist of different methods for determining the weights that are implicit within the distribution rule.

In a recent article Escapa and Gutierrez (1997) demonstrate how different bargaining rules generate very different distributional consequences for the distribution of the gains from the Climate Change Convention. They look at three possible distribution rules: (1) the equal distribution of bargaining power derived without reference to the non-cooperative outcome – the first-best (FB); (2) the Nash bargaining solution (NB) (derived with reference to the non-cooperative solution); and (3) the Kalai–Smorodinsky (KS) solution (a distribution rule with differential weights applied in reference to the non-cooperative solution). Their simulations of the impact of the various distributions of gains are shown in Table 6.5.

This table demonstrates how the conflict point drives the bargaining in a particular direction, and it also illustrates how different the final bargains can be with different weights on the various bargainers' positions. In this simulation the first-best outcome is achieved when all of the various states (here sets of states: China and India, EU, Rest of Developed World, Former Soviet Union and Rest of World) undertake uniform abatement of 2.45 per cent. In that case all of the various bargainers' returns receive an equal weighting (0.166 each), and the total world benefit is maximized (at 0.2592). On the other hand the Nash and KS solutions are based on different weighting formulas applied to bargaining frontier defined by the Nash conflict point.

Table 6.5 *Percentage of carbon emissions abatement and distribution of gain from cooperation (applying various rules of distribution)*

	Percentage Emission Abatement					Distribution of Gains				
	x^{NC}	x^{FB}	x^{NB}	x^{KS}	w^{FB}	$\%^{FB}$	w^{NB}	$\%^{NB}$	w^{KS}	$\%^{KS}$
USA	0.277	2.459	1.827	1.820	0.166	0.0062	0.19	0.1319	0.196	0.1297
CHI I	0.138	2.459	1.201	1.312	0.166	−0.9132	0.289	0.7456	0.271	0.626
EU	0.386	2.459	2.769	2.815	0.166	0.2688	0.125	0.2053	0.126	0.1927
ROD	0.322	2.459	2.712	2.919	0.166	0.2901	0.128	0.2406	0.122	0.206
FSU	0.384	2.459	2.253	2.200	0.166	0.2003	0.154	0.2516	0.162	0.2623
ROW	0.987	2.459	3.100	2.955	0.166	0.7325	0.112	0.2697	0.120	0.3560
TOT	0.525	2.459	2.387	2.364		0.2592		0.2285		0.2355

Source: Escapa and Guitierrez (1997).

These bargaining concepts yield very similar weights and benefits for the various states, but both are very different from the first-best distribution. In addition they both aggregate to similar totals, less than the first-best social benefits. The simulations in Table 6.4 illustrate how the bargaining defined by the point of non-cooperation gives very different results from the first-best, irrespective of the rule of distribution that is applied.

Note that the aggregate gains from cooperation are highest in the FB but that this is the only case in which the gains to an individual country might be negative; this is because the other distribution rules disallow the consideration of distributions which are worse than the non-cooperative outcome. In all cases the USA is a low achiever, and this is because it is currently the state closest to pursing the non-cooperative outcome (and acquiring free-rider rents). Note that different emissions abatement targets are required in order to achieve a more equal distribution of the gains (compare FB to NB).

What about the instrument that will be used to achieve these gains, and then distribute them? How will the choice of instrument impact on distribution of the gains? This point has been made in other articles concerning the possible imposition of greenhouse taxes and the complicated distributional considerations that arise. For example Whalley and Wigle (1991) demonstrate the alternative impacts from imposing carbon taxes at the producer and the consumer level in order to achieve a 50 per cent reduction in carbon emissions (see Table 6.6). The global tax is a tax collected at the international level, and then redistributed on a per capita basis. Although the fiscal impact on the world economy is the same under all of these taxes (–4 per cent), the distributive impact varies widely (for example the oil exporters gain 4.5 per cent under a producer-imposed tax system and lose 18.7 per cent under a consumer-imposed tax system).

In general this last study illustrates a number of interesting points. First, the development status of individual countries is very significant in the determination of the distribution of costs. Second, there may be some groups of states which incur disproportionate amounts of costs and benefits due to their physical characteristics. Finally, the distribution used (per capita entitlements under the global tax above) will have profound implications for the distribution of benefits. All of these points will be examined again in the chapters ahead. For now it is worth while to point out the generality of these principles in international bargaining.

6   Development status and environmental management

The literature discussed thus far is based on the idea that a certain distribution is required in order to induce the individual state away from the non-cooperative equilibrium, and towards the cooperative one. One important question concerns the path that would be taken by different countries in the future,

Table 6.6 *Distributive impact of the instrument used to manage climate change*

Region	Production Tax	Consumption Tax	Global Tax
EU	−3840	−1006	−3724
	(−4.0%)	(−1.0%)	(−3.8)
North America	−5494	−4576	−12 442
	(−4.3%)	(−3.6%)	(−9.8%)
Japan	−1459	214.3	−366
	(−3.7%)	(0.5%)	(−0.9%)
Rest OECD	−487	−440	−939
	(−2.3%)	(−2.1%)	(−4.4%)
Oil Exporters	1191	−4901	−3416
	(+4.5%)	(−18.7%)	(−13%)
Developing World	−9392	−8994	2371
	(−7.1%)	(−6.8%)	(1.8%)
World Total	−19 482	−19 704	−18 516
	(−4.4%)	(−4.4%)	(−4.2%)

Source: Whalley and Wigle (1991).

given non-cooperation. This non-cooperative path is the *baseline* against which all abatement must be measured. In order to understand the derivation of a baseline path, it is first of all essential to understand the general nature of the relationship between development and unilateral abatement efforts.

Several studies have investigated the empirics of the relationship between environmental degradation and economic development; most of these studies have investigated how environmental degradation relates to the development status of various countries. The studies usually take the form of investigating how a given type of injurious emissions (for the air, water, atmosphere and so on) relate to the economic structure of a range of different countries.
So, for example, following Grossman (1995), the relationship between aggregate emissions of a given type and national income may be broken down as follows:

$$E_y = \Sigma_i a_{it} s_{it} Y_t \tag{6.4}$$

where:

Y = aggregate GDP of investigated unit (country, city)
s_i = the share of output represented by activity i

a_i = the rate of emissions per unit of activity i

Then over time the rate of change in aggregate emissions will change according to:

$$\hat{E} = \hat{Y} + \Sigma_i \lambda_i \hat{s}_i + \Sigma_i \hat{\lambda}_i \qquad (6.5)$$

where:

(hat) = rate of change in the variable
λ_i = share of aggregate emissions generated by activity i

This indicates that the change in emissions with growth/development may be attributable to one of three factors:

1. *Scale* – the impact of growing scales of human activities on the environment. This is the factor which classical economists feared, and which Daly *et al.* (1991) continue to cite.
2. *Restructuring of economy* – the impact of changes in the structure of the economy with increasing development. This is the factor which results from economies moving from traditional structures to industrial to service-based structures, and beyond. As an economy moves through these phases, within the contexts of what other economies are doing, the structure of its output will alter considerably.
3. *Technological change* – the impact of changes in technology (industrial, managerial and institutional) on the rate of emissions per unit of output. This is the factor which results from expanded knowledge, with the passage of time, concerning the capacity to limit harmful by-products of the development process.

Together these studies demonstrate what is termed an 'inverted U relationship' between GDP per capita levels and harmful emissions (Grossman, 1995). This is the case both within the USA and across much wider sample groups. These studies demonstrate a quadratic form of relationship between GDP and emissions (and stocks where this information is available); income has an initial positive linear impact on the accumulation of environmental damage, but there is also a negative quadratic effect as well which ultimately overtakes the initial effect. The relationship between emissions (environmental use) and income levels is therefore modelled as a quadratic relationship:

$$E = \alpha + \beta Y - \gamma Y^2 \qquad (6.6)$$

Since the squared (quadratic) term eventually must overtake the linear term in income, the relationship that is discovered is this 'inverted-U' shaped curve (Figure 6.3).

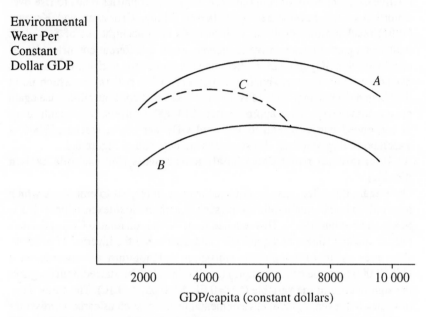

Figure 6.3 Income and environmental usage

6.1 Different literatures analysing this 'inverted U' relationship

(a) National (USA) cross-sectional data/local environments (air pollution)

This quadratic effect may be discerned from cross-sectional data applied to the USA alone. Even at much higher levels of income there is sometimes this same non-linear relationship between economic activity and environmental degradation, that is lower income levels in the USA demonstrate higher levels of environmental usage per unit of economic activity. Note however that there is little evidence of this effect registered in regard to a couple of pollutants that are regulated only at the national level: lead, for example.

(b) International cross-sectional data/local environments (particulates and sulphur dioxide)

Grossman and Krueger's analysis shows that the positive impact on income growth overtakes the negative impact in terms of air pollution at around US$5000. In a cross-section study involving 80 countries Lucas *et al.* (1992) found that there was a inverse-U relationship between GDP per capita and total toxic emissions relative to GDP, with the pollution intensity of economies increasing until a certain point, beyond which emissions fall. This relationship is also borne out by time-series studies which indicate that the relative toxic intensity of economies in individual countries tends to rise over a portion of the development path before falling. Grossman and Krueger (1991) reach similar results in their analysis of concentrations of SO_2, dark matter and particulates relative to income levels in different countries. It was concluded that SO_2 and dark matter concentrations tend to rise until countries reached a GDP of approximately \$5000 (1985 US dollars), at which point they began decreasing. The study also indicated that concentrations rise again once income levels reach approximately \$14 000. Conversely concentrations of suspended particles tend to fall until GDP per capita reaches \$9000 at which point they stabilize. These results are depicted in Figure 6.3.

(c) International panel data/global environments (for example carbon dioxide)

Once again this effect may be detected even with respect to emissions which have only international implications (such as carbon dioxide emissions) (Holz-Eakin and Selden, 1995). This reduced form estimation related CO_2 emissions only to income (linear and quadratic) and discovered the inverted-U relationship once again (although the emissions did not turn downwards until US\$30 000 (outside of the sample) (see Table 6.7). The starred items register the significance of the variable (***=0.01, **=0.05, *=0.10). The study demonstrates that even a global environmental problem such as carbon emissions is clearly embedded within a regular developmental process. In short the level of development indicates the expected level of carbon emissions that a country will generate.

Table 6.7 CO_2 emissions on GDP

	Levels	Logs
Intercept	0.31797*	−0.40682**
	(0.18224)	(0.17531)
Linear Term	0.15212***	0.52037***
	(0.013671)	(0.05039)
Quadratic Term	−0.002152***	−0.02895*
	(0.00034)	(0.01949)
R^2	0.75	0.84

Source: Holz-Eakin and Selden (1994).

6.2   The nature of the relationship between income levels and environmental usage

The argument is that income growth drives the demand for reduced environmental degradation. Richer countries have preferences for less environmentally intensive forms of industry and they implement these preferences by choosing: (a) to engage in industries that are less environmentally intensive (restructuring); (b) to apply technologies that are less environmentally intensive (technological change); and (c) to manage resource utilization more actively to keep it less environmentally intensive (environmental management). In essence this analysis indicates that there is a regular relationship whereby most peoples in the past have chosen to forego a high quality environment at low levels of income in order to industrialize and increase income levels, but once income levels reach a certain point there are in-built preferences for environmental quality which result in the reversal of this process.

6.3   Development-induced resource management

All of these studies develop a single point: whether resources are managed or not is a choice variable that will be determined from the perspective of the governments concerned with regulating them. And this perspective will hinge crucially upon the development status of the state concerned. At certain levels of development, certain resources are not the focus of sufficient concern to warrant adequate management to assure their 'optimal utilization' (from other country's perspectives) but that this is the result of a trade-off based on that particular country's level of development. For this reason resources will be degraded until such time as their scarcity value increases (or the general level of development increases) in that country so as to warrant the investment of that society's resources in their management. Management of a particular environmental problem will occur when a country's development status reaches the level that it becomes a high enough priority (relative to the other problems that the country has to solve).

7   Development status and global public goods – a case study of CFC management

This analysis of the relationship between environmental management and development status is crucial to the understanding of the appropriate starting point for environmental negotiations, that is the *baseline path* from which gains/burdens are assessed. It indicates that the assessment of unilateral management efforts (that would have been undertaken along the NC path) should be netted out prior to the assessment of cooperative gains.

The problem of ozone degradation is the classic instance in which economic analysis indicates that national interest might drive unilateral efforts at management (Barrett, 1994). In fact one recent study claims that the entirety of the abatement effort undertaken between 1986 and 1993 (WRI database) may be explained by reference to unilateral environmental management and not the intervening Protocol. These authors imply that the Montreal Protocol did not move the parties off the non-cooperative path of CFC emissions (Murdoch and Sandler 1997).

This study fails to take into account the dynamics between development status and unilateral management efforts. This can only be ascertained by considering what would have occurred in the absence of the Montreal Protocol. This can be done by looking at the levels of CFC abatement that occurred between the time of the discovery of its impact on the ozone layer (approximately 1970) and the agreement of the Protocol itself (in 1989). The behaviour of individual countries in this interim period would indicate how CFC management occurred in a non-cooperative context. The analysis of the available data from this period by Swanson and Mason (1998) reveals a significant relationship between national income levels and both domestic CFC production and consumption (and hence implicitly CFC abatement): the national production of CFCs increases with income and then begins to decline at the level of about US$15 000 per capita while national consumption falls off at around US$12 000 per capita (Table 6.8).

Table 6.8   Estimated CFC production and consumption related to income and income squared

Production	Estimate	Standard error
Constant	−0.335	0.222
GDP	3.564	2.026
GDPSQD	−0.111	0.073
Consumption		
Constant	−0.523	0.269
GDP	0.300	0.087
GDPSQD	−0.012	0.005

Prior to the Montreal Protocol, a cross-sectional analysis of the available data demonstrates a relationship between a country's income level and its CFC emissions – the 'inverted-U' relationship discussed previously. The initial increase in CFC emissions is seen in the positive coefficient on the linear term for national income, while the negative coefficient corresponding to the quadratic term indicates that it must ultimately decline. This implied 'inverse-U'-shaped relationship is indicated in Figure 6.4.

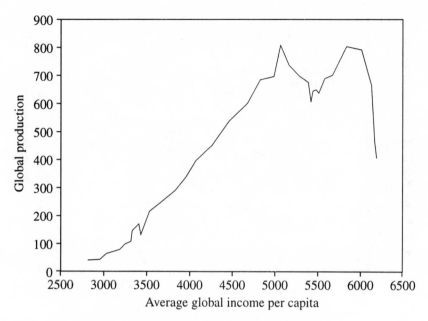

Figure 6.4   Global CFC production v. income per capita

The first point to note from this study is that the finding of unilateral management efforts *does not* necessarily imply the solution of an environmental problem in the absence of cooperation. It is predictable that the rates of unilateral management will be inadequate in the case of a global public good, precisely because it requires cooperation to provide a public good. For example, in the case of CFC emissions, unilateral management would not result in an aggregate reduction in the rate of emissions be the case that the rates of management in the state of non-cooperation will find that (in the absence of the Protocol) global CFC emissions would continue rising precipitously through at least the year 2050 (see Figures 6.5 and 6.6). The aggregate baselines for CFC production listed in those Figures demonstrate that in the absence of the Montreal Protocol CFC emissions would rise by a factor of five over between 1990 and 2050.

Contrary to the static analysis contained in Murdoch and Sandler (1997) the relationship between national income and CFC production/consumption identified here indicates that aggregate CFC emissions would rise for many decades across a wide range of assumptions. National incomes in the countries with the largest number of people remain low enough that their expanding production/consumption of CFCs would swamp all unilateral abatement efforts for years to come. The Montreal Protocol, if monitored and enforced to

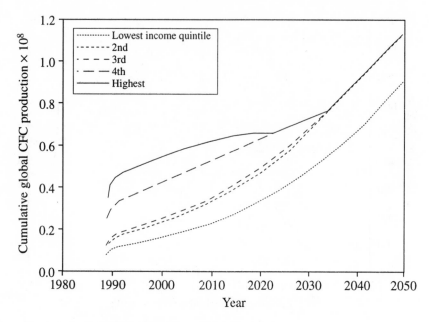

*Figure 6.5   Forecast cumulative global CFC production (by income
grouping)*

bring its terms into effect, will reduce aggregate CFC emissions to zero
during a period in which they are forecast to be rising fivefold (see Figure
6.7).

The observed induced management of CFCs in higher income countries is
therefore incapable of solving the ozone depletion problem but it is important
for the purpose of assessing relative responsibilities under that accord. This
relationship is important for any analysis of burden-sharing because it indicates the expected path that *unilateral management efforts* would have taken
in the absence of any multilateral undertaking. This means that countries will
undertake management of pollutants in their own self-interest once particular
levels of income have been attained, and these efforts need not be taken into
consideration in the computation of efforts supplied to a multilateral regime.
They are the *baseline* against which country efforts should be measured.

For example the analysis of the period 1976–88 indicates that the richer
countries followed a path of continuing to produce and consume products
containing these pollutants at increasing levels but decreasing rates until
they reached an income level of about $12 000, at which point their
consumption of CFCs began to decline. This would imply that inexpensive
CFC-based refrigeration and solvents have been chosen by these societies

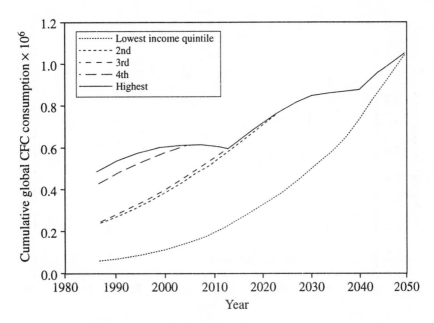

Figure 6.6 Forecast cumulative global CFC consumption (by income grouping)

in preference to ozone management until they become 'rich enough' (in this case about $12 000 per capita) to consider the higher-priced substitutes. This means that countries whose income levels are above this level are making little additional contribution to ozone protection than they would in their own self-interest, while countries whose incomes are well below that level are taking action against self-interest even when they only increase their production/consumption by less than they would otherwise. This is the importance of developing a 'baseline' which incorporates development status; the management that each country takes unilaterally is crucially dependent upon its current development level. Requiring all countries to undertake abatement of CFCs by 2010 places the vast majority of the burden for supplying the ozone layer squarely upon the shoulders of the least developed countries.

8 Conclusion: the economics of IEAs
This brief introduction to the basic economics of IEAs illustrates the fundamental nature of the problem we are discussing. At base this is simply a problem of distribution that must be resolved before movement from the non-cooperative situation to the cooperative. It is in the best interests of all of the

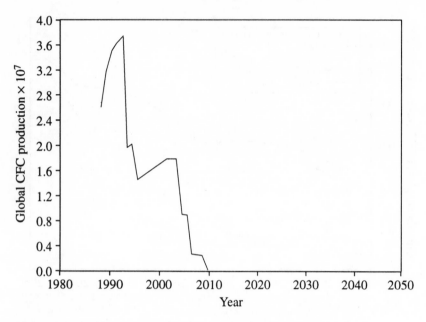

Figure 6.7   CFC production under the Montreal Protocol

various states to recognize their interdependence, and to enter into joint management of the common resources; however, this recognition alone is not enough to move from non-cooperation to cooperation.

Between the recognition of inefficiency and the movement to an efficient management regime lies the problem of institution-building. Many times it is assumed that it is the absence of institutions that prevents efficient resource management at the international level, but this is not the case. These institutions may be created, and the rewards are there for their creation. The problem of institution-building that must be resolved is the distributional one rather than the administrative one.

This chapter has also illustrated one approach to the resolution of the distributional problem, that is the approach based upon the path of non-cooperation or baseline behaviour. Different countries will have undertaken different levels of management in the absence of cooperation, and this level of management provides the baseline against which cooperative contributions are then measured. Since management of environmental problems is so clearly linked to income levels, this means that the baseline level of environmental management on international resource problems should be related to the development status of countries: more developed countries should be expected to contribute more management.

Even if there is agreement on the determination of baselines, this still leaves plenty of room for disagreement on the distribution of the burden of cooperation. Should it be based on individual rights (population levels)? Or, natural endowments (resource abundance or scarcity)? Or, historical rights (prior appropriation of the resource)? Different countries will come to the table with different proposals and alternative approaches for implementing them.

The remainder of this part of the book investigates in greater detail these problems of distribution and their resolution in international institution-building. These are the problems that must be resolved at the foundations of effective international environmental law.

7 Negotiating international environmental agreements: bargaining problems over common resources

1 The nature of the holdout problem:

Vous etes un peuple de brigands![1]

In 1884 the International Union for the Protection of Industrial Property was ratified by most of the then-industrialized (or industrializing) world.[2] The purpose of the Union was to provide some common principles regarding the use of intellectual property.[3] Two states elected to remain outside of the patent union. Those two states were Switzerland and The Netherlands. Switzerland remained outside due to the uncertainties regarding its capacity to enter, given its federal constitution, but did in fact enter the Union by 1888. The Netherlands, on the other hand, had previously elected in 1869 to pursue industrialization in a patentless environment; it had repealed its previously existing patent statute at that time. The Netherlands was determined to continue this policy even after the Paris Convention, thus inciting the wrath of the other delegates (as indicated by the above quotation from one conference delegate). The Netherlands was, perhaps, the first ever example of the 'holdout problem' in international resource law. And it established a quite remarkable benchmark in the field of international footdragging by remaining outside of the Union for nearly 30 years.[4]

Of course the Patent Union is not unique in this regard. Most international conventions subsequent to the Patent Union have been plagued by significant hold-out problems. There is no international resource convention which has been accepted by all states; very few have been accepted by as many as 50 states. Most conventions are subject to significant exceptions; many conventions have been accepted by only a handful of states.

At first glance it is apparently straightforward to deduce the rationale for being a 'hold-out'. As has long been recognized in the domestic public sector, the hold-out is simply pursuing its individually perceived first-best option in a multilateral bargaining game: attempting to secure the others' undertaking while individually pursuing the unconstrained optimum.[5] In this case the hold-out is simply 'free-riding' on the agreement of the other parties. This is apparently the view taken by the delegate to the 1884 Paris Convention regarding The Netherlands position, when that delegate made the above-referenced allegation.

On further reflection, however, it is possible that the source of the difficulty might be the terms of the proposed contract itself, rather than the attitude of the non-accepting state. It might be the case that the terms of an international resource convention impose an unequal burden on the various affected states.[6] In this instance it is the behaviour of the proponent, rather than the 'holdout' states which might be unreasonable. This is, apparently, the view taken by the less-developed countries concerning the application of a uniform CFC ban regarding the use of the ozone layer.

Therefore the nature of the international hold-out problem itself is difficult to elucidate. It could be of the nature of the domestic 'hold-out problem', long known in the public economics literature. Or, it might be analogous to the 'adverse selection' problem much discussed in insurance economics; that is, it might be the result of the offering of a single set of contract terms to a heterogeneous group of states.

In sum it appears that the nature of the hold-out problem in international resource law is generally analogous to a multilateral bargaining problem, which has been addressed primarily in two other contexts: free-rider (in public finance) problems and insurance contracting problems. These contracts have been the subjects of entirely distinct literatures, and they have evoked very different responses. In the former literature the solution has been deemed to be the creation of a power of eminent domain in the public entity, so that 'involuntary' transactions may be commanded. In the latter the solution has been the generation of different charges/standards for the various parties to the contract. Therefore the two literatures reach entirely opposite conclusions: one requiring agreement without special compensation, the other requiring individualized compensation prior to agreement. The reconciliation of these opposing themes must be a precondition to the understanding of the nature of this problem, and thus to its solution. The next section attempts to unify these various strands of thought in a framework for analysing international bargaining problems.

2 A general theory of bargaining over international environmental agreements

The failures of international environmental agreements have been entirely predictable because they are derived from the peculiar combination of both the nature of the problem (the regulation of open access resources) and the nature of the process which has been applied to its resolution (multilateral contracting). In essence the nature of problem and process together generate predictably high bargaining costs, which prevent the gains from joint management being achieved.

The costliness of contracting in this context is attributable to three factors. First, there is the nature of 'international resources'. These are generally *open access* resources available to the entire international community for use, which therefore require the cooperation of all users (existing and potential) for resolution. Second, there is the nature of 'international lawmaking' the *contractual* nature of international law requires that each state finds the proposed convention to be in its own interest before acceptance is possible. Third, another facet of international lawmaking is its multilateral character, this makes the possibility of *sequential acceptance* (as opposed to simultaneous commitment) a real possibility, which generates a system of incentives which runs contrary to agreement.

These next two sections develop the reasons why these three factors result in predictable regulatory failures. This section will investigate the capability of regulation to operate effectively in the presence of all three of the factors above. In section 3, the third assumption (regarding sequential acceptance) is dropped, and then the comparative costliness of international contracting in either situation is examined in section 4.

2.1   International law as a multilateral bargaining problem

The peculiar difficulties of international resource agreements may be conceptualized as multilateral bargaining problems. A *bargaining problem* is a situation in which a joint gain is clearly achievable by virtue of moving from non-cooperative to *cooperative behaviour*, but it is not realizable until agreement is reached on how such a gain should be distributed. In the context of an international environmental agreement, the gain from joint management would result from the implementation of the aggregate optimal rate of use of the resource, and the issue of distribution concerns the allocation of shares in the international resource once joint management is achieved

Bargaining problems of a bilateral nature can be difficult and costly to resolve, but where many parties are involved ('multilateral contracting') the problem is raised to a higher order of difficulty; such joint management problems have been discussed under the rubric of 'collective choice problems' in the domestic context (Olson, 1970). This is because multilateral contracting affords the possibility of sequential acceptances. That is, in bilateral contracting, there are only two options: the parties are either in a state of disagreement or agreement; the potential for gain from agreement provides the impetus for movement from the former state to the latter. In multilateral contract there is the added possibility that some subset of the necessary parties will agree to the standard while some other subgroup will not. It is this third option which generates the distinct set of problems associated with international resource conventions.

2.2   The impact of sequential acceptance – free riding

The international lawmaking process generally operates as follows. First, there is an international conference on the subject at which a text is agreed and published. Second, the text, or 'convention', is then left open for signature and ratification, usually for several months or years. Third, the text comes into effect for ratifying states once a sufficient number (as indicated in the text of the convention) have ratified. Fourth, the convention remains open for subsequent acceptance by other states, should they choose to later 'accede' to the laws. Therefore the entire process is usually geared to the non-contemporaneous acceptance of the convention's standards.

Sequential acceptance essentially affords the possibility for the bargaining problem to continue in existence even after the agreement has been signed by some of the necessary parties. The terms of the international resource convention will prescribe an initial standard which will expressly or implicitly determine the distribution of the relative shares of the gain from coordinated usage. The effect of hold-outs is primarily redistributive; that is, a hold-out reallocates shares away from those parties which have agreed the standard and towards itself. Therefore, in the context of sequential acceptances, international resource conventions afford the possibility of continuing the bargaining process (and hence its costliness) even after the terms of the convention have been established (by their acceptance by some subgroup of users).

The essentially redistributive effect of sequential acceptance of international resource convention standards is easily illustrated. This would be analogous to the situation in which any subgroup of users of an open access resource were to undertake unilateral restraint. Consider a fishery, for example, which is being depleted through competitive harvesting. If a number of the fishing vessels undertook voluntary restrictions on their catches, there would not necessarily be any effect on the aggregate level of the use of the resource, as the unconstrained harvesters could simply absorb the surplus stocks made available by the others' constraints. On the other hand, in this scenario, there would be significant redistributive effects. Voluntary constraints on the part of some users merely transfer their share of the resource rents to those users who decline to assume the constraints (Hoel, 1991).

The combination of *open access resource* and *sequential acceptance* is the source of this free rider problem which is inherent in all attempts to contract in this manner with regard to the use of an international resource. The resulting system of incentives is such that the first-best option in multilateral contract bargaining will always be the pursuit of unconstrained maximization while other users assume binding constraints. This is another example of the general problem of opportunism, or rent-seeking, in contracting when appropriable rents exist (Williamson, 1986).

This problem of opportunism, or free-riding, may be depicted in a simple bilateral game matrix which shows the consequences for each player given the actions of the other. In this scenario each player has the choice of accepting or not accepting the proposed constraint, where universal acceptance will produce the jointly maximized outcome (S*) and total non-acceptance will result in the wastage of the resource, an inferior result (W*). Since there is an assumption of equal and open access, both players will acquire an equal share of the inferior outcome (W*), but under a managed outcome (S*) they must agree a distribution of the resulting rents.

All players could do better under S* than W*, because this is the essence of a cooperative gain or managed outcome. The bargaining problem is to determine a system by which the players are able to agree on the distribution of (S*), in order to avoid the default situation. The point we are making here is that this bargaining problem is rendered more difficult in the context of sequential acceptance. This is because the individual first-best result is to 'not accept' the constraint if the other player is already committed to 'accept'. Sequential acceptance allows states to determine their share of resource rents by virtue of their place in the order of acceptance. Assuming that the aggregate rents from sequential acceptance are the same as from non-management in this example, it is possible that the order of acceptance would generate a substantial asymmetry in the distribution of those rents. For example the unconstrained player might receive the vast majority of the available rents, say, 0.75W* while the constrained player receives only 0.25W*. This is the appropriable rent available from acting opportunistically (see Table 7.1).

Table 7.1   Opportunism and the incentives to non-acceptance

		Player 2	
		Accept	Not Accept
Player 1	Accept	(S*)	0.25W*, 0.75W*
	Not Accept	0.75W*, 0.25W*	0.5W*, 0.5W*

The incentive structure within this framework is such that the continued wastage of the resource is inevitable, when sequential acceptance is the method of contracting. Individual incentives exist which drive the international community away from agreement.

It is sequential acceptance which might at first be attributed with the responsibility for these incentives to disagreement. Sequential acceptance by itself makes available the possibility of an individually determined distribution rule rather than a jointly agreed distribution of S^*. Where this unilateral appropriation of rents is available, the result is often non-acceptance by some necessary party and the continued wastage of the resource: W^*. It is for this reason that most economists advocate the adoption of *ex ante* bargaining and simultaneous acceptance as the solution to these international contracting problems (Maler, 1991).

In addition it is worth noting that the incentives to non-acceptance actually increase when the context is altered from two parties to many. This is because the incentives to free-ride, in this framework, actually increase with *each* successive acceptance. The transfer of one more user from the unconstrained group to the constrained makes available more of the resource for the remaining hold-outs. These states actually face an increasing opportunity cost from acceptance of the standard. Therefore multilateral contracting with sequential acceptance increases the incentive to free-ride on other users' unilateral restraint; it makes the possibility of moving ultimately to the jointly managed outcome even more costly (for individual states) and hence more unlikely (Barrett, 1990).

2.3 An alternative source of hold-outs – heterogeneous parties

What motivates an individual state to become a 'hold-out'? One possibility, described above, is opportunism, but this fails to indicate why some states are and others are not hold-outs. There is no distinctive trait which determines the capacity to receive 'free-rider rents'. Any state which is successful at being other than first to assume the constraint is able to appropriate a larger share of the resource rents. In fact the last state to hold-out would have the capacity to command the entirety of the gains from agreement in return for its accession. Within this analysis it is difficult to understand why *any* states would elect to accept a binding standard.

Opportunistic behaviour is not the sole motivating force behind the hold-out problem, however. Another predictable source of hold-outs is the rational reaction of diversely situated parties to a proposed uniform standard. This is known as adverse selection within the economics literature (Rothschild and Stiglitz, 1976). In short any proposed standard, no matter how uniformly presented, will have widely varying impacts. This is because states are heterogeneous, and their heterogeneity implies that even a uniform constraint has differential impacts. There must be a spectrum of costliness related to any proposed constraint, depending upon the development status and investment context of the particular country.

The difference in the set of incentives facing two parties may once again be illustrated in a simple game matrix. In this case it will be assumed that the distribution of the rents from agreement are inherent within the terms of the rule. Although the rule may be uniform in its application (for example all states to discontinue the use and production of CFCs), the costs of alternatives and the wealth of the states may determine differential impacts for different countries. This would mean that the managed outcome is still jointly preferable to the unmanaged outcome ($S^*>W^*$) but that the distribution of S^* is inherent within the proposed management regime just as the distribution of W^* is inherent within an open access regime (see Table 7.2).

Table 7.2   Heterogeneity and the incentives to non-acceptance

		Player 2	
		Accept	Not Accept
Player 1	Accept	0.25S*, 0.75S*	0.25W*, 0.75W*
	Not Accept	0.75W*, 0.25W*	0.5W*, 0.5W*

The capacity of a given standard to divide the group of users into two sets is illustrated by the entries in the matrix. The 'natural' bias in the two states' preferences makes it likely that the two will prefer different outcomes. In short, player 1 in Table 7.2 would strictly prefer 'non-acceptance' if its share in that situation (either 0.5 or 0.75W*) were greater than its expected share under an efficient management regime (0.25S*); in this case, it is said that the strategy of non-acceptance is *strictly dominant*. Player 2 on the other hand has a natural tendency towards 'acceptance'; its expected pay-off from efficient management of the resource (0.75S*) clearly exceeds its highest available pay-off under non-acceptance (0.75W*). Although not strictly dominated the strategy of acceptance outweighs the benefits from being opportunistic for this player (0.75S* > 0.75W*), and so this player has a substantial incentive to encourage cooperation and discourage opportunism.

Therefore the proposal of a standard, no matter how uniformly presented, will have the effect of presenting different incentive frameworks to different countries. This much is inherent in the differential development and investment status of different countries. And, as illustrated in the example above, it is even possible that a uniformly presented standard will have the effect of dividing the users into two groups: those perceiving net benefits from its acceptance and those perceiving net benefits from its non-acceptance.

This matrix also illustrates the interaction between heterogeneity and opportunism in the multilateral context. For example a state that is biased towards non-acceptance would receive substantial benefits from others' acceptances and would then perceive these benefits as an opportunity cost to acceptance as well. Sequential acceptance only enhances the problem of heterogeneity. Conversely a state naturally inclined to acceptance would see a dramatic increase in its relative share if it did free-ride (a doubling from 0.25W* to 0.50W*) but this still might remain below its expected return from efficient management (0.75S*). Thus the availability of sequential acceptance magnifies the benefits of non-acceptance for those naturally inclined to reject the standard.

3 The nature of alternative solutions to the hold-out problem

Therefore there are two potentially very different sources of hold-out in international resource contracting. One is the set of incentives to act opportunistically with regard to any constraint for which sequential acceptance is a possibility, these incentives are depicted in Table 7.1. The other is the wholly reasonable reaction of diversely situated states to a proposed uniform standard; these incentives are depicted in Table 7.2.

The nature of the solution to the hold-out problem is also very different depending on the ultimate source of the problem. Hold-outs sourced in heterogeneity require side-payments in order to equalize shares. Individual incentives based in share redistribution are the necessary basis for agreement. Hold-outs sourced in opportunism, on the other hand, must be convinced of their incapacity to procure side-payments by means of their recalcitrance. Incentives based in the firm refusal of share redistribution are the necessary basis for agreement.

These two solutions may be demonstrated by reference to Tables 7.1 and 7.2. With regard to hold-outs sourced in opportunism, as depicted in Table 7.1, the efficient solution is readily obtained once the option of opportunistic is removed; this is the means by which changes in the law in domestic regimes are effected. This may be accomplished by placing a 'ban' on the choice of non-acceptance, while specifying a date by which all states will move simultaneously (or not at all) to that new equilibrium. The requirement of simultaneity removes the jointly dominated, but individually profitable, strategies from consideration (Schotter, 1986).

On the other hand the required approach to the problem of state heterogeneity is *ex ante* bargaining and redistribution. Under this scenario the states benefiting disproportionately from efficient regulation must share their benefits with those disproportionately burdened in order to secure the latter's agreement to the change. In Table 7.2 this would require that player 2 transfer some of its gain to player 1 in return for agreement; for example player 2 might agree to transfer 0.25S* to player 1 (as compensation for its disproportionate burden), resulting in a joint pay-off to agreement of 0.50S*, 0.50S*. This is the idea of creating a system of side-payments, which will generate the cooperative solution.

It is very difficult to regulate international resources using either of these methods. First, it remains impossible to enforce codes of behaviour against individual states, unless that state adopts the code voluntarily. This is the essence of national sovereignty. Since this means that it is not possible to force parties to contract in a certain manner with regard to the use of a global resource, the domestic solution of declaring an activity illegal is unavailable. Secondly, it is virtually impossible to segregate entirely between the effects of heterogeneity and opportunism. At one level it is usually very difficult to determine where the recalcitrant state's desire for compensation leaves off, and its pursuit of free-rider rents sets in. As developed in Table 7.2, a state inclined to non-acceptance will see the benefits derived from others' acceptances as another cost of compliance; therefore, this state's 'reservation price' may come to embody *both* transfers sourced in differential burden and in opportunism.

Third, and more fundamentally, it is sometimes the case that the distinction between 'compensable burden' and 'free-rider rent' is not very clear-cut. The information is not always available to separate between the two different motives; even the logical distinction between the two becomes confused given the dependence of current costliness upon choices that the state itself made much earlier (regarding sunken investments and courses of development). In the context of Table 7.2 this indicates that the natural biases in a party's pay-offs is in fact dependent upon prior choices made regarding the use of a resource, for example whether to invest in more or less intensive use. Then those who have recently been investing heavily in an inefficiently utilized resource are those with the largest claim for compensation. In that case some sort of arbitrary judgement must usually be taken concerning the point in time at which previously reasonable non-acceptance becomes transformed into an act of opportunism.

These last two points are the primary contributors to the costliness of *ex ante* bargaining. The indivisibility of compensable burden and opportunistic rents means that there is no objective basis for agreeing the 'scientifically correct' shares. In addition the fuzziness of the line separating the two categories of costliness results in excessive demands on the resource. Each state's price of agreement usually includes a component of both; hence the aggregate shares often add up to more than the carrying capacity of the resource. These difficulties are at the core of the costliness of *ex ante* bargaining, and they will be elaborated upon in section 4.

Between these two 'purist' solutions (of imposed laws or *ex ante* bargains) lies a third range of possibilities. These result from the combination of uniform standards and sequential acceptance. When this combination exists the states perceiving the proposed standard as a net benefit will accept it immediately, while those perceiving it as a net burden will not. For the latter group of states the option of 'tailoring' the agreement to their individual characteristics remains open, despite the uniformity of the standard. That is through *ex post* redistributions it is possible for these states to receive a very different allocation of the resource than that which is set forth under the terms of the governing convention. The bargaining problem, consisting of tailoring individual shares to individual characteristics, is resolved in this situation via *ex post* redistributions (that is after the convention has come into existence) rather than *ex ante* bargaining. This is the method of *ex post* bargaining which is used to regulate many global resources today.

In this book we refer to *ex ante* bargaining as negotiation, and we refer to *ex post* bargaining as evolution; however the point to be made here is that both are parts of the same problem: the generation of universal agreement to a new regulatory institution.

4 Negotiating IEAs: differentiating between bargaining positions

This theory of international contracting states that hold-out problems are sourced in one of two areas: free-rider problems and/or heterogeneity. The creation of an effective IEA will require that the source of a state's demands be identified, and that the appropriate policy then be pursued. That is the country should receive a side-payment if the demands for differential treatment are sourced in differential impacts based on heterogeneity, or the country should be sanctioned if its demands are based on rent-seeking and opportunistic behaviour. In theory this separation is possible, in practice it is far more difficult.

4.1 The Netherlands and the Patent Union: the importance of development status

As was discussed in the introduction The Netherlands was one of the first 'hold-outs' in international resource convention history. It managed to remain outside of the Patent Union for nearly 30 years. It is quite straightforward to see why this was a desirable strategy on the part of this (or any other) state. Under the terms of the Convention a non-signatory was entitled to patent protection for any innovation which was registered in a foreign state, while retaining the right to imitate all patented inventions at home. That is, international information bases are open access resources, just as are many natural resources. Therefore any given state had an incentive to attempt to be the 'last' state to accept the convention; this strategy allowed the unilateral appropriation of the rents of this resource.

How did The Netherlands fare as the lone Western 'hold-out' from the International Patent Union? Very well indeed; the 'authoritative' work on Dutch Economic History labels the period of 1870–1914 (coinciding almost precisely with the patentless period) as the 'era of industrialization' in that state.[7] How much did this depend on the exploitation of their nonconformant status in the Patent Union? Two examples will suffice to relate the impact.

The first involved the marketing of the American innovation, the Edison electric lamp, for which Edison had acquired patents in all European states by 1881. Edison licensed two German corporations as its sole licensees within Europe; they were (the predecessor corporation to) A.E.G. and Siemens & Halske, both licensed in 1883. For the next decade they spent much of their time and efforts contesting their rights as against various potential competitors throughout Europe, winning five court rulings confirming their monopoly rights. In The Netherlands Gerard Philips started unlicensed production of incandescent electric lamps in a small business in Eindhoven in 1891. By 1913 it was the largest manufacturer of lamps in Europe (selling 6.4 million in that year). It went on to become the Philips corporation, diversifying into the production of many electronic goods.

Another example of the benefits accruing to The Netherlands occurred in the margarine industry. In this field the patents were held by a French chemist, Mege Mouries, dating to 1869. Two Dutch butter merchants, Jurgens and Van den Bergh, obtained the formula for the butter substitute (which was available due to disclosure requirements in the patenting process) and went on to commence unlicensed manufacture of the commodity in 1871. The two firms quickly became the leading producers in Europe, exporting vast quantities of margarine to Britain, later merging to form the Unilever corporation.

Therefore this would appear at first glance to be the prototypical case of free-riding on others' constraints with regard to an international resource. The Netherlands' 30 years as an international renegade in the field of industrial technology made a significant contribution to its development as a modern industrialized state, and established large corporations which dominate their fields to this day. Although international pressure ultimately prevailed in causing this state to accede to the Union, in the interim The Netherlands amply demonstrated the value accruing to the last 'hold-out' under an international resource convention. The Netherlands appropriated vast quantities of rents through their access to the international resource. It will never be possible to determine the precise extent to which their 30 years of nonconformance resulted in underinvestment in the resource, but the cost must be at least equal to the amount of The Netherlands' gain.[8]

As would be predicted there was another force in favour of nonconformance in the case of The Netherlands. Economic historians report that, as of the date of the convention, The Netherlands was one of the most industrially backwards of European states.[9] For example one study reports the following measure of industrial development in Europe at the mid-nineteenth century (Table 7.3).

Table 7.3   Availability of steam power in 1850 (hp)[10]

UK	France	Belgium	Prussia	Netherlands
500 000	67 000	51 000	43 000	6500

The effect of the Patent Union would have been the recognition of the other states' proprietary rights in their technical know-how (and the corresponding responsibility of The Netherlands to license the same). For some states with substantial stocks of technical knowledge, the benefits of this convention were self-evident; for example, the UK and the USA were significant proponents of the treaty. The net benefits to a relatively backwards state, such as The Netherlands, were less evident. Although the proposed standard on face value appeared to be a uniform constraint, it was clearly much more binding on some states than on others, given their varying states of technical development. It simply was not in the self-interest of a state such as The Netherlands to agree to such a 'uniform' constraint in the absence of some form of compensation.

Therefore it is not clear even in this instance whether the appropriate remedy for non-agreement was sanction or compensation. On the one hand The Netherlands engaged in what now appears to be flagrant piracy of numerous pieces of almost universally recognized industrial property. On the other hand there was no real consideration offered to The Netherlands in return for its accession to this treaty, and hence for its recognition of others' holdings of this new form of property (since it had no property of like kind to be recognized in return). The development status of The Netherlands was very different from the others within the treaty, and so the net benefits from the uniform codes of conduct were of a very different order. This demonstrates that the regulation of a joint resource will always have a differential impact on differing countries, given their differential development status.

It also demonstrates that it is irrational for the treaty's proponents to expect net losers to accede, and it is unreasonable to accuse them *ex post* of piracy. In fact The Netherlands simply exercised its option to redefine the terms of exchange through the existing international lawmaking procedure; it unilaterally appropriated from the international resource until it had achieved some manner of parity of consideration for contracting. The Netherlands engaged in *ex post* bargaining, to cause the convention to evolve into something from which it received a substantial share of benefits.

However, as indicated in the discussions above, the failure of the *ex ante* bargaining approach to the Patent Union would have severely reduced its aggregate benefits. The rents appropriated by The Netherlands were extracted from the returns generated by the information created by Edison and the other inventors. The expectation of reduced rewards would, in theory, reduce the efficiency of the entire system, and hence reduce the investment in the generation of such industrial information. Although The Netherlands defined a share that it was willing to accept, the cost was incurred by reason of the inefficient management occurring under the entire system.

4.2   Western Europe and the Helsinki Protocol ('club of 30 per cent'): physical attributes

In 1979 the states of Europe adopted the Convention on Long-Range Transboundary Air Pollution (LRTAP) at a high-level meeting of the Economic Commission for Europe (ECE) in Geneva.[11] It is a remarkable treaty in that it was the first multilateral convention regarding air pollution control, and because it acquired acceptances by all parties to which it was open: the states of Western and Eastern Europe as well as the USA and Canada.[12]

This latter point is not so remarkable when the terms of the treaty are reviewed. There is no standard enunciated within this convention which could be interpreted as binding on any potential party.[13] For example the sole obligation of the parties regarding pollution control is 'to endeavour to limit and, as far as possible, gradually reduce and prevent air pollution including long-range transboundary air pollution'.[14] In terms of meaningful restrictions on the use of the resource (that is the European airspace), this means that the net benefit of acceptance of the convention was zero; the parties did it solely as a gesture.

It is more interesting to compare the accession record of the Helsinki Protocol of 1985 with that of the 1979 convention.[15] The Helsinki Protocol set a strict standard with regard to air pollution controls; it required that the parties reduce their national annual sulphur emissions or their transboundary fluxes by at least 30 per cent (of 1980 levels) by 1993. To observe how such a 'uniform' standard of emission controls would impact the various European states, consider the following diagram (Figure 7.1) produced in 1986 by the ECE's Cooperative Program for Monitoring and Evaluation of Long-Range Transmission of Air Pollutants in Europe (EMEP).

Figure 7.1 illustrates that the states in Europe with the most significant air pollution problems arising from foreign sources were those in the East. Those in the West (Italy, Spain, Portugal, the UK and Ireland) are relatively well-insulated from foreign deposits by the prevailing winds from the west. Therefore the benefits from the imposition of a standard regarding emissions largely flow from west to east in Europe.

The reactions to the standards contained within the Helsinki Protocol divided almost precisely along these lines. The dichotomy between those perceiving a net benefit from the treaty, and those perceiving a net cost, divides neatly between west and east (Table 7.4).

Sulphur concentrations and acidity in Europe

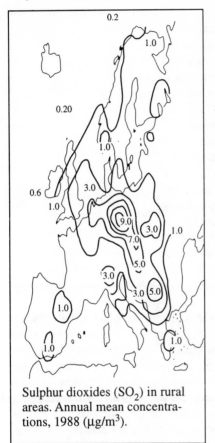
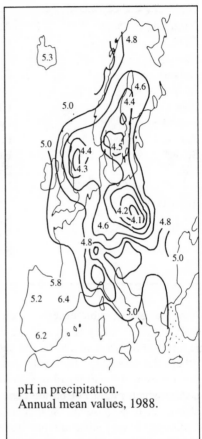

Sulphur dioxides (SO$_2$) in rural areas. Annual mean concentrations, 1988 (µg/m^3).

pH in precipitation. Annual mean values, 1988.

Source: UNCE (1991).

Figure 7.1   Sulphur deposition in Europe[16]

The states which stayed outside of the so-called 'club of 30 per cent' were largely those same states for which foreign-sourced sulphur deposition was not the major problem; those within the group corresponded closely to those for which such deposition is the primary source of sulphur within their borders.

Table 7.4   1985 Protocol acceptance compared with 1979 convention accession (as of 1 January 1989)

Out	In
Belgium	Austria
GDR	Bulgaria
Greece	Canada
Iceland	Czechoslovakia
Ireland	Denmark
Italy	Finland
Poland	France
Portugal	FRG
Spain	Hungary
UK	Lichtenstein
US	Luxembourg
Yugoslavia	Netherlands
	Norway
	Sweden
	Switzerland
	USSR

Note the two possible exceptions on the 'out' list: Belgium and Poland. In both of these states foreign-sourced deposition appeared to be a major problem (up to 59 per cent and 58 per cent, respectively), yet neither deigned to accept the protocol; why would this be the case? This is indicative of the possibility that the protocol standard might be significantly binding on these states, which might not be the case with regard to many of the accepting states (such as those in Scandinavia where energy production is largely hydroelectric and other non-coal-based sources). These states thus face significant costs, and opportunity costs, from the convention. The sole reason to accede to the protocol in that case is in order to modify the behaviour of another state with significant impact on your own use of the resource. In the case of Belgium this state was probably the UK, and in the case of Poland it was probably the DDR Acceptance by Belgium and Poland, without contemporaneous acceptance by the other two, would simply render further benefits to the two nonconformants (by increasing the stock of resource available for them to exploit), thus supplying disincentives to acceptance by the remaining hold-outs.[17] Sequential (noncontemporaneous) acceptance of a convention standard might create pressures within other fora, but it only increases the incentives to 'hold-out' in the use of the principal resource.[18]

Consider what would occur if the standard that was adopted was based on the achievement of the optimal level of sulphur dioxide in the European landmass. That is, what would be the incentives for the various countries to adopt a standard that was calibrated to balance the benefits and the costs of sulphur emissions from various countries? Once again the heterogeneous impact of the movement of air across Europe generates very different incentives for the various countries on that continent. The result of such a standard is a spectrum of net costs and benefits distributed across the European states, ranging from a net cost of −336 million DM for the UK to a net benefit of 1505 million DM for the USSR (Table 7.5). The primary losers are again in the 'west' (Italy, Spain and the UK); the primary beneficiaries to their east (Scandinavia, Poland, The Netherlands, France and the USSR).

Table 7.5   The full cooperative solution to the acid rain problem in Europe

Country	Percentage Reduction in Sulphur Dioxide	Net Benefits (Millions of Deutschmarks)
Bulgaria	43	−7
Czechoslovakia	75	152
Finland	14	−2
France	10	879
German Democratic Rep.	80	11
Germany, Federal Republic of	86	328
Italy	33	−83
Netherlands	62	565
Poland	27	599
Soviet Union	2	1505
Spain	14	−29
Sweden	4	606
United Kingdom	81	−336
All Europe	39	6290

The single standard applied to each of the states in this simulation was the equivalence of the marginal (aggregate) benefit from abatement of sulphur emissions to the marginal (internal) cost of abatement. Due primarily to the direction of the airflow this single standard required abatement in excess of 80 per cent of current emission levels in the UK, former DDR, FRG, Greece and Denmark, but required abatement of less than 5 per cent in Scandinavia and the USSR.

Thus the appearance of fairness from the adoption of 'uniform standards' can often be misleading. In the context of multilateral contract a single standard will usually have a significant redistributive component to it, even though its primary motivation is the achievement of proper administration of the resource.[19] This is particularly apparent when the above simulation is reiterated in the absence of the 'net losers': Italy, Spain and the UK. There are two basic results to note. First, the total benefits to the group drop by almost 15 per cent, from 6290 to 5180 million DM. Second, and more interestingly, there is a new group of states whose involvement in the idealized convention is rendered a net loss; GDR, Hungary, Ireland and Portugal would no longer have any reason to remain within the convention (Table 7.6).[20]

Table 7.6   The incentives to non-cooperation in the acid rain context

Country	Emission Reduction (%)	Net Benefit Millions of Deutschmarks
Cooperating Countries		
Czechoslovakia	75	125
German Democratic Republic	80	−47
Germany, Federal Republic of	86	78
Poland	27	544
Soviet Union		1372
Sweden	3	478
Total for cooperators	37	4933
Defecting Countries (Non-participants in Solution)		
Italy		150
United Kingdom		87
Total		237
Total for Europe	28	5180

Source: Maler in Helm (1991).

In the context of the Helsinki Protocol, it is now apparent why the various countries responded to its terms in the manner that they did. The terms of that Protocol had a very different impact on the different countries, depending on where they fell within the European landmass. Their response to the Protocol, as indicated by each country's acceptance or non-acceptance of its terms during its initial phase of operation, was predictable given this heterogeneity.

4.2.1 The Second Sulphur Protocol and the US trading system: two different approaches to heterogeneity After the Helsinki Protocol the Economic Commission for Europe went to work on their next attempt to devise a system that would take the heterogeneous impacts of sulphur dioxide into consideration. At the same time the Americans were devising their own approach to the problems of acid rain. Contrasting the two approaches provides an interesting case study on the way in which different approaches to the same environmental problem weigh different policy goals differently.

The US system incorporates the use of tradable emission permits with relatively unrestricted trading. Such a system effectively assumes identical impacts from each emission, rather than heterogeneous impacts that occur in reality. The European system could not be more different. The European system incorporates 257 different 'zones' with different impacts, and effectively prohibits trading by virtue of requiring that emissions meet each of these different standards. One approach is ignoring environmental heterogenity, while the other is ignoring cost heterogeneity. It is the reconciliation of the very different priorities of different parties that makes environmental institution-building complex and difficult.

4.2.2 The US acid rain regulation programme In the USA the 1990 amendments to the Clean Air Act requires that electricity generators reduce SOx emissions within the USA by 50 per cent, to 9.8 million tonnes per annum. This is to be accomplished by means of a five million tonne reduction between 1995–2000 and a further five million tonne reduction thereafter. The key to accomplishing this 50 per cent reduction in SOx has been the determination of an annual aggregate quota of emissions, and its allocation among existing emitters (on the basis of historical fossil fuel consumption). The emitters are then allowed to trade their emissions permits among each other. The EPA has put in place a continuous monitoring system on all stacks, in order to match up actual emissions with permits. The total cost of attaining this 50 per cent reduction is estimated to be $700–1000 million less than in the absence of the allowed trading regime.

4.2.3 The European approach – taking heterogeneity into account The problem with the US approach is that it treats emissions from two different sites as equivalent in their impact as acid rain depositions. This is clearly not the case in Europe, and not in the USA either. At the extreme an emission from an electricity generator in Scotland has virtually no impact as acid rain, given the prevailing westerlies and the surrounding sea, while the same emission in Germany is very likely to heap significant damage on the forests of its neighbours to the east. The impact of acid rain varies greatly depending upon how much of it falls, and what it is falling upon (Table 7.7).

Table 7.7   European acid rain (pH average)

Germany/Poland	UK	Southern France/Italy/Iberia	Rainwater	Pre-IR
4.1	4.3	> 4.9	5.6	6.0

4.2.4   Critical loads standards   The system used to regulate heterogeneous impacts across Europe is known as the 'critical loads' standard. This is a system based on the ecological characteristics of the soils across Europe. Critical load is the level of acidity in precipitation that the soil in an area is able to absorb before it begins to run-off into surrounding surface waters. In effect it is a standard that controls directly for the contribution of acid rain to damage to surface waters (such as lakes), and indirectly for any other form of damages. The Second Sulphur Protocol committed the member states to the attainment of depositions not in excess of critical loads across the land mass of Europe. As a regulatory standard critical loads has been translated into 257 distinct zones within which the different standard must be met. This would imply, within a trading system, that any given sulphur emission would be required to have a permit for the amount of deposition that it implied in each of the 257 zones. There are several different problems with this approach to location-based effects. This emphasis on geographical heterogeneity has dis-allowed the consideration of other important forms of heterogeneity, such as differential costs of abatement or different development levels. Even more importantly this standard does not allow for the actual damages of sulphur deposition to be taken into account, because of its emphasis on the one form of damages (Table 7.8).

Table 7.8   Acid rain damages

Soil Runoff	Forests	Buildings etc.
Surface water damage	Deforestation	Corrosion and repairs
$38 m. p.a. Scandinavia	$25 bn. p.a. Germany	$18.7 bn. p.a. Europe

Source: Newbery (1992).

4.2.5   How should the gains to European cooperation be distributed?   One
of the biggest hurdles to successful problem solving is agreeing on the
distribution of these gains (bargaining). In many environmental contexts the
instrument used to solve the problem will itself determine the shares that are
to be received; this is because environmental problems may be conceived as
the need to establish some sort of institutional structure with regard to a
resource. The objections to how this resource will ultimately be distributed
under the new institution often suffices to keep the resource unmanaged (that
is within an open access regime) which is, of course, to the benefit of no one.

Under the critical loads standard the real winners in the European regulation of sulphur dioxide were the Scandinavian states. The system places a
tremendous amount of emphasis on the control of soil run-off, with a consequent benefit (primarily to the pristine lakes of Scandinavia) of about $38
million per annum. The other costs of acid rain are not so well-regulated to
the costs of many states in the east who bear them. Other approaches would
have had very different impacts on the distribution of benefits across Europe.

*4.2.6   Alternative decision rules available for determining allocation of SOx
emissions*   For example, consider the many different ways in which the amount
of sulphur commensurate with critical loads might have been allocated. If
critical loads are to be attained this implies a reduction of European sulphur
dioxide emissions of about half to around 10 million tonnes per annum. The
critical load standard itself dictates where these emissions must occur (by
reason of dictating where the depositions may fall), but it is interesting to
note how alternative allocation rules might have distributed this same set of
entitlements. That is, how might an alternative rule (other than the critical
loads standard) have distributed the same amount of sulphur emissions across
the European states?

Consider the following alternatives that might be argued for in the context
of SOx. Critical loads allocate this amount of emissions to the states of
Europe in the manner indicated in the rightmost column. You will note in
Table 7.9 for example that Denmark has its lowest possible allocation under
this criterion, because of the substantial impact its emissions have on
Scandinavian lakes. Another possibility would be to allocate this same quantity of sulphur emissions by reference to each country's development level.
This is represented by the column denominated 'income' in which each
country's entitlement is weighted inversely in accordance with its per capita
income. In this column the countries of Eastern Europe fair much better than
the more developed countries of the west. Another possibility would be to use
a criterion based upon population level, on the rationale that each citizen of
Europe is entitled to an equal right to emit sulphur. In this case the larger
countries in Europe, France, Germany and the UK fare relatively well.

Table 7.9   Alternative entitlement rules for allocating aggregate SOx emissions

Country	Nature (appropriation)	Individual Rights (population)	Income (GDP/person)	SSP (critical loads)
Austria	0.50	1.89	2.73	0.52
Belgium	1.52	2.36	2.82	1.65
Czech	9.97	3.74	15.18	11.55
Denmark	1.08	1.24	2.29	0.60
Finland	3.07	1.21	2.45	0.78
France	10.94	13.77	2.57	8.09
Germany	13.38	15.40	2.22	8.46
Hungary	6.29	2.48	13.04	5.96
Iceland	0.11	0.06	2.24	0.04
Ireland	1.31	0.85	4.41	1.03
Italy	9.31	13.63	3.00	12.12
Luxembourg	0.04	0.09	2.00	0.07
Netherlands	1.02	3.64	2.83	0.71
Norway	0.61	1.03	1.93	0.22
Poland	11.54	9.21	19.56	17.16
Portugal	2.60	2.37	8.67	2.08
Spain	13.40	9.38	4.93	11.60
Sweden	1.33	2.08	2.23	0.69
Switzerland	0.23	1.66	1.77	0.40
UK	11.64	13.89	3.14	16.27
Total	100%	100%	100%	100%

Finally you could base the standard on the natural propensity of the nation to emit sulphur, that is its historic rate of high-sulphur usage. This would be equivalent to a 'historical rights' or prior appropriation sort of standard. This once again rewards the more developed countries relative to the less.

Any of these standards is arguably the correct one in a particular context, or it may be that the best standard would be a combination of all of the above. The object of this example is simply to demonstrate that there are a wide range of feasible criteria, any one of which is as worthy as the next, and all of which generate a wide range of possible allocations. It is this indeterminacy that generates the long-running disagreements about distributions and entitlements that undermine so many international environmental agreements.

4.3   Fisheries quotas and NEAFC: the importance of investments

Another source of heterogeneity between countries lies in the investment paths they have taken. When resources are regulated one of the immediate impacts is that their value is increased. This is of course the entire object of the regulatory exercise – the enhancement of the value of the resource through better management – but it also implies an increased cost to the users of the resource. Heavier users of the resource will perceive an increased cost to introduction of restrictions on its use. Heavier users are often those users who have made sunk investments in capital for the purpose of accessing the resource. One of the reasons that some countries claim a disproportionate burden from the introduction of a global management regime is the fact that they have invested heavily down a path that assumed a low cost of access.

The short-lived regime of the North East Atlantic Fishing Commission (NEAFC) is a disproportionately colourful example of this sort of negotiation. During the years 1974–76, when it was apparent that the herring fishery was under tremendous pressure, this commission adopted four different quotas in order to attempt to regulate the resource. Despite these repeated attempts at regulation, the stocks of herring suffered enormously during this period; the sustainable harvest recommended by the scientific committee fell from 310 000 tonnes in 1974 to 0 in 1976 (Underdal, 1980).

Why did the NEAFC fail so abjectly in its attempt to regulate the resource under its jurisdiction? This is clearly an example where the states could have benefited jointly from cooperative behaviour; the fishing quotas (if properly managed) could have been maintained relatively constant forever. The failure of the commission resulted in the degradation of the fishery, and the dissipation of the rents implicit within it.

Closer examination of the negotiations indicates that the various parties were arguing for different shares of the fishery based upon different criteria for distribution. In the deliberations at the NEAFC, the 12 different parties broke down into three identifiable camps: (1) those states arguing that the individual quotas failed to give enough weight to 'historical rights' (Poland, Sweden, Russia); (2) those arguing that the individual quotas failed to give enough weight to 'industry problems' (Denmark); and (3) those arguing that the overall quota must be kept low irrespective of individual demands (the UK and Norway).

The 'historical rights' group were those states that were exercising recent restraint, and demanding that quotas take that into account. The state arguing for 'industrial problems', Denmark, was the recent investor in this case; it was stuck with heavy new sunk investments in North Sea fishing capital. The third group was the group that expected to benefit most from the new 200-mile exclusive fishing zone then proposed under the Law of the Sea Convention; that is, they were the future owners of the property that NEAFC was then regulating. In addition to these arguments Russia and Poland also argued that they were entitled to additional consideration on account of their development status.

Based on the scientific committee's evidence, the agreed overall quota was 400 000 tonnes while the sum of the individual shares demanded in this round of negotiations was 572 000 tonnes. This latter figure was clearly unsustainable as it was greater than the total estimated biomass of the fishery in that year. Ultimately the states caved in to Denmark's demands (giving it a 42 per cent share of the fishery, higher even than its recent catches), but the overall quota adopted was still in excess of the scientific committee's recommendation.

The next year's negotiations were even more interesting. From the outset the states that had practised unilateral restraint were out to restrict Denmark's quota. They pushed uncompromisingly for individual quotas that would require the greatest sacrifice from the big users: Denmark, Norway and Iceland. Their argument rings familiar: those countries responsible for the deteriorating state of the fishery should bear the brunt of the cutbacks required to protect the resource. The proposed quota required that 92 per cent of the cutbacks fall on these 'big users'. The measure was passed by a predictable margin (8–3), and then, just as predictably, ignored by the minority. The 'enacted quota' was for 254 000 tonnes while the actual harvest was 365 000 tonnes; the share captured by Denmark in that year actually increased by almost 33 per cent over the previous year, when the other states had capitulated to all of Denmark's demands. Following these abject failures in negotiations, the fishery collapsed and there was no further need for the NEAFC.

The elucidation of the NEAFC saga demonstrates the extent to which history insists on repeating itself in the context of IEA negotiations. The disproportionate impact of resource management regimes often derives from positions that the parties have themselves chosen in the past. Investments that are based upon previously low costs of access to the resource render the imposition of strict management regimes untenable. This is because these investments assume one price for the resource, while the entire object of resource regulation is to render the resource more valuable.

It would be easy to take the position that such investments are based upon inefficient resource values and so they should go uncompensated. There are two problems with this approach. First, the country with these sunk investments feels these costs in a real and concrete manner, and so they are something that must be dealt with if an international agreement is going to emerge. Second, the timing of investment is often closely correlated with the development status, and so there is a confusion here of the two factors. In many instances it is the richest and most developed countries that have the least investments sunk in a problematic industry, while the later developing countries are often those which have made the problematic investments. Then it is a case of compensating the differential burden for the right reason.

5 Conclusion: the role of baselines

In this chapter we have identified three important sources of heterogeneity between nations: development status, investment choices and physical locality. The latter factor implies that many countries will have differential impacts from common resources simply because of their physical location, proximity to the resource or relative ease of access to it. So, for example, countries located near the poles will have differential impacts from the depletion of the ozone layer. Low-lying countries experience differential impacts from sea-level rise. Countries with long seaboards have differential access to oceanic resources. There are very few resources, if any, for which there is not some physical attribute that determines some heterogeneity of impact on the various countries.

Development status is an even more prevalent source of heterogeneity. Development and wealth accumulation are processes that occur across time, and at any given point in time different countries will be at different points in their development. Every country will perceive the same resources, and even the same levels of costliness, differently. This is because different levels of development, and wealth, imply different trade-offs that will be made by those countries. People in countries with large stocks of wealth tend to be relatively satiated on consumer goods and the like, and this allows them to place a greater proportion of their marginal income into commodities such as health, nature and aesthetics. The high-income elasticity of these sorts of fundamental commodity has been demonstrated often, and it is for this reason that citizens of the richer countries have a higher willingness to pay for environmental and health-related resources. In contrast there is no reason why a poorer country should perceive the need to invest in these commodities to the same extent as a rich country; these poorer countries are simply at an earlier point in the same process.

This point leads on to the next step in the analysis. The differing perspectives of different countries should be able to be related to a common *baseline*: an underlying relationship between human development status, physical location and that person's valuation of the environmental resource. The commonality of humanity provides that different people will feel the same about the resource, so long as they stand in the same place in space and development. This commonality allows for these relationships to be developed and applied across the whole range of a country's perspectives.

The role of such baselines is to determine the base against which various country's efforts should be measured. Then different countries can be allotted different requirements, given their development status.

Notes

1. The quote is from E. Shiff, *Industrialisation Without National Patents*, Princeton University Press, Princeton, NJ: 1971. It was addressed to the delegation from The Netherlands at the Paris Convention on Industrial Property in 1883.
2. See *The role of patents in the transfer of technology to developing countries*, report of the Secretary General, United Nations, New York: 1964 (history and principles of the International Patent Union).
3. One of the fundamental principles agreed was the 'unconditional treatment of foreigners as nationals', which applied regardless of the treaty status of the foreigner's state. See Schiff, *supra*, n. 1, at 22.
4. In fact The Netherlands was wholly without domestic patent legislation between 1869 and 1912, a period of 43 years; however, the International Union only existed for 29 of those years.
5. The hold-out problem in public economics has been discussed in the domestic context for many years. The problem lies in the ability of any necessary contractor to 'free-ride' on the agreement of others; for this reason, as more parties enter into an agreement concerning a common resource, the opportunity cost of doing so rises for all remaining non-signatories. See Olsen, M., *The Logic of Collective Action*, Chicago: 1974. In the international sphere, this same point has been made by Barret, S., 'On the nature and significance of international environmental agreements', *Oxford Economic Papers* (1993).
6. This is analogous to the problem of 'adverse selection' in the insurance economics literature. This problem results from the offering of a single set of contract terms to a large pool of heterogeneous persons. Obviously some of the persons will find the offered terms to be more valued than others.
7. See Brugmans, I.J., *Paardekracht en Mensenmacht*, Den Haag: 1971.
8. Theoretically the expenditures on industrial innovation will be equal to the expected rewards from winning the 'patent race'. Since The Netherlands' strategy substantially reduced the amount of these rewards, the corresponding investment must have been likewise reduced. See Arrow, K., 'Economic welfare and the allocation of resources for invention', in R.R. Nelson (ed.), *The Rate and Direction of Inventive Activity*, 1962.
9. See Mokyr, J., 'The industrial revolution in the low countries in the first half of the nineteenth century: a comparative case study', *The Journal of Economic History*, vol. 31, p. 1 (1974) (failure of the Dutch to industrialize in the first half of the nineteenth century under several indicators of technical development: distribution of labour force, incidence of innovation, steam power and so on).
10. Extracted from Griffiths, R.T., *Industrial Retardation in The Netherlands: 1830–1850*, Martinus Nijhoff, Den Haag: 1979.
11. Misc. 10 (1980), Cmnd. 7885.
12. See Gundling, L., 'Multilateral co-operation of states under the EEC Convention on long-range transboundary air pollution', in Flinterman, C. (ed.), *Transboundary Air Pollution*, Martinus Nijhoff, Den Haag: 1986.
13. *Id.*, at 27. ('Obligations to take measures for a reduction of trans-boundary air pollution are laid down only in general terms, and they are, in addition, lined to a number of "escape clauses". There is no obligation, under the convention, to reduce specific air pollutants, like sulphur dioxide, by a specific period of time.')
14. Art. II.
15. The Protocol to the 1979 Convention on Long-Range Transboundary Air Pollution on the Reduction of Sulphur Emissions or their Transboundary Fluxes by at Least 30 Per Cent, Helsinki, 8 July 1985.
16. Extracted from Wetstone, G. and Rosencranz, A., *Acid Rain in Europe and North America*, Environmental Law Institute, Aspen: 1983.
17. The prototypical example of this concept is the history of the exploitation of the whale population. As international pressures forced more of the participants from the field (in sequential fashion), the exiting states not only left the resource open to unconstrained exploitation by the remaining harvesters but even sold them their whaling fleets for that

purpose. Therefore these partial and non-contemporaneous acceptances provided no incentives, in themselves, for later acceptances. See Birnie, P.

18. Thus the principal means by which remaining whaling states have been caused to conform with the standards enunciated by the International Whaling Commission has been the threatened withdrawal of (wholly unrelated) fishing rights within US territorial waters. The 'Pelly Amendment' allows the certification of states failing to conform to international conservation conventions, and the subsequent withdrawal of fishing rights in territorial waters. The threat of this certification has been sufficient to pressure conformance by several states which had previously given notice of reservation or withdrawal; for example Chile and Peru in 1981, and Japan in 1985.

19. Another instance in which this disparate impact is readily apparent is in the current movement to amend Appendix I of the Convention on International Trade of Endangered Species of Flora and Fauna in order to ban the trade in African elephant products. The movement is spurred by the rapid decline in continental elephant populations, which have been halved in each of the past two decades; however the population changes have varied widely between individual states (depending on both poaching pressures and the investment in anti-poaching efforts). For example Southern African populations have remained relatively stable recently while East African populations have plummeted. See Ivory Trade Review Group, 'The ivory trade and the future of the African elephant', report prepared for the Second Meeting of the CITES African Elephant Working Group, Gaborone, Botswana, July 1989 (proposing the placement of the African Elephant on Appendix I). Of course it is predictable that the Southern African states do not perceive the proposed ban as a 'net benefit' from their standpoint. See Department of National Parks and Wildlife Management, 'International moves to ban the legal trade in raw ivory', June 1989 ('Zimbabwe does not support the current moves to ban the ivory trade ... Zimbabwe will enter a Reservation before the proposal is debated'.)

20. *Id.*, at 12.

8 The evolution of international environmental agreements: negotiations after negotiations

1 Problems after the creation of international environmental agreements

In Chapter 7 we saw that the pursuit of agreement in international environmental law was complicated both by the individual state's pursuit of resource rents and by its pursuit of fairness. States perceive that the equal treatment of unequals does not equate with fairness, but their pursuit of fair treatment becomes intermeshed with other states' pursuit of resource rents. The process through which these various demands are negotiated sometimes results in an initial text for an international environmental agreement (IEA).

However, the development of this text, and even its acceptance by many states at an initial international convention, is often the beginning of the long road toward resource management, not the end of it. These texts are often phrased in a very vague fashion, so as to garner sufficient acceptances to give them effect, or (if not) they imply commitments that many states find unacceptable. States then have available intermediate options such as signing the convention but refusing to ratify it, or signing it with reservations in regard to specific articles, or signing it without any observable implementation of its implied commitment. Therefore, even after an international environmental agreement comes into existence, there continues to be a very long process of evolution towards bringing it into actual effect. Remember that the point of an IEA must always be to impose restrictions on the use of some common resource and, until these restrictions are brought into effect, an existing environmental agreement has no real impact.

The problems of bargaining and distribution underlie this process as much as it did the negotiation process described in Chapter 3. The problems concerning the effectiveness of existing IEA are still sourced in the problems of inducing acceptance and compliance with the resource management regime. These acknowledged inefficiencies of the IEAs stem from the costliness of the solution to the 'bargaining problem'. That is all of these difficulties in international law are traceable to the problem of agreeing on the distribution of the gains realized by agreement. A state which feels aggrieved about its allocated share of the resource under the convention standard has available to it any of these options for the unilateral appropriation of additional shares of the resource. One of the fundamental costs of this system of bargaining is that agreed laws are subject to unilateral restructuring; hence the perception that international agreements have little substance is perpetuated.

The most direct impact of non-agreement (whether in explicit or tacit form) is a much less effective system for administering the international resource. Irrespective of the avenue chosen, the costs are the same: the overexploitation and deterioration of the resource stock to the detriment of all.

2   Characteristics of a binding resource management agreement

The fundamental problem to resolve in international resource law is how to create an optimal resource management regime via an international agreement which is concrete, universally binding and enforceable. This requires that the contract contain each of the following elements:

1.   *efficiency*: optimal aggregate usage level
2.   *distribution*: concrete individual shares
3.   *implementation*: a monitoring system for share enforcement and sanctions to deter evasion of the monitoring system.

These are the necessary characteristics of a binding agreement, that is one that is concrete and enforceable. In addition, in order to negotiate a universally binding agreement, it will be necessary to construct the terms of the agreement in such a manner so that it induces simultaneous acceptance by each and every state.

This is the precise implication of an *ex ante* bargaining procedure; that is the object of *ex ante* bargaining should be to achieve the *simultaneous* movement of all potential users to the cooperative equilibrium, by constructing an agreement in such a way as to create the incentives for this move. This is a difficult task to comprehend in the context of a single instrument. This section investigates the difficulties involved in solving all four parts of the *ex ante* bargaining problem. In the remainder of this part of the section, we outline the essence of parts (1) and (3) of the problem, and in the next part we focus attention on the distributional hurdle.

2.1   Sanctions: the necessity of self-enforcing conventions

One source of contractual costliness is the necessity of a self-enforcing contract. In the international context there is no overarching authority in place for the enforcement of bargains, as there is in the case of domestic contracts (that is the judiciary and the police). This does *not* imply that such contracts are unenforceable; it merely implies that enforcement must be supplied as part of the contract, since it is not automatically supplied elsewhere. This means that the contractual terms must not only induce agreement at the time that the bargain is struck; these terms must also induce perform-ance of the agreement throughout its life as wen.

Most contracts in private relations are in fact of this nature. It is prohibi-tively costly to access the governmentally supplied enforcement mechanism, so enforcement must be provided on a private basis to supplement the public mechanism (Williamson, 1986). This is often done by providing for third party mediators, or by making contracts within the framework of a repeating relationship. To the extent that these private contractual mechanisms are successful, this success is attributable to the existence of reciprocal sunk investments in the relationship. Sunk investments are any expenditures which will only yield a return through the performance of the terms of the contract. They are the 'bonds' provided to assure performance of the agreement. To the extent that all parties have roughly equivalent bonds riding on the perform-ance of the original bargain, the freedom to engage in unilateral restructuring of that contract is limited.

This means that an international resource agreement must not only deter-mine shares of resource use, but also that such shares must be allocated over a certain period of time and bonds instituted for the enforcement of this bargain. Otherwise changed conditions will alter individual perceptions of the distribution of the benefits and burdens of coordination, and the agree-ment will collapse. Therefore the bargaining problem in the international resource context is further complicated by the addition of this dynamic di-mension to the negotiations over resource shares.

2.2   Implementing a credible international monitoring system

A monitoring system is a fundamental component of a system of joint man-agement. The resolution of the bargaining problem has little impact unless the performance of the agreement is observable. Each party receives its 'implicit return' from personally foregoing the opportunistic strategy by means of observing that all other parties are reciprocating. Without monitoring, the parties to the contract are returned to the 'Prisoners' Dilemma'.

One of the fundamental problems with international law has been its reli-ance upon state self- implementation of international obligations. This manner of monitoring is doomed to failure, not because states are necessarily oppor-tunistic but because there is no observable return to self-enforcement. The return to enforcement must come from observing other states' enforcement efforts, that is international monitoring.

2.3   Efficiency: determining optimal aggregate use

The determination of the optimal aggregate level of use is problematic be-cause it becomes easily intertwined with the issue of share determination. For example those parties desiring larger shares often do so through the mechanism of arguing for a *pro rata* share of a larger aggregate quota, thereby implying that the burden of optimal management will be left to fall upon other states. This argument for individualized treatment often takes the form of the presentation of 'scientific evidence' supporting a high level of aggregate use; then those supporting lower aggregate rates of access may be made to absorb the majority of the impact of the position which they are supporting. Therefore there exist incentives to distort the objectivity of the process even at the level of determining aggregate usage.

2.4 Distribution: determining individual shares

As we have already seen in Chapter 3 this is the core of the problem of the negotiation process. There are no obvious or easily calculated methods for determining individual shares, and the confusion between burdens and opportunism renders the bargaining even more difficult. This section considers why several possible 'focal point' solutions fail to work well in solving the bargaining problem in the international resource context.

2.4.1 The problem of uniform share allocations

One means of solving the distributional problem would be to use the 'rule of equal treatment' to allocate equal shares in the global resource to all states. It has been argued by some that this rule appeals to 'the sense of fairness', especially in regard to the use of international resources (Young, 1989). This principle is in wide usage in the formulation of most international resource conventions.

But it is a singularly unhelpful approach, as is any approach which attempts to treat unequals equally in a contractual context. The construction of a contract must take into consideration the incentives its terms create for its own acceptance; otherwise it is doomed to failure. Uniform standards ignore the fact that the 'sense of fairness' is not shared by all (certainly not by those affected unequally) and this results in the predictable failure of the regulatory mechanism, because international resource regulation requires the agreement of all potential users.

Importantly these concepts of fairness have been developed within an entirely different institutional environment. In the domestic context the multilateral bargaining problem no longer arises because a distinct layer of institutions has evolved to deal with multilateral contract situations. Domestically contract has been largely relegated to the bilateral spheres of activity, and multilateral contracting has been largely managed through 'political' processes, such as representative government and majority voting. These additional institutions provide the means by which heterogeneous parties may be pooled within a contract with a uniform set of standards. To apply 'senses of fairness' acquired within the domestic context to the international is counterproductive because the latter has evolved ways of dealing with these problems which the former has not.

2.4.2   The problem of allocation under objective criteria   In theory it should be possible to ascertain *objectively* the individual cost of compliance, but this is a very difficult task to accomplish in a multilateral setting. Such a determination is usually unnecessary in bilateral bargaining, where it is possible instead to rely on the individual's 'reservation price', that is the user's own subjective determination of its individual costliness of acceptance. The costs from otherwise remaining in the (uncoordinated) state of disagreement create incentives for truthful revelation in that context. This is of course not the case in multilateral contracting. The 'costs of disagreement' in this context are often the 'benefits from free-riding' on others' restraint, if sequential acceptance occurs. Therefore, in multilateral contract, there is little incentive for the state to truthfully reveal its perceived costs.

In fact the hold-out state itself might not be aware of the true source of its recalcitrance in this situation; when sequential adoption occurs, the two phenomena, individual costliness and free-rider benefits, will be necessarily interrelated. As a sequence of states curtail the use of a resource (or potential users abstain), the hold-out will increase its rate of access in pursuit of rents. This increased rate of usage will, however, simply increase the costliness to this state of future accession to the agreement. Thus differential dependence on the resource is itself a symptom of the pursuit of 'hold-out rents'.

This leaves two avenues for the allocation of shares in the resource after coordination. The first is to attempt an 'objective' (or scientific) determination of the relative costliness of accession. To a large extent this is merely a reformulation of the initial task (of securing some basis of agreement on shares) by means of involving a group of third party intervenors. In the international regulation context the reference to scientific criteria usually leads to pitched battles along these lines, as each state then arms itself with its own 'expert testimony' as to its individual burden. Even if a scientific consensus is developed there is no reason why any one state must necessarily submit to that tide of opinion, especially as it can usually be predicted that the consensus was developed with the backing of those states whose interests are advanced by that particular perspective.

A variant on this theme is the establishment of a 'scientific committee' under the international regulatory mechanism, whose recommendations as to shares are vested with some presumption of validity. In these regimes the fundamental battles are then waged in regard to the manner by which appointments to the scientific committee are occasioned.

2.4.3   The problem of allocation by prior appropriation   Alternatively the individual shares of the resource could be determined by reference to some point in time; that is shares can be frozen by reference to use at that time.

Such entitlements procured through first use are known in the domestic context as rights by 'prior appropriation'.

Although the principle of 'prior appropriation' has been used quite extensively with regard to common resources in the domestic context (for example oil pools, minerals, water, wildlife and so on), it has been demonstrated that this doctrine results in the same wastage in that context that can be anticipated to occur in the global. Prior appropriation as a legal regime is hugely inefficient with regard to the exploitation of domestic open access resources (for example oil pools) and it has resulted in the complete dissipation of the resource rents in the form of wasteful overcapitalization in these industries (for example domestic fisheries) (Libecap, 1989).

2.4.4   The problem of paying the polluter   Furthermore it makes even less sense to create a general system of incentives to encourage investment in international resources in this way. An international resource management system which is constructed so as to compensate disproportionate investments in the appropriation of some global resources will have the effect of encouraging those investments with regard to other international resources. That is the dynamic efficiency of 'paying the polluter' is doubtful. It will, perhaps, result in a binding universal agreement with regard to one global resource only at the expense of encouraging further the overexploitation of other such resources.

This range of problems regarding the determination of individual shares is the fundamental problem of *ex ante* bargaining. There is no obvious criterion for determining shares under an international resource agreement. Yet shares must be determined on an acceptable basis in order to acquire universal agreement. It is the resolution of this paradox which is at the base of the fundamental costliness of *ex ante* bargaining.

3   The alternative of *ex post* bargaining: the evolution of IEAs

The allocation of concrete shares of an international resource and the construction of a mechanism for their enforcement is no small task. The costliness of the bargaining to accomplish this would not be inconsequential in any case.

Clearly, *ex post* bargaining is also a very costly approach to resource regulation. The failure to agree enforceable shares *ex ante* implies the adoption of the sequential acceptance mechanism for attempting to achieve the jointly managed solution. This in turn implies substantial redistribution of shares through the mechanism of free-riding on others' unilateral restraint. Ultimately, this method of *ex post* bargaining over shares may also lead to universal agreement; however it entails its own costliness during the period in which 'hold-outs' exist.

This 'hold-out problem' underlies many of the reasons for allegations concerning the ineffectiveness and insubstantiality of international law.[1] These perceptions are largely attributable to the peculiar infirmities of international law, deriving from the now familiar factors: textual ambiguity, non-accession, reservation and non-implementation. These are the sources of most concerns about the efficacy of international law.

Each of these failures derives from the same fundamental problem; each is a method used to appropriate greater shares of the resource than would be allowed under the convention. Non-acceptance of the treaty, via failure to sign, ratify or accede, is of course the classic form of 'hold-out'. Equally damaging is the party that formally accepts the treaty, but makes a significant reservation with regard to its use of the resource.[2] The lack of concreteness in convention language is often necessary for consensus, but also renders the convention largely unenforceable against any state.[3] Finally the acceptance of the convention in all respects *de jure* while (owing to severe monitoring problems) the state continues using the resource without regard to its international obligations *de facto* has the same impact as each of the preceding practices.[4]

There are good reasons to prefer an *ex ante* bargaining solution to an *ex post* one. First, the *ex post* solution implies delayed coordination in the use of the international resource. This is an irretrievable deadweight loss. In addition it is possible that the continued overexploitation of the resource may result in an additional loss by reason of its extinction. With regard to most natural resources, once exploitation has reached a certain level, the resource cannot be retrieved. This implies additional losses regarding future 'options' and generations.

Another reason to prefer the *ex ante* solution concerns the external effects of *ex post* redistributions on other international regulatory regimes. These redistributions are often undertaken in the form of express disagreements and the refusal to sign or ratify the convention. More often, however, these redistributions occur in the context of tacit disagreements which do not, in writing, appear to rise to the level of total non-acceptance, but in practice have the same effect. These forms of tacit disagreement are often countenanced in the pursuit of nominal 'consensus', but do a great deal of harm to both the administration and the reputation of international resource regimes.

Each of these forms of disagreement, express and tacit, addresses the same *ex post* bargaining problem; that is each is a method used to enable individual states to appropriate greater shares of the resource than would be allowed under the terms of the agreement. Non-acceptance of the treaty, via failure to sign, ratify or accede, is of course the classic form of 'hold-out'. Equally damaging is the party that formally accepts the treaty, but makes a significant reservation with regard to its use of the resource. The lack of concreteness in convention language is often argued to be necessary for consensus, but this also renders the convention largely unenforceable against any state. Finally the acceptance of the convention in all respects *de jure*, while (owing to severe monitoring problems) the state continues use without regard to its international obligations *de facto* has the same impact as each of the preceding practices.

These acknowledged inefficiencies of international resource lawmaking are various manifestations of the costliness of the solution to the 'bargaining problem' in this context. That is all of these difficulties in international law are traceable to the problem of agreeing on the distribution of the gains realized by agreement; a state which feels aggrieved about its allocated share of the resource under the convention standard has available to it any of these options for the unilateral appropriation of additional shares of the resource. One of the fundamental costs of this system of *ex post* 'bargaining' is that 'agreed' laws are subject to unilateral restructuring; hence the perception that international agreements have little substance is perpetuated.

Therefore there are fundamentally sound reasons to prefer a system of *ex ante* bargaining concerning international resource regimes as opposed to the *ex post* form that has developed. Of course an *ex ante* system would itself not be costless; the preceding section indicated that there would be substantial costliness involved in solving the bargaining problem on this basis. However the costliness of bargaining over shares exists, whether accomplished on an *ex ante* or an *ex post* basis, while the benefits to coordinating usage of the resource are achieved earlier in the former case. In essence international resource agreements are an example of the 'shrinking cake' bargaining game, where the parties lose forever the benefits from agreement when it is deferred (Rubinstein, 1988). In this framework, it will always be more efficient to pursue the *ex ante* approach.

4 The costliness of *ex post* bargaining

There are four different avenues by which *ex post* redistributions can occur, even after a convention has been adopted for the regulation of an international resource: (1) non-signatories; (2) reservations (signing but with explicit rejection of one or more parts of the agreement); (3) textual ambiguity (signing agreement with no concrete terms); and (4) non-implementation (signing but refusing to comply with the agreement). In this section we outline some examples from the marine context to demonstrate how these are used to appropriate resource rents to individual states.

4.1 Non-signatories

The collapse of international regulatory regimes by reason of the refusal of users to accept the standards of the convention has occurred widely. Most recently the United Nations Law of the Sea Convention, developed through 25 years of continuous negotiations, failed to gain wide acceptance. Although open for signature since 1982 it has still failed to obtain sufficient accept-ances (60 states) to come into effect. Among the significant non-signatories are the FRG, the UK and the USA. In fact even though 159 states signed the convention within its two-year signature period, as of 1987 only 32 had ratified.

The primary reason that this convention has failed to secure the acceptance of these important signatories is its provisions for regulating the one area of the oceans which are retained exclusively in international jurisdiction, that is the deep seabed. The vast majority of states declared this region the 'common heritage of mankind', and the LOSC provides that any working of this region is to proceed through an international body known as the enterprise, or its licensees [LOSC, Art. 134 *et seq.*]. This provision proved unacceptable to most of the developed states (including the non-signatories listed above), whose firms had already invested over $250 million in the development of deep seabed technology and exploration.

An eleventh-hour attempt to save the Law of the Sea Convention was launched in 1982, by the adoption of a compromise resolution which vested exclusive rights to seabed areas of up to 150 000 square miles in each of eight 'pioneer investors' for a period of eight years. Obviously this was a last ditch attempt at some true *ex ante* bargaining, but the offer was declined; the seabed mining states instead entered into a reciprocating states regime under which they recognized one another's claims to certain areas of the seabed.

This was perhaps one of the most recent, and most famous, incidents in a long line of international regime failures. The very first attempt at regulation of oceanic resources was subject to the same difficulty. In the latter part of the nineteenth century the taking of fur seals at sea by US and Russian fleets had resulted in the near decimation of this species; in about 1885 these two states agreed to undertake the unilateral restraint of forbidding their fleets from taking fur seals at sea. The response was immediate; Canadian and Japanese sealers swarmed into Alaskan and Siberian waters, respectively. In 1893 the USA and the UK (for Canada) finally agreed a ban on all pelagic ('at sea') sealing, which of course only opened that part of the seas to Japanese exploitation as well. By the turn of the century the fur seal populations were reduced to a small proportion of their original size, and Japanese sealers had appropriated a much greater share of the harvest by reason of the unilat-eral restraint of the other sealers.

In general the history of the international fisheries commissions was ren-dered an unhappy one by the appearance of the long-distance trawlers on the scene in the 1960s. This entry by a few states with large factory-sized ships rendered nascent agreements by territorial states unworkable in a large number of regulated fisheries: the Inter-American Tropical Tuna Commission; the International Commission for the Northwest Atlantic Fisheries; and the International Pacific Halibut Commission are examples. In fact the last-named commission had, through 40 years of cooperation between the USA and Canada, just achieved maximum sustainable yields when the large trawlers arrived on the scene. The trawlers tended to be from one of a few states (Japan, the USSR, Korea and East or West Germany) at that time, but the identity was of little consequence. The arrival of these trawlers was predictable, as the unilateral restraint of bordering states began to pay off in higher yields; these large ships were simply the technologically determined manifestation of the fisheries' free-riders under these circumstances.

All of these fisheries were hugely overfished in the period leading up to enclosure. Although the worldwide fish harvest remained roughly stable during this period (at about 68 million metric tonnes), this was being achieved primarily by substituting less-demanded species for overfished ones; for example, the worldwide catch of haddock had been reduced from 910 000 tonnes to 240 000 tonnes in the decade of the 1970s. In addition many fisheries have made substantial recoveries in the period after enclosure (Keen, 1988). For example the Pacific halibut catch has increased from 13 500 tonnes to 34 400 tonnes between 1976 and 1988. Effective regulation of many of these resources is now occurring.

4.2 Reservations

The taking of a reservation or objection is simply the means by which an existing member of a regulatory commission is allowed to individually opt out with regard to a proposed regulation. Such reservations occur predictably when the negotiations over shares have concluded unhappily for a particular state.

An example of the use of a right of reservation in order to redistribute shares is the short-lived regime of the Northeast Atlantic Fisheries Commission (NEAFC). As was described previously, during the years 1974–76, this commission adopted four different quotas in order to regulate the resource. The first quota was adopted (under the prevailing code of majority rule) by a vote of 9–2, but the two states in the minority simply took reservations and ignored the quotas. The next quota was passed by a vote of 8–3, but only two of the three objecting states took official reservations. The penultimate quota was actually passed by consensus, and no reservations occurred. The final quota, before enclosure occurred, was passed by a vote of 7–2, with both objecting states taking reservations. The sum total of this regulation was that, in three years of regulation constituted of scientific fact-finding and continuous negotiations, a set of binding quotas were only in effect for six months. The stocks of herring suffered accordingly; the sustainable harvest recommended by the scientific committee fell from 310 000 tonnes in 1974 to 0 in 1976 (Underdahl, 1980).

4.3   Non-implementation

Perhaps the most notorious of all hold-outs, are the so-called 'flags of convenience' states in international shipping. A flag of convenience is, in effect, a state which is not adequately regulating its fleet of registered ships. All such states are non-signatories of the High Seas Convention, which requires genuine links between a ship owner and the registering state (in order to provide that state with jurisdiction over that person and his assets). In addition, many of these states, even though signatories to a number of conventions regarding safety standards at sea, implement a lax and ineffective regulatory regime. The offering of registration to non-resident owners together with the implied laxity of standards allows these states to appropriate a disproportionate share of the shipping trade, and consequently the registration fees which are attached. Liberia, Panama and Cyprus are all flag of convenience states, and they together represent about 25 per cent of the world's registered shipping tonnage.

The oceanic resources which are overexploited as a result are the waters and shorelines which are polluted as the consequence of potentially avoidable tanker accidents. The ship owners do, of course, have incentives to undertake sufficient safety measures to protect the value of their vessels, but they have little regard for the potential losses inflicted upon others by reason of the loss of one of their vessels. As exemplified by the Torrey Canyon, the Amoco Cadiz, or the recent Alaskan oil spill, these external effects can in fact be quite substantial; perhaps far greater than the value of the vessel itself. Therefore the protection of these third parties (to tanker accidents) requires the international regulation of the resource, and the appearance of 'flag of convenience' states is the predictable response to the development of such regulations. These states are simply acquiring the hold-out rents from lax implementation of the various navigational safety conventions; they are the unavoidable consequence of the failure to create an adequate international monitoring scheme.

The impact of these hold-outs on the resource is observable from the differential accident rates experienced by the various flag states. For example between 1980–83 flags of convenience accounted for only 27 per cent of shipping tonnage but for 37 per cent of all lost tonnage. In 1985 the serious accident rate per tonnage was 2 per cent for Panama and 0.7 per cent for Cyprus (both 'flag of convenience' states); the corresponding rate for the other large shipping countries (Japan, the UK and the USSR) was well under 0.1 per cent for each. In sum nearly a third of the world's shipping tonnage was being regulated by regimes whose accident experience rate was 10–20 times that of the other major shipping states (Churchill and Lowe, 1989).

Non-implementation is a far more pervasive phenomenon in international regulation than is indicated by even this one fairly spectacular example, but by its nature it is not that readily observable. Where agreements are made, but enforcement is left in the hands of each of the individual states on the high seas, there is little reason to expect that their terms are honoured. An example of this would be the International Whaling Commission which established Antarctic whaling quotas for 30 years, which went largely ignored. The same is true of many of the fisheries commissions; the Inter-American Tropical Tuna Commission continued setting annual quotas after the entry of numerous long distance fishing states, even though the declining stocks clearly indicated that these quotas were being ignored (Keen, 1988). In short, although the evidence is sparse, it is apparent that strict self-implementation of the terms of an international resource convention is the exception rather than the rule.

4.4   Ambiguity

The ambiguity of the terms of an international resource convention can allow for *ex post* redistributions, by permitting a wide range of interpretations to be given to the shares implied by the agreement. Sometimes it is the case that a convention is rendered a nullity by reason of overly vague language. For example the initial Convention on the Continental Shelf failed to achieve agreement on the delimitation of the shelf (which is an ambiguous concept in itself) and settled instead on vesting full sovereignty in the adjacent submarine lands 'to where the depth of the superjacent waters admits of the exploitation of the natural resources of the area'. This was not the vesting of property rights in an international resource, which is a viable approach to regulating previously open access resources; it was simply the enshrining of the resource's open access status. The convention was so ambiguous that it became a non-statement. This is often the case with the language of international law texts, which frequently broadly admonish states to behave properly and do right.

Another form of ambiguity is the 'loophole'; a purposefully inserted ambiguity whose initial intent was perhaps narrow, but whose interpretation can be extended so as to swallow up the whole of the restrictions in the text. A good example of such a loophole is the 'scientific whaling' exception in the International Whaling Convention. Because the convention was intended to regulate the more significant commercial whaling sector, it exempted the scientific takings from its regulatory requirements on the assumption that such removals were too insignificant to affect stocks. When the commercial whalers were subjected to zero quotas by the commission in 1984, suddenly a new and substantial scientific whaling industry sprang up; Japan gave notice of the taking of 800 whales under this exception and Iceland gave notice of the taking of 400 immediately after the moratorium was introduced.

Similarly when the USA and Canada had achieved success in their regulation of the Pacific halibut fishery after 40 years of management, the USSR and Japan sent long-distance trawlers into the waters. When it was unanimously agreed that the halibut fishery was already operating at full capacity, the two new entrants agreed to fish outside of halibut waters and to 'abstain' from halibut fishing when in those waters. The 'abstention' loophole allowed the long-distance trawlers into the halibut fishery, and the US/Canadian harvest of halibut collapsed over the next 15 years (to a third of its previous volume) until the fishery was enclosed and the interlopers ejected.

In sum these are all examples of the ineffectiveness of agreeing regulations, which are then subject to unilateral *ex post* restructuring. The deterioration of these resources under these regimes was evidence enough of the inefficacy of this approach.

5   The evolution of wildlife trade regulation: the case of CITES and the African elephant

The population of the African elephant declined dramatically over the decade of the 1980s. The stock of elephants fell from over a million to around half that number between 1981 and 1989. Simultaneously the number of regulatory measures instituted for the conservation of the African elephant was rapidly increasing. For example most of the range states introduced bans on the unauthorized hunting of elephants and on the trade in ivory.

However more often the attempts at regulating the elephant population in Africa in the recent past were international in nature. This international regulation has occurred in the context of the biennial meetings of the parties to the Convention on the International Trade in Endangered Species of Wild Flora and Fauna (CITES). The international trade in African elephants, or any 'derivatives', has been regulated since the initial meeting of the Conference of the Parties in 1976. At that time the African elephant was included on Appendix II of the Convention, requiring a CITES permit for trade in the products of the species.

It was generally agreed between the parties that the trade in elephant ivory was important to the maintenance of this species on the continent. Elephants live for 60–70 years, and require a substantial amount of good grazing land for their sustenance (approximately 0.5 square kilometres each); hence the commitment to maintain a half-million of these animals on a poor continent implies substantial resources. The parties to CITES agreed that the trade in ivory could be an important source of such resources.

As the status of the elephant population continued to decline, the parties introduced another regulatory regime at the Buenos Aires Conference of the Parties in 1985. By Conference Resolution 5.12 they agreed to implement a 'management quota system' for the control of the African elephant. The

CITES management quota system put into effect by Resolution 5.12 was then in place for the calendar years 1986, 1987 and 1988. This regime was a last ditch effort to save the ivory trade, by means of demonstrating that it could be regulated effectively; however it failed abysmally as the elephant population continued to plummet as the unrestricted ivory trade continued unabated.

In response the Seventh Meeting of the Conference of the Parties in 1989 was focused on the possibility of 'uplisting' the African elephant population to Appendix I, which would have the effect of prohibiting all trade in elephant ivory for 'primarily commercial purposes'. This was problematic on account of the widely varying population trends across range states; for example, during the past decade, Tanzania lost about 70 per cent of its approximately 200 000 elephants while Botswana increased its initial population of 20 000 by nearly 300 per cent to 60 000. Although there was a downwards trend in aggregate, many of the African states' elephant population were moving in the other direction. What was often simplistically presented as a uniform and continent-wide problem of uncontrolled poaching and population declines was in fact a complex and widely varying set of problems related to underfunding and mismanagement.

Despite these complexities, the African elephant was moved to Appendix I at the Seventh Conference of the Parties, effectively removing its ivory from international trade for all of the range states. This disallowed all of the countries in Africa from benefiting from the trade, those who managed their elephants and those who did not. In effect the countries of Africa were penalized for the failure of the international community to adequately control the trade.

Why did the management quota system fail? Why is it not possible to introduce effective international regulation even when it is essential for the protection of the resource? These are the questions addressed here in the context of the case study of the 1980's elephant ivory trade debate.

5.1 Description of the CITES management quota system

The system regulating the trade in the African elephant between 1985–87 was the management quota system adopted under CITES. The CITES treaty was signed by 21 states in 1973 and came into force in 1975 with the subsequent ratifications. There are now 99 signatories to the convention, and it is the primary international mechanism for the management of most wildlife and its products; however there are numerous other treaties which deal solely with species which primarily inhabit international territories or waters.

Two very important points are recognized in the preamble to the convention. First, ' ... States are and should be the best protectors of their own wild fauna and flora ...'; ultimately the management of a resource which lies wholly within national boundaries must be conducted by that nation. Second, 'international cooperation is essential for the protection of certain species of wild fauna and flora against overexploitation ...' That is it is recognized that it is possible to utilize joint action to conserve the stocks of certain domestic resources. Together these precepts define what should be the overarching objective of the international regulation of national wildlife: the recognition of joint incentives and the utilization of international trade institutions to correct distortions within internal resource management institutions.

The mechanism which the treaty provided for the accomplishment of this international regulation is the CITES permit system. Species listed in the appendices to the convention must receive pre-clearance from the exporting state's management authority prior to export; the authority issues an export (or re-export) permit if the conditions for trade are satisfied. Each importing state is under obligation to ensure that each specimen is accompanied by such a permit. The parties must then submit annual reports to the Secretariat detailing the trade which has occurred in listed species.

The conditions for importation vary depending on the Appendix listing. The import of Appendix I listed species is not allowable if it is 'to be used for primarily commercial purposes'. The burden of proof is on the importing party to demonstrate a non-commercial purpose, and importation is authorized only in exceptional circumstances.

An Appendix II listing merely requires that the importer 'require prior presentation of either an export permit or a re-export certificate'. Several states have required import certificates as well, as a means of ascertaining the flow of ivory shipments. The African elephant was listed on Appendix II at the initial Conference of the Parties in 1976.

Given the rate of exploitation of the resource, it received more attention very soon thereafter. At the third meeting of the parties, in New Delhi 1981, Conference Resolution 3.12 made the initial attempts at tightening the international regulation of the elephant. It provided for the marking of ivory by punch-die and for the licensing of international traders ('where possible'). It further provided that no importing state should allow raw ivory to enter without mentioning the state of origin in the CITES documentation, and even then not unless 'the Party is satisfied the ivory was legally acquired in the country of origin'. Finally it exhorted all parties to comply with the earlier procedures regarding Appendix II commodities, that is the provision of annual reports.

As the situation continued to worsen, the Conference of the Parties in Gaborone, 1983, by Conference Resolution 4.14, directed the Technical Committee 'to draw up guidelines for controlling the trade in worked ivory as quickly as possible ...' The African parties qualified this authorization with the proviso that further international regulation should be directed toward their realization of the maximum benefits from the resource. The preamble to this Resolution provides, in part, that international regulation should not reduce the profitability of trade but rather that it should provide for the sustainable utilization of the resource.

The result of Resolution 4.14 was the introduction of the management quota system via Conference Resolution 5.12 at Buenos Aires in 1985. This system, devised within a consultancy report provided by Rowan Martin, attempted to formulate the international enforcement mechanism for the implementation of domestic management programmes. Its basic components are as follows. Each range state was to formulate a management programme for the utilization of its elephant stock and then submit an annual 'quota' of tusk production to the CITES Secretariat. The exporting nation should inform the Secretariat of any authorized exports, transmitting copies of the permits and details of the tusk markings.

The CITES Secretariat was to fulfil the role of the information conduit within the trade network. It was to receive all information from the exporting states: management quotas, export permits and annual reports. With regard to reports and quotas, it was to make reports to all parties in order to provide information on which states were legal exporters. It was to provide information to importers on request as to the legitimacy of received export documents.

Importing states were to accept ivory only from states (party or non-party) with a non-zero quota, and then only after verifying the authenticity of the export documents through the Secretariat or the exporting management authority. Imports from re-exporters were to be accepted only if the re-exporter provided the correct information with regard to the country of origin.

All states were to avoid trade with any state not conforming with the ivory quota system, as so deemed by the Secretariat. Quotas were to be submitted by 1 December of the year prior to implementation; the first year of the system was to be 1986.

The Ottawa Conference of the Parties in 1987 focused closely on necessary amendments to the management quota system, producing six separate resolutions regarding the ivory trade. Resolution 6.11 proposed pressuring countries 'continuing to allow illegal trade in ivory, in particular Burundi and the United Arab Emirates ...' Resolution 6.12 recommends that 'the Parties ... fully comply with the quota system ...' It proposes that the Parties 'assist the range states to improve their capacity to manage ...', and that 'the states be encouraged to offer rewards' in order to arrest and convict illegal traffickers. Resolution 6.13 urges 'contributions on a voluntary basis to the Secretariat for ivory trade control co-ordination'. Resolution 6.14 recommends the establishment of 'a system of registration or licensing, or both, for commercial importers and exporters of raw ivory ...' in each state, and suggests that the ivory carving industry be similarly organized as well. Resolution 6.15 makes official the use of ink rather than punch-dies in the marking of tusks and allows the import of 'small' (under one kilogram) pieces without marking; it also recognizes the legitimacy of imports from re-exporters where the information on the country of origin is not provided, 'when there is justification given for this omission ...' Resolution 6.16 officially adopts the Secretariat's view that worked ivory is 'readily recognizable' as a regulated specimen under CITES.

This constitutes a very brief synopsis of the international regulations that pertained to the trade in ivory. In brief the idea was to have each range state submit a 'management quota' of tusks to be produced in the upcoming year as a result of that state's wildlife management policy. The enforcement of the state's quota was to be made possible through the marking of the tusks, and the requirement of proper documentation (and the verification of the authenticity of this documentation) by any state importing (or re-importing) the ivory.

5.2   Failure of implementation

This section concerns the natural appeal of the CITES system to each of the range states; that is it concerns the system's tendencies toward self-implementation. To the extent that a system appeals to the self-interest of the regulated parties, it has in-built incentives for implementation. To the extent that a system fails to invoke self-interest, and still relies on individual efforts for implementation, then the entire system hinges on external enforceability (which will be discussed in the next section).

The CITES system failed to create adequate incentives for the internal implementation of resource management systems. This was because it failed to recognize the source of the range states' joint interest, and thus did not provide the mechanism for the implementation of that mutual interest. Within the CITES system each range state acts unilaterally in the creation of its own resource management programme. The sole incentive to act is the mechanism of international enforcement devised within the quota system framework.

The failure of the CITES incentive system to induce action by the range states is amply demonstrated by reference to the Secretariat's statistics on implementation. Of the 34 range states (23 of which are parties to the convention), the following numbers performed in accord with the new system (Table 8.1).

As 30 of the range states had indicated their willingness to comply with a system of regulation of the ivory trade, these data demonstrate the minimal incentives towards compliance which the system generated.

In fact these figures overstate compliance with the system. The purpose of the quota system was to provide a requirement that each state develop a management system from which it would then derive its production quota. Only 6 of the 18 states submitting quotas in 1986 or 1987 accomplished this

Table 8.1   Implementation of CITES by range states

	1986	1987	1988	1989
Quotas Submitted	13	17	14	10
Annual Reports Received	6	0	0	0

objective; the remainder tendered illogical or nonsensical management quotas. This is not meant as an indictment of the range states' performances; the recognized value of a system is demonstrated by its 'take-up rate'. For example motorists drive on the left or the right in various countries not because of the importance of following the written law, but rather because of the obvious self-benefit accruing from conforming with the dictated norm. Likewise the failure to conform with the dictated norm is evidence that there is little recognition of the benefits from compliance.

The major problem with the management quotas submitted was the extent to which ivory quotas were derived from 'confiscated ivory'. Many of the forms listed illegal killing as the major source of ivory within their management system. The CITES Secretariat has attempted to confront this problem by interpreting Resolution 6.12 to prohibit the inclusion of more than 50 tusks taken by confiscation on the quota submission forms, thereby requiring additional notice of subsequent confiscations. In essence, however, the CITES system has failed to create the incentives necessary to cause domestic elephant management responsibilities to be removed from the poachers; the submitted quotas simply recognize that production within the current environment will be operated by others than the range states themselves.

Finally the failure to adopt the ivory marking system was itself evidence of unwillingness to invest in the CITES system by the range states. Despite multiple exhortations to undertake the small investment required for indelible marking, the import of Resolution 6.14 is that punch-die marking is no longer an element of the system, adopting the standard practice of ink-marking instead.

The record of CITES quota system implementation by the range states makes clear that it does not appeal sufficiently to the self-interest of these states to be internally implemented. In this case, as in most instances, some manner of external enforcement is necessary.

5.3   Failures of enforcement

Much of the failure of this system must lie ultimately with its unenforceability. Even if the system contained few incentives for implementation by the range states, it might still be implemented through strict control of the international trade through external mechanisms, and the compliance which these controls would then induce within the range states. The CITES system, however, contains general enforcement mechanism deficiencies which renders strict external control of the trade impossible.

These deficiencies in enforceability, the incentives to exploit them, and the continuing underinvestment in the resource, are all interlinked in a cycle of systematic evasion which maintains the rate of exploitation of the African elephant. First, the trade identifies and exploits one of a number of loopholes (which are attributable to the deficiencies discussed below). Second, as any particular loophole is addressed by the Secretariat (such as the control of raw ivory imports into Japan), another springs up (such as the development of carving factories in 'free trade zones' and the export of worked ivory). Third, the obviousness of these deficiencies contributes to the feeling of lack of efficaciousness, and the perceived lack of benefits flowing from the system; hence the range states are unwilling to invest resources which are dependent upon the system for a return. Thus the internal investment deficiencies remain substantially unaltered. Fourth, these same investment deficiencies are the source of the incentives for overexploitation of the resource, by reason of open access to the asset. Finally, this unauthorized exploitation of the resource then creates the demand for loopholes for the conduct of the ivory trade, and the cycle is reinitiated.

5.3.1   Non-range states   States, which are not range states, were able to evade the system to some degree on account of two basic sources of 'systemic flexibility'. First, each 're-exporter' is capable of 'authenticating' questionable export documents, and then sending the shipment along under its own documentation. This leaves the final importing nations at a loss with respect to the examination of the originating permits; under the CITES system it is permissible to re-export ivory without its original documentation. Second, as discussed below, any state is a potential situs for a portion of the ivory carving industry, and is therefore capable of importing illegal raw ivory and rendering it into largely unregulated worked ivory. Therefore there is flexibility for any state wishing to exploit the system to do so without the cooperation of any other state involved in the industry; all that is necessary is for the trader to locate itself in some jurisdiction willing to accomodate its business interests.

Under the CITES regime, the unit of regulation has been the raw ivory tusk itself, quotas are to be stated in tusks in order to internalize incentives for efficient tusk harvesting. That is, the member state would then choose to satisfy its own quota from larger tusks as this would create the greater ivory value, while concomitantly serving the conservationist's purpose of harvesting solely from the older stock.

There are two problems with this regulation. First, this is an attempt to distort the internal management incentives without first attempting to identify the source of management deficiencies; these sorts of 'arbitrary restriction' often produce bizarre results. For example this regulation provides no incentive to invest properly in elephant management (which would involve culling from all ages of the population distribution), only to truncate the upper reaches of the population. It is unlikely that this regulation has had this impact on the harvesting strategy (as it is unlikely that the range states are in control of the harvesting strategy), but the impact that it might have had would have been far from the intended one. Hence it is very important to identify the distortions which are creating the undesired internal management problems and then to directly address them; unnecessary amendments to the parts of incentive schemes which are not obviously deficient may in themselves create distortions. Second, and more importantly, the choice of the ivory tusk as the regulated unit renders the post-manufacture sector of the industry unregulatable; this has very important implications for enforceability.

The ivory industry involves three necessary components: harvesting, carving and consumption. For the most part the first and the third are fixed spatially, the first restricted to the range states and the third restricted to those states with substantial international purchasing power. The second component, although traditionally fixed in the Far East (Hong Kong, China and Japan in particular), is far more mobile than the other two. The essence of the non-cooperator's solution has been to move the cutting and the carving of the tusks closer to the production and further from the consumption (where the bulk of enforcement occurs) and then ship the ivory in some roughly worked, and unregulated, form. The essence of the regulator's response to the problem has been to attempt to close the worked ivory loophole, first in the Far East and then generally by the adoption of Resolution 6.16.

The regulator's approach cannot ultimately succeed within this framework, because the quota system still regulated only the number of tusks. It is not possible, with worked ivory, to determine whether the originating raw ivory shipment was sufficient to generate the entirety, or merely a fraction, of the subsequent shipments attributed to it. This flexibility within the system renders strict regulation infeasible, although other more serious deficiencies currently overshadow its significance, in the final analysis this manner of flexibility must be removed for serious regulation. The unit of regulation must be equally applicable from the point of production to the point of final consumption, otherwise manipulation of the system remains possible by transfer of the point of manufacture, or by the falsification of numbers on documents.

5.3.2 Range states A more fundamental source of flexibility in the system was the range states themselves, as there was no real constraint placed on the activities of any ivory producing state. It is perfectly consistent with economic self-interest for the individual range states to provide CITES permits to stockpilers of illegal ivory. There is an individual benefit realized from the sale of such permits and the joint cost (of encouraging the illegal taking of ivory) will be realized in any event since one of the range states is bound to succumb to the temptation. Hence it was entirely rational for the range states to sell these permits to willing buyers, and the supply was unlimited as the range states were individually responsible for the establishment of their quotas. There was one example of a range state which found it necessary to increase its original quota before selling its permits in blank. Parker estimates that about 250 tonnes of ivory (one-third to one-half of the annual harvest) was processed in this way during each of the initial two years of the management quota system. Hence a re-exporter securing the cooperation of a range state has *carte blanche* for unrestricted trade in African elephant ivory.

This manner of evidence is consistent with the incentives generated by the CITES scheme of regulation pertaining to the range states. This response to the system is entirely predictable. In essence the system has created a piece of paper that is valuable for foreign exchange on the international market at little or no direct cost to the selling states; it would be unusual for such incentives not to generate the observed response. Since non-compliance with the formal system is not directly observable or punishable while it is individually beneficial (though jointly detrimental), it is to be expected that non-compliance would be the general result in this system.

This willingness to 'cheat' on the joint agreement accounts for the greatest amount of flexibility in the CITES system. It is consistent with economic incentives that vast amounts of poached ivory be surreptitiously shipped into Dubai, for example, to be later transformed into licensed imports from even those African states where the ivory was poached.

The important point is that it is the international system which is the source of this ludicrous state of affairs; the role of the entrepôt is minimal. This is because the entropôt acts only as a 'matching up' point between illegal ivory and legal permits. Any state in the world could perform this function; the only constraint on fungibility is the proximity of the state to the fine which implicitly links producers and consumers.

Hence 'diplomatic efforts' to close the entrepôt in the ivory trade are largely wasted efforts. The closure of one 'matching up' point eliminates only one from dozens of possibilities. The trade had initially sought out those bastions of non-interference known as 'free ports', but these are inessential characteristics of the entrepôt; the trade has amply demonstrated its resilience with regard to its trade route. Thus there is no real meaning to the closure of one among many options, so long as so many totally fungible substitutes continue to exist.

Even if the task of securing the cooperation of every entrepôt is accomplished, these efforts cannot succeed because this system ultimately fails on account of the incentives for non-compliance on the part of the range states themselves. Range states have little reason to invest in a system which is so lacking in mutual verifiable commitments; it is a bad result (from each state's perspective) to have all range states fail to implement the system, but it is a worse result (from each state's perspective) to be the only state incurring the expense to implement an ineffective system. This is the source of the problem with speculative permit sales alluded to earlier, and in its most pernicious manifestation it could result in the sanctioning of transboundary poaching expeditions between the range states. Hence, so long as the system makes it so easy to cheat, it cannot pay to be honest. Therefore the patchwork attempts to remedy the CITES system cannot succeed until the system is amended to provide the correct incentive structure for the range states themselves.

In general a system of regulation is usually required because the 'natural' order creates individual incentives which are at odds with the jointly recognized preferred state of affairs. The simple agreement of all concerned parties does not solve this problem; the incentives to individual defection remain. For this reason sole reliance on internal incentives for implementation is misplaced. The CITES system fails *ab initio* because it has no effective external enforcement mechanism. As this is the case, and it is readily recognizable as being the case by the range states, it makes little sense for any individual state to adopt the system unilaterally; thus the entire system of regulation stands largely unimplemented.

5.4   The failure of the management regime in CITES

The CITES management quota system did not work, in the sense of altering the management programmes of the range states. It required huge amounts of effort and resources to accomplish what it did; that is the accumulation of information on the trade in ivory. So it was not the lack of genuine good intentions and sound efforts, it was the failure of the scheme of incentives and enforcement within the system.

The management quota system could not be effective in assisting domestic management of the resource because it did not address the needs of the range states correctly. Its failure to do so was evident in the low implementation rate by the range states. More importantly it was evident in the lack of real impact which the system had on the ivory industry during the years of its operation.

The system failed most fundamentally because it did not constrain the range states, even when such constraint would be in the mutual interest of all of the range states. It is true that a management system for each state should be in its own interest, and an external enforcement system which reinforces the domestic system would enhance those incentives; however it is even more appealing to have such a system and then sell permits to your neighbours' resources. Since the management quota system failed to constrain this manner of discretion, or to provide a mechanism for detecting those who engage in it, there was little incentive to invest in the system. If the system is unimplemented it has little impact on the original investment deficiencies which were contributing to the resource's mismanagement.

In short the lack of binding constraints and commitments within the management quota system created a management regime with too much room for manoeuvre on the part of the states involved. These states made predictable use of the flexibility within the system for the purpose of routing the resource rents towards themselves. Burundi nearly managed to corner the trade in ivory while having a single elephant within its borders! These sorts of failures of international environmental agreements bring all of international law into disrepute, yet they are simply the consequence of the failure of the parties to reach agreement on the shares to be received under a concrete and enforceable regime. In lieu of the adoption of such a regime, the parties opt instead for these vague and unenforceable systems which allow each party to pursue its own share of the rents. These sorts of system cause great harm to both the environment and international law.

6   Conclusion: evolving international environmental agreements
The elements of an effective resource management regime are easily listed: efficiency (in aggregate quota); distribution (of agreed shares); and implementation (of concrete and enforceable system). The difficulty lies only in achieving agreement of the member states to such a regime.

The difficulties of negotiating the adoption of such a regime from the outset were discussed in Chapter 3. Here we have outlined the problems that result when states attempt to pursue resource management in the absence of effective agreement. The result is invariably rent-seeking, mismanagement, and resource degradation. The examples discussed from the marine context, and the case study of the ivory management quota system, demonstrate just how easily the frailties of international environmental agreements can be exploited. It is essential that effective international environmental agreements be pursued from the outset.

It is not impossible, or even incredibly difficult, for international environmental law to have substantial and important impacts. The creation of enforceable resource management regimes is simply a matter of achieving agreement to such between the parties. Monitoring and enforcement can be achieved; it is simply a matter of acceptance on the part of the states involved. At base the real problem of effective international agreements is the same – the development of an approach that is recognized as fair and accepted in a concrete and enforceable fashion.

Notes
1. See Akehurst, M., *A Modern Introduction to International Law*, 6th edn, 1985. ('The popular belief is that international law is not really law'.)
2. The 'right of reservation-consensus' trade-off is also recognized in the literature. See Zemanek, K., 'Majority rule and consensus technique in law-making diplomacy', in MacDonald, R. and Johnston, D. (eds.).
3. There is a substantial international law literature discussing the 'concreteness-consensus' trade-off. See, for example, Monnier, 'Observations sur quelques tendencies récentes en matière de formation de la volonte sur le plan multilateral', *Annuaire Suisse de droit international*, **31**, p. 31 (1975); Jenks, 'Unanimity, the veto, weighted voting, special and simple majorities and consensus as modes of decision in international organisation', in Jennings, R. (ed), *Cambridge Essays in International Law; Essay in Honour of Lord McNair*, 1965.
4. This is the case in regard to the Elephant Ivory Management Quota System adopted under the Convention on International Trade in Endangered Species. Although about 30 of the 33 range states are parties to this convention, only about half of these states even met their obligations to establish a quota under the system in the years 1986 and 1987. Of these only four or five were established in conformance with the system guidelines. In fact there was virtually no adherence to the system although it was almost universally subscribed.

9 Developing international environmental law: a case study of CITES and trade regulation

Introduction

Wildlife trade regulation can be seen from very different perspectives. Some people would like to see it as a first step toward the containment of wildlife utilization, and the prevention of the decline of individual species in other countries. Others would like to see it as a license to use the wildlife trade for the purposes of social development, and they may view other objectives as infringements upon national sovereignty. Is there any prospect for the regulation of the wildlife trade to accomplish a broad set of objectives consonant with this wide range of perspectives: the encouragement of growth and development and also the avoidance of wildlife depletion? Or, will it always remain necessary to embrace one of the two polar positions: a trade proponent or a trade protectionist?

The argument of this chapter is that it is not only possible to achieve this common objective but that it is a necessary objective to pursue. International environmental law will become rationalized once it takes a shape that positively encourages trade and development down particular pathways, rather than simply banning or discouraging a few of these. The fact is that the shape development takes in various countries does matter to others, and they are willing to pay to help direct that development. This is the reason why millions of residents in the northern hemisphere give tens of millions of dollars each year to organizations whose self-proclaimed objectives are to promote the conservation of the wildlife resident in the southern hemisphere (see the discussion on environmental values in WCMC 1992). People do have preferences regarding the form of development that occurs in lands that are not their own, and these preferences may be transformed into a willingness to subsidize particular pathways toward development.

Do such preferences constitute unwanted interference in the decisions that rightfully belong to other peoples? Of course not, because every purchase by every person on each and every day has the same sort of impact, whether it is done through ignorance or not. Flows of funds from consumer purchases shape the world, and taking this impact into consideration is the thoughtful, rather than the neglectful, thing to do. National sovereignty can always be protected in matters of trade, because trade requires the consent of all of the parties to the commerce. In order to protect sovereignty a trade regulation mechanism should not disallow particular forms of trade, it should simply encourage those forms which meet the combined objectives of the purchasers. That is, a trade mechanism should have as its object the combination of the consumer good and the production process into a single package. Thus, when people care not only about the good they are buying (say, a wildlife product such as ivory) and also the process which created it (free range versus factory production, for example), then it is possible to sell the good/process in a single package and charge more for it. This is the objective of mechanisms such as 'eco-labelling' they provide the consumers with the information necessary to discriminate between the various production processes underlying otherwise indistinguishable products. Then the consumers are able to affect the development choices of producers through their informed purchases, while continuing to allow producers to choose their own development path.

There is another reason why it is important for trade regulation to move in this direction. International trade regulation can 'work' only if it is devised in a manner that takes both sets of perspectives into account. Otherwise one side or the other will have little incentive to adhere to the treaty, or to support its objectives. Trade regulation created only from the perspective of one side of the exchange is doomed to failure.

In this chapter I would like to demonstrate these general points within the context of a case study of the Convention on International Trade in Endangered Species (CITES): the convention which regulates trade in wildlife and bans it when it becomes threatening. In this context it will be easy to show that the initial system of international regulation had little to offer one side to the exchange, but that for this reason the system (to become effective) has had to evolve increasingly towards the middle ground. This is because many so-called global environmental treaties are of little relevance to the needs and concerns of the vast majority of the peoples on the earth. They are instead constructed from the perspective of the residents of a small number of 'Northern' nations, with little understanding of the perspectives of others. However, to address and especially to solve global problems requires international cooperation, and thus over time the nature and direction of a treaty can change significantly if some sort of constructive effect is to be achieved.

This is what is occurring with regard to the CITES. It is evolving towards the middle ground between the Southern 'wildlife producing' states and the Northern 'wildlife consuming' states. At the same time it is moving towards becoming an international regime that 'works' it will establish the means and the mechanism through which poor countries will be able to afford to conserve wildlife within their territories. This will allow them to develop down a pathway consistent with the retention of their wildlife. CITES has taken 20 years to reach a juncture closer to the middle ground between the parties involved in this trade. By learning from this process, it should be possible to develop other international regulatory regimes that have a prospect of becoming effective and useful from the outset.

1   The control structure within CITES as drafted

Of the large number of international environmental conventions, CITES has probably the single most detailed control structure. It was the first international wildlife treaty to provide for both express obligations and international monitoring. Therefore, CITES represents an important step along the road towards making substantive international law with concrete impacts. The purpose of this analysis is, however, to ascertain the capability of the convention to address, as drafted, the developing world's perspective on the endangered species problem. Other authors may be consulted for a detailed analysis of the specific workings of CITES. (Lyster, 1985; Wijnstekers, 1988).

CITES was signed in March 1972 and came into force three years later. The argument of this chapter is that CITES was drafted with little attention to the problems of the developing countries in maintaining their species. It focused instead on the identification of endangered species and the withdrawal of the trade in the same. This might make sense from the perspective of persons resident in the Northern hemisphere; however, for those who share their lands with the vast majority of the remaining wildlife, it is not at all a constructive approach.

CITES functions as a potential trade control mechanism primarily through the operation of two Appendices, on which potentially endangered species are listed. Appendix I is intended as a list of those species which are currently threatened with extinction [Art. II(1)], while Appendix II contains a list of species for which there is some indication that they might become threatened [Art. II(2)]. The Conference of the Parties to CITES makes these determinations at its biennial meetings.

Once a species is listed on either of the CITES Appendices, it becomes subject to the permit requirements of the convention. An Appendix I species may not be shipped in the absence of the issuance of an 'export permit' by the exporting state [Art. III(2)]. Furthermore, this permit may not be issued, under the terms of the convention, unless both the exporting state certifies that the export will not be detrimental to the species and the importing state certifies (by the issuance of an import permit) that the import will not be used for commercial purposes [Art. III(3)(c)]. Therefore, an Appendix I listing acts as an effective 'ban' on the trade in those species and, even if exporters wish to continue the trade, the importing states have a duty to deny all commercial imports.

An Appendix II listing, on the other hand, leaves the decision on trade control wholly to the discretion of the exporting state. That is, there is no role for the importing state, other than to ensure that an export permit is issued for each specimen [Art. IV(4)]. These permits are issued only as long as the exporting state itself certifies that the export will not be detrimental to the survival of the species within the exporting state [Art. IV(2)].

The other important responsibility of member states is to provide annual reports to the CITES Secretariat on the amounts of trade in listed species [Art. VIII(7)]. The Secretariat also sometimes acts as the intermediary between exporting and importing states, in order to confirm the authenticity of trade documents for example.

2   The nature of the extinction problem in developing countries

CITES was constructed with a 'backward looking' perspective on resource utilization by Northerners, that is, Europeans and North Americans. In the past, direct human overexploitation has been the primary contributor to species extinctions (Diamond, 1989). And, most of the documented extinctions have occurred outside of the tropical zones. In prehistorical terms much of the megafauna of the northern temperate zones was simply hunted to extinction. This has also been a problem in regard to some oceanic species exploited by Northerners (for example, the near extinction of the blue whale and the severe reduction of various fish species). Therefore, it is not surprising that those in the developed world fear the worst out of wildlife exploitation; our record demonstrates that we are capable of nothing but that.

This is not so much the case with regard to many of the peoples of the developing world and their wildlife. In many cases these countries have a long history of coexistence between people and wildlife. Partly on account of this, most of the world's remaining diversity of species resides in these developing countries.

However, at present and in the future, there is a very serious threat to these species looming in these same countries. Yet it is still not the threat of overexploitation which most endangers the species of these countries. It is the loss of the habitat on which these species rely that is likely to be the more significant factor contributing to species extinctions in these lands.

The countries with the most species are facing unprecedented development and population pressures. In these areas a doubling and redoubling of the human populations is a virtual certainty over the next 50–100 years. Kenya, for example, has a current population growth rate of about 4 per cent, which implies a doubling of the human population every 18 years. This is not exceptional; population growth rates of 3–4 per cent are the norm throughout much of sub-Saharan Africa, Latin America and Southeast Asia.

In addition to human population growth, there is also great pressure for development in these regions. Of the 15 countries which feature prominently in terms of diversity of 'higher species' (reptiles, birds and mammals), none has an average annual income greater than $2000 (MacNeely *et al.*,

1990). In fact, most of the countries listed register average incomes which are amongst the lowest in the world, around $200–$500 per annum. In essence, the world's 'wealth of species' lies within the 'poorest of nations' (Swanson, 1992).

It is the pressures of human populations and development needs in these poorest of countries which currently represent the greatest threat to species. As population and development pressures continue to mount, they result in the conversion of massive quantities of previously available wildlife habitat (Wilson, 1988). The felling of tropical forests and the extension of the frontier into these regions relieves some of these pressures temporarily, but at a tremendous cost in terms of the loss of species. From the perspective of the developing world, these are the base problems of species extinctions.

Therefore it is still the human factor which is extinguishing species via habitat conversions, but now the greater threat is that it will do so *indirectly*. Species are finding themselves undercut when the resources on which they rely are converted to human uses.

The problem with CITES is that it is a global treaty built on a Northerner's perspective. A policy for the reduction of species extinctions *must* address *both* of these sources of losses: overexploitation and habitat conversions. Efforts at 'saving species' from overexploitation, where the resources of developing countries are concerned, may actually be only exercises in shifting them from the one column of the extinction ledger to the other. Since the vast majority of global wildlife exists within the developing world, a global treaty really must focus upon the needs of this sector.

Over almost two decades of operations under CITES, the parties have become aware of the dual nature of the endangered species problem. It has been recognized within the context of the conferences of the parties that CITES must evolve to meet both prongs of the problem. And the direction of change is slowly being revealed.

3   The path down which CITES must develop

In order to address both facets of the extinction problem, it is necessary to do two things. First, it is necessary to route funds to those countries with large numbers of endangered species, so that they might then provide habitat for these species and closely manage the exploitation of those species. Second, it is essential that there is assurance that the funds supplied are directed to the purposes indicated, namely the conservation of endangered species. The provision of funding alone is no solution. There must also be incentives in place to encourage the investment of the funds in species and habitat conservation. This is because terrestrial species reside almost without exception within the borders of particular states, and ultimately the question of conservation concerns the motivation of the 'range states' involved.

For these purposes a strategy of wildlife utilization by local peoples has much to commend itself as a conservationist tool. That is, using the unique characteristics of wildlife habitat to generate funding (through tourism, wildlife products trade, subsistence harvests) can itself act to conserve that same habitat. It creates revenues for species conservation and it creates incentives for the application of those funds to that purpose. People are willing to abstain from converting habitat that is valuable in its current state. It is the fact that it has this combination of capacities, that is, fund-raising and incentives-generating, that makes a policy of wildlife utilization so appealing. However, it is also historically apparent that unregulated wildlife utilization is a threat as well as a potential benefit. With the diffusion of new technologies and the decay of old institutions, overexploitation has come to endanger the wildlife of developing countries as well (Luxmoore and Swanson, 1992).

The major problem with this approach is the creation of a system for the sustainable management of natural habitat and its resources. This is an expensive proposition on account of the unregimented nature of such habitat. Most developing countries are unequal to such a sophisticated, and expensive, management task in the context of rapidly changing (and often deteriorating) conditions. Therefore, as a possible direction for the evolution of CITES, the regulation of trade to achieve this goal is one possible approach to the dual problem of extinction.

Another possible direction for the evolution of CITES is the movement towards 'captive breeding' of wildlife for trade. Captive breeding is a term defined under CITES which means the maintenance of a number of individuals as breeding stock completely segregated from the wild population. Then, under such a regime, the progeny of the breeding stock are available for trade, even when the wild variety of the same species are not. Obviously the captive breeding policy is addressed to the problem of overexploitation. If captive bred animals (such as the fur-bearing animals: minks, otters, foxes), are provided in adequate numbers and at low enough prices, then the pressure on those same species in the wild is reduced.

However, captive breeding does nothing to address the problem of habitat conversions. In fact, to a large extent, it worsens this situation. This is because captive breeding operations are usually operated in the consumer states, where the bias is towards intensive farming methods of production. Therefore, a shift from wild harvests to captive breeding methods is largely a movement of the 'wealth of species' from the developing countries to the developed. Once the wildlife species valued by the developed countries are established under farming regimes in the North, the natural habitats of the South are truly rendered 'valueless' in the eyes of those living on the frontiers of these wildernesses. Then, there is no deterrent to the law of the chain-saw (Swanson, 1992).

Another possibility is to preserve habitats as 'parks', while preventing overexploitation through captive breeding or a similar policy. This has in fact been attempted throughout much of the developing world. In the 1970s and the first part of the 1980s vast areas of land were designated 'protected areas'. Today nearly 4 per cent of remaining wilderness has received some sort of protected status. There are a number of reasons why this policy is not effective. First, parks without funds are not protected areas in any sense of that term. It has been found that the levels of poaching in African game parks is directly related to the level of expenditure on the parks. A figure of nearly $200 per square kilometre was necessary for effective prevention (Leader-Williams and Albon, 1989). Most parks in the developing world exist almost wholly on documents alone. There is no funding available for such extravagances in lands where infant mortality rates are high and literacy rates low. Most of these are 'paper parks' only.

Second, the prevalence of poaching points out the contradictory nature of the policy. None of these 'natural habitats' evolved without a human component within them. The local peoples have usually used the lands and appurtenant resources over centuries, if not thousands of years. These attempts at halting all utilization, which are as old as the colonial legacy in these regions, introduce conflicts between local peoples and local wildlife which were never there before (Marks, 1984).

Finally, all these problems could be sorted out if substantial sums of money were forthcoming from the international community for their resolution. However, in general, there is a lot of good intentions and little solid support from this sphere. The pledge of financial support following the ban of the ivory trade never came to fruition. The developed world, through the mechanism of the Global Environmental Facility (about which there is much current clamour), pledged $200 million per year over the first half-dozen years of that programme for the resolution of the problems of global biodiversity. The scale of this funding is large compared with past contributions, but it is nothing compared with the value of the resources at stake. To put this amount into context, $200 million is roughly the amount that the developed world pays the producer states for raw reptile skins alone each and every year.

This quick review of the current option indicates that the route that holds most promise in addressing the developing world's species conservation problems is that of *controlled* wildlife utilization. The use of the wildlife trade to generate incentives for species conservation in the developing world would be effective if the developed world routed its custom only to those countries which demonstrated sustainable management of its natural habitat. This form of environmental conditionality would punish unsustainable exploitation while encouraging sustainable exploitation and investment in habitat, while simultaneously providing the funds for the same. It would provide the incentives for movements down development paths compatible with existing natural resources, while refusing to fund some countries' campaigns to mine their natural environments out of existence.

This would allow the 'trade' between affected countries to benefit both the producers and consumers of goods plus those interested in the manner of development taking place in the producing state. For example, northern consumers could buy certified products (say, ivory) safe in the knowledge that they had not only acquired a beautiful natural product but also helped to conserve the habitat of the African elephant. This is the sort of international regulation that can only be beneficial to the participants to trade: it is sorting out the 'lemons' amongst competing producers of natural products, and this allows the interested 'green consumer' to support the trade for reasons associated with the production process as well as the product itself.

It is down this path that CITES had to evolve if it was to become a workable system of international regulation. Over a period of 20 years it has achieved much in the development of systems that discriminate between different producers and allot quotas to those which are the most effective investors in their wildlife. There have been abject failures as well, but the important message here is that future international regulation must learn from both the failures and the successes of previous regimes. The remainder of this chapter will trace the path of the evolution of CITES into a form of 'constructive trade control' mechanism.

4 The convention as a trade regulation mechanism

As originally drafted, the CITES convention provided little in the way of a 'constructive trade control mechanism'. The history of the CITES convention has witnessed many species progress from Appendix II to Appendix I, as potentially unsustainable trade levels raise concerns about the viability of the species. Most recently, this has occurred in the well-publicized case of the African elephant, for which a 12-year listing on Appendix II ended in 1989 with its 'uplisting' by the Conference of the Parties.

Such a progression from 'potentially threatened' to 'endangered' is predictable, given the structure of the CITES convention. This is because an Appendix II listing gives little in the way of a wildlife trade control framework. An Appendix II listing leaves each range state operating independently, with no international assistance to perform the additional tasks that are required of the parties or producer coordination to provide the incentives to conservation. Therefore, an Appendix II listing provides only additional tasks, and no real incentive framework, for the control of the trade in listed species. What an Appendix II listing certainly does accomplish is to publicize the potential rarity of the listed species. For some species this might actually result in an increase in consumer demand (for example, with regard to the exotic pet trade). Therefore, the consumer-side impact of an Appendix II listing is uncertain, and it could range quite widely.

Where Appendix II listing does encourage speculative purchasing, the combination of additional demand pressures with negligible control structures is a threatening one for Appendix II listed species. Since most wildlife species exist in unmanaged circumstances, it is usually difficult to handle the existing, let alone any increased, pressures. Thus, the progression of species from listing on Appendix II to 'endangered' status is not unforeseeable; for some species, it is entirely predictable. An Appendix I listing promises much more in the way of international cooperation; however, the efforts are put to no constructive effect. That is, once the regulated species completes the progression from virtually uncontrolled Appendix II species to endangered Appendix I species, the international community then launches into concerted action to 'ban the trade'.

Of course, this will address the problem of possible immediate extinction from overexploitation which might arise during an Appendix II listing; however, it does nothing to provide resources for the management of the species or the conservation of its habitat in order to avoid extinction in the medium term. For the endangered species of the developing countries, the withdrawal of value necessarily hastens the process of its elimination. They are under threat from both overexploitation and habitat conversion. To address either of these forces, in anything other than short-term circumstances, requires management and finances.

In the worst cases, the situation has gone from bad to worse; with the uplisting to Appendix I, the traded species is protected from short-term extinction from overexploitation, while simultaneously hastening the medium-term extinction of its habitat. Now what is lost is not only the single species generating consumptive value, but also many of the related species and systems whose shared habitat could be subsidized by this value.

Therefore, CITES as drafted provides for a peculiar sort of international regime of trade controls. For traded wildlife species it initially provides virtually nothing in the way of an international control structure, together with a global notice of 'potential rarity value' (with the posting of an Appendix II listing), while following that with the withdrawal of developed world purchases of the wildlife product (via an Appendix I ban) if the population then comes under even greater pressures. The former, at best, provides no positive incentive framework; the latter provides no possible constructive use of wildlife value.

5   The convention – attempts at innovation

The Conference of the Parties to CITES has been taking steps towards a more constructive approach, with the attempted development of various sorts of constructive utilization systems. Although these are still in their formative stages, they represent the initial steps towards the recognition of the producer countries' perspective on the problem. At various times important, but not always effective, steps have been taken towards the construction of a rationalized international control structure.

5.1   The recognition of the need for constructive utilization

As early as 1979 the delegates from developing countries brought the anomoly of 'indirect extinction in lieu of direct overexploitation' to the attention of the Conference of the Parties. In San José, Costa Rica, they argued that there must be an economic benefit from the controlled species if they were to be able to justify protecting their habitats from development. These concerns gave rise to the first step towards the reform of CITES, with the adoption of Conference Resolution 3.15 at the New Delhi Conference of the Parties in 1981. This resolution provides for the downlisting of certain Appendix I populations for the purposes of sustainable resource management. The criteria which specify how Appendix I species may be utilized in order to procure compensation for their habitat are known as the 'ranching criteria', and each Conference of the Parties usually sees a large number of such proposals for review and possible acceptance. The first ranching proposal accepted involved the transfer of the Zimbabwean population of Nile crocodile to Appendix II in 1983 (Wijnstekers, 1988).

Ranching proposals tend to be focused on a particular state, or operation, and do not constitute mechanisms for the constructive control use of the entire trade. In essence, they continue the 'ban' in effect while allowing very limited, individual operations to recommence. While being of some utility, they do not constitute attempts at harnessing the value of an entire species for its own conservation.

In 1983, a species-based approach was first adopted with regard to the exploitation of the African leopard. Although listed on Appendix I, it was recognized in Conference Resolution 4.13 that specimens of the leopard could be killed 'to enhance the survival of the species'. With this, the Conference of the Parties approved an annual quota of 460 specimens, and allocated these between the range states. In 1985 this quota was then increased to 1140 animals, and in 1987 to 1830.

This approach to trade management was then generalized in 1985 with Resolution 5.21, which provided for the systematic downlisting of populations where the countries of origin agree a quota system which is sufficiently safe so as to not endanger the species. Under this Resolution five different species have been subject to quota systems: three African crocodiles, one Asian crocodile, and the Asian bonytongue for which the Indonesians were allowed a quota of 1250 specimens (the latter being a fish much admired by the Japanese as a wall hanging).

None of these ranching systems went any further than the development of species-based quotas. In particular, no external control structure was ever implemented, this being left to the discretion of producer states. Thus, predictably, these quotas can be abused. For example, Indonesia is believed to have issued permits for about 140 per cent of its first year's quota of bonytongues (TRAFFIC, 1991).

At the Seventh Conference of the Parties, in Resolution 7.14, this scheme for developing quota systems was made time-limited, so that no quota system could continue beyond two Conferences of the Parties. The argument there was that CITES should encourage a movement away from general quota systems, and towards specific ranching regimes. This, however, is closely linked to the 'captive breeding' movement. It is important to recall that it is only the farmers who benefit from farming what was formerly wildlife; conservation benefits accrue when harvests occur in the wild (Luxmoore and Swanson, 1992).

The third avenue of innovation under CITES, and the most concentrated effort thus far in the development of an international control structure within the system, was the creation of a management quota system (MQS) for the African elephant populations under Resolution 5.12. This system was founded upon the ideas of management-based controls with consumer-based enforcement. Annual quotas were to be constructed at the outset of each year, and producer states were then to issue permits not exceeding these quotas. Then consumer states were to disallow all imports unless accompanied by a MQS permit.

This did not result in an effective control system for one very important reason. The system provided no external checks on the discretion of the producer states. The determination of annual quotas and the issuance of MQS permits was within their unsupervised discretion. There were no externally enforced incentives for sustainable use. This resulted in most states basing their annual 'management quotas' of ivory on the 'expected' confiscations from poachers. In addition, there were also no disincentives for cross-border exploitation, since consumer states were allowed to import ivory unquestioningly from any exporter issuing permits. Thus, Burundi, with one elephant, became the largest exporter of ivory in Africa under this control regime (Swanson, 1989).

The Management Quota System failed as a consequence of these clear inadequacies, resulting in a collapse of public confidence in the capacity for trade controls to work (Barbier, *et al.*, 1990). These control system failures are not costless. It is essential that an effective control system is developed and implemented before all consumer confidence is permanently lost in the potentially constructive capacity of wildlife trade. What is clearly indicated as a requirement is an external means of enforcing sustainability on the developing countries' use of their wildlife resources.

Nevertheless, despite the lack of enforceability, there is the germ of a good idea represented within these attempts. The use of national quotas, which are linked to the sustainable offtakes from wild harvesting, is one way of controlling the use of natural habitat. The substitution of trade monitoring for habitat monitoring is probably the only way to make utilization compatible with wilderness.

5.2 The evolution of environmental conditionality

What continues to be necessary is a means for the establishment and enforcement of a sustainable quota system. A system that has been evolving in connection with, but not directly within CITES, addresses this need. This has occurred under the European Community Regulation 3626/82, which effectively requires (under Article 5) an import permit for all Appendix II species. More importantly, for certain specified species (listed on Appendix C2 to the Regulation) there is an affirmative obligation on the exporting party to demonstrate that the export will not have a harmful effect on the population of the species in the country of origin.

This Regulation has acted to move the enforcement of sustainability from the producer to the consumer states (in regard to the EC), where its enforcement is affordable. Producer states find it desirable to mine their natural resources precisely because it is far more expensive to manage the production process than it is to mine it (Swanson, 1994). That is why there is a widely noted positive relationship between development (income) and environmental management: the management of production processes requires resources that are not often available in the poorest of countries (see for example Beckerman, 1994). Resource management is a rich country's occupation.

If rich countries care about effective resource management and they are willing to provide the funds to support it, then there is no reason why they should not do so within the context of an international trade regime. Their interest in the manner in which the flow of natural goods is provided (and their willingness to pay more for a flow that derives from a particular sort of production process) give them the right to contract for a particular production process. This willingness to pay then allows for the imposition of the sort of 'conditionality' that is required for constructive use of the wildlife trade. The EC does in fact negotiate, on a country by country basis, the terms upon which it will remove that country's populations from Appendix C2. From this conditionality arises the possibility of state-by-state quotas created by the import permit obligation, and enforced by the EC customs inspectors.

In practice the EC scheme operates by cancelling all trade in Appendix II species unless the exporter state meets its CITES Article IV obligation of demonstrating that the harvest is sustainable (or 'not detrimental to the wild population' in the language of CITES). When the exporter approaches the EC about the removal of the ban, the EC suggests a worldwide quota which would satisfy them as to the sustainability of the trade from that state. If the exporter agrees, then trade is resumed until the annual quota is satisfied.

This regulatory system provides for many of the necessary parts of a successful trade regulation mechanism. Its drawbacks lie almost wholly in its piecemeal approach. That is, optimal quotas require that the entire potential production of the species be considered. Furthermore, the most successful incentives for sustainability require that all the major consumers enforce conditionality; otherwise, supplemental conditions and enforcement by one consumer will often shift trade to others. In essence, however, the evolution of CITES into a constructive trade control mechanism must involve the rationalization and globalization of the EC regime of 'environmental conditionality' across all of the major consumer states (the USA, Japan and the EC).

The one objection to the EC regime is its inroads into the realm of national sovereignty. As mentioned in the Introduction, the reason that a trade regulation should be non-controversial is that there is no reason why trade need ever be disallowed, only encouraged down particular pathways. The EC regime does not conform to this tenet, instead it disallows certain types of trade that should be within the sole discretion of another country. For example, is there any equitable basis for disallowing the Latin American states from trading in their tropical hardwoods, by countries which have cleared most of their hardwood forests long ago? If a country chooses to pursue a relatively hardwood-less development path (as many 'Northern' countries have done long ago), this should be its right.

In order to preserve the development choices of the producer state while allowing consumers to have their say in the making of that choice, the trade regulation mechanism should act as an information system. That is, it should allow consumers to make informed choices about product/production process combinations rather than requiring producers to make only one combination if they wish to trade. Then, consumers may induce particular combinations by means of their willingness to pay higher prices for them. For example, a country which sustainably manages its elephants should be allowed to sell its ivory through a mechanism such as an 'exchange', where consumers come to pay higher prices for the combined product (ivory/sustainable management); while a country which is rapidly removing its elephant populations should be allowed to sell its ivory but only at the prices which unmanaged ivory is able to fetch. It is this discrimination between the two types of products which will allow every producer country to make its choice of development approach, while consumers are allowed to choose how much they wish to pay to influence those choices.

Finally, even if this approach is undesirable from the perspective of many of the parties to CITES (who might view trade regulation as an unsavoury idea), there is little alternative in the medium run. In the future the various international environmental treaties must be brought into conformity with the GATT/WTO process, and this is what will be required. The WTO has expressly ruled that only multilateral regulation is allowed when production processes (rather than traded products) are the object of the regulation. When this principle is finally recognized in the case of CITES, it will be necessary for both producer and consumer states to agree a set of trade regulations. This does not bode well for the current consumer-led approach of enforced bans. The future of CITES is likely to be determined rather by the need to develop regulations from the producer states' perspectives than the consumers', and this indicates the need for the recognition of the right to choose all sorts of development paths. In the future, CITES will have to become much more flexible in order to allow producer states the choice of whether to trade within CITES (and receive whatever premium that confers), or not.

6 Conclusion: the development of CITES

International regulation can only 'work' if it is developed from the perspectives of all the parties concerned. This might not seem a possibility in some cases. From the perspective of the average resident of a developed country, it would appear that the exploitation of wildlife is inconsistent with the conservation of wildlife. To a large extent, this perception is derived from a relationship with nature that has seen the extinction of a large part of the flora and fauna in the northern temperate zones. Other peoples in other parts of the world have not historically demonstrated the same relationship. For them, what we perceive as wildlife resources are in fact their primary resources. Many of them rely on diversity and natural habitat in the same way that we rely on a few species such as cattle, sheep and domesticated fowl. For example, in many parts of rural Africa the vast majority of protein consumed still derives from wildlife sources. (Prescott-Allan and Prescott-Allan, 1982). Given these differences in relationships, we have found ourselves in a polarized world. The Northerners have few remaining species; those in the tropics have the vast majority of the global total. Coincidentally, the countries with most 'species wealth' also have the least 'material wealth'.

This is the classical basis on which comparative advantage and gains to exchange are based. The difference lies in the fact that the developed world would be interested in paying countries in the developing world for the conservation of its stocks of natural resources as well as for the uniqueness of its flows. In that case it is not enough to have trade; it is also necessary to have a trade regulation mechanism which will inform consumers which flows derive from sustainably managed stocks. Then the consumer is able to pursue both forms of trade at once: purchase of the relatively unique natural product together with the conservation of the region from which it came. A welfare enhancing contract between North and South would enable both forms of exchange to occur.

CITES does not currently perform this role, but it is developing in that direction. The treaty was initially drafted solely from a Northerner's perspective. It provided for punitive measures against the trade when a species became endangered. It provided for no regulation, only monitoring, otherwise. The logic was simple, and Northern: species endangerment equates with overexploitation. Thus, all users of wildlife were punished, the sustainable with the unsustainable, when a species became endangered.

This logic ultimately led to the absurd result at the 1989 Conference of the Parties when Zimbabwe, with a long and unquestioned history of sustainable elephant ivory utilization, was penalized along with the other ivory traders for the substantial decline of the African elephant population in a handful of states. The indiscriminating application of Appendix I resulted in the equal treatment of Zimbabwe (whose elephant population increased by 10 000 in the 1980s) with Tanzania, Central African Republic, Zambia and Sudan (whose joint elephant losses equalled about 500 000 during the same period) (Swanson and Pearce, 1989; Barbier *et al.* 1990).

The development of CITES requires two fundamental changes. The developed countries must learn to appreciate the perspective of the developing countries; wildlife utilization need not be inconsistent with wildlife conservation. Then, CITES must be reformed to discriminate between the constructive and the unconstructive use of the wildlife trade. That is, the objective is a constructive trade control mechanism which penalizes unsustainable utilization (relatively) by subsidizing the sustainable. The fundamental importance of all of the recent developments surveyed in this chapter (that is, ranching, quota and conditionality regimes) is that they represent a search for this 'middle ground' between the Appendix I and Appendix II regimes. That is, they are the embodiment of the parties' recognition that international regulation of wildlife trade may be turned to constructive effect in the developing countries. Furthermore, they represent the first, halting steps toward the implementation of a contract that will recognize all of the parties' trade objectives as legitimate. A trade mechanism should discriminate between differing trade flows, in order to inform consumers about what is happening in regard to the producer countries' stocks. In this way the consumers are fully informed about the entire package of goods and services that their custom represents. This is the essence of effective and useful international trade regulation. It must be seen as regulation that will enable more complicated forms of exchange to arise, not simply as regulation to disallow the less desirable forms of trade.

PART III

PRINCIPLES OF INTERNATIONAL ENVIRONMENTAL LAW AND LAWMAKING

Sam Johnston – Secretariat of the CBD

10 Principles of international environmental law

Among the earliest international environmental agreements were the Regulations adopted by the Arbitral Tribunal established to resolve the dispute between the USA and Great Britain over the exploitation of fur seals in the Pacific. The USA had sought to prevent British vessels from overexploiting Pacific fur seals in international waters of the Bering Sea. The Regulations adopted by the Tribunal provided for the 'proper protection and preservation' of fur seals outside jurisdictional limits, which prohibited killing during certain seasons, limited methods and means of fur sealing, and included exceptions for indigenous activities. These Regulations have served as an important precedent for the subsequent development of international environmental law.[1]

Since the 1893 award adopted by the Tribunal, international environmental law has come a long way, and a basic structure of institutions, principles and standards is now in place. The international community's recognition that environmental problems transcend national boundaries has resulted in the development of the important new field of international environmental law. It recognizes that *ad hoc*, disparate and reactive policy responses by individual states or local communities cannot effectively address the growing range of environmental problems faced by the international community. These have grown exponentially with advances in technology, industrialization and scientific understanding. As a consequence environmental law – itself a relatively new field – has necessarily grown from a body of national or bilateral rules into an area increasingly governed by regional and global obligations.

Overexploitation of natural resources, loss of biological diversity, ozone depletion, climate change, acid rain, deforestation, desertification, air and marine pollution, toxic and other waste and a population explosion are but some of the threats currently facing the planet. At the United Nations Conference on Environment and Development (UNCED), held in Rio de Janeiro in June 1992, poverty and international debt were added to the official list of the root causes of global environmental degradation, further expanding the issues properly considered to be concerns for international environmental law. Each of these areas requires international measures, and hence a central role for international law and organization. Indeed it is already clear that the combination of scientific evidence about what *needs* to be done, public pressure over what *should* be done, and political action as to what *can* be done, has already led to an explosion of new international laws addressing environmental issues. They have gained increasingly wide acceptance, are increasingly broad in their scope and sophisticated in their approach, and penetrate issues which, until recently, were thought to lie beyond the range of environmental legislation and activism.

This part of the book is divided into three parts: section 1 (Introduction) briefly describes the context of the subject, its historic development, the primary sources of obligation, the institutional arrangements, and the traditional legal order within which environmental challenges fail to be addressed. Section 2 identifies the basic principles of international environmental law, including general principles and specific topics which have been addressed. Section 3 addresses compliance, including implementation, enforcement and dispute settlement.

1   Introduction

1.1   The international legal order

International law and organizations provide the central basis for international cooperation and collaboration between the various members of the international community in their efforts to protect the local, regional and global environment. At each level the task becomes progressively more complex as new actors and interests are drawn into the legal process: whereas just two states, representing the interest of local fishing communities, negotiated the early fisheries conventions in the middle of the nineteenth century, more than 150 states negotiated the 1992 Climate Change Convention and in so doing represented a comprehensive range of economic and industrial interests.

In both cases, however, the principles and rules of public international law, together with the international organizations that have been established thereunder, are intended to serve similar functions. The overall objective of the international legal order is to provide a framework within which the various members of the international community may cooperate, establish norms of behaviour and resolve their differences. The proper functions of international law are legislative, administrative and adjudicative functions. The legislative function serves as the basis for the creation of legal principles and rules which impose binding obligations requiring states and other members of the international community to conform to certain norms of behaviour and to follow certain required practices. In relation to the environment these obligations place limits upon the activities which may be conducted or permitted because of their actual or potential impact upon the environment. The impact might be felt within the borders of a state, or across the boundaries of two or more states, or in areas beyond the jurisdiction and control of any state.

The administrative function of international law allocates tasks to the various actors to ensure that the standards imposed by the principles and rules of international environmental law are carried out. The adjudicative function of international law aims, in a limited way, to provide mechanisms or fora to allow the pacific settlement of differences or disputes which arise between members of the international community involving the use of natural resources or the conduct of activities which will impact upon the environment.

1.2 Sovereignty and resources

The international legal order thus regulates the activities of an international community which comprises states, international organizations and a broad range of non-governmental actors. States continue to play the primary and dominant role in the international legal order, both as the principal creators of the rules of international law and the principal holders of rights and obligations under those rules. As the dominant actor in the international legal order states are sovereign and equal, which means that they have equal rights and duties as members of the international community, notwithstanding differences of an economic, social, political or other nature. The sovereignty and equality of states means that each has jurisdiction, which is prima facie, exclusive over its territory and the natural resources found there. Additionally each state has a duty not to intervene in the area of exclusive jurisdiction of other states.

The sovereignty and exclusive jurisdiction of the 190 or so states over their territory means, in principle, that they alone have the competence to develop policies and laws in respect of the natural resources and the environment of their territory, which comprises:

- land within its boundaries, including the subsoil
- internal waters, such as lakes, rivers and canals
- territorial sea, which is adjacent to the coast, including its seabed and subsoil
- airspace above its land, internal waters and territorial sea, up to the point at which the legal regime of outer space begins.

Additionally states have more limited sovereign rights and jurisdiction over other areas including: a contiguous zone adjacent to their territorial seas; the continental shelf, its seabed and subsoil; certain fishing zones; and 'exclusive economic zones'.

As a result of these arrangements certain areas are left to fall outside the territory of any state and in respect of which no state has exclusive jurisdiction. These areas, which are sometimes referred to as the global commons, include the high seas and its seabed and subsoil, outer space, and, according to a majority of states, the Antarctic. The atmosphere is also considered to be a part of the global commons.

This apparently straightforward international legal order apparently worked satisfactorily as an organizing structure until technological developments permeated national boundaries. The structure does not coexist comfortably with an environmental order which consists of a biosphere of interdependent ecosystems which do not respect artificial territorial boundaries between states. As an ecological matter, if not a legal one, many natural resources and their environmental components are shared, and the use by any one state of the natural resources within its territory will invariably have consequences for the use of natural resources and their environmental components in another state.

This is self-evident where, for example, a river runs through two or more countries, or living resources migrate between two or more sovereign territories. What is less evident, and has only become apparent in recent years, is that apparently innocent activities in one country, such as the release of chlorofluorocarbons, can have significant effects upon the environment in areas beyond national jurisdiction with consequential harmful effects within the territory of a state. Ecological interdependence therefore poses a fundamental problem for international law, and explains why international cooperation and the development of shared norms of behaviour in the environmental field is indispensable: the challenge for international law in the world of sovereign states is to reconcile the fundamental independence of each state with the inherent and fundamental interdependence of the environment. A further matter arises as a result of existing territorial arrangements which leave certain areas outside any state's territory: how can the protection of areas beyond the national jurisdiction of any state be addressed?

1.3 International actors

Although states remain far and away the most important actors, the history of international environmental law reflects the central role played by international organizations and non-governmental actors in the legal order and its associated processes. The environmental field provides clear evidence that international law is gradually moving away from the view that international society comprises only a community of states, and is increasingly extending its scope to encompass the persons (both legal and natural) within and among those states. This feature is similar to the human rights field, where non-governmental actors and international organizations also have an expanded role. This new reality is now reflected in many international legal instruments, especially the Rio Declaration on environment and development and Agenda 21 adopted at UNCED, which recognize and call for the further development of the role of international organizations and non-governmental actors in virtually all aspects of the international legal process which relates to environment and development.

These various actors have different roles and functions, both as subjects and objects of international environmental law. These functions and roles include, principally: participating in the lawmaking process; monitoring implementation, including reporting; and ensuring enforcement of obligations. The extent to which the different actors contribute to that process turns upon the extent of its international legal personality and the rights and obligations granted to it by general international law as well as the specific rules established by particular treaties and other rules. The Rio Declaration and Agenda 21, as well as an increasing number of international environmental agreements, envisage an expanded role for international organizations and non-governmental actors in virtually all aspects of the international legal process.

1.3.1　States　States are the primary and principal subjects of international law. It is still states which create, adopt and implement international legal principles and rules, create international organizations and permit the participation of other actors in the international legal process. There are currently 181 member states of the United Nations (UN), and another dozen or so are not. Broadly speaking they are divided into developed and developing countries. Developed countries include the 24 member states of the OECD and the 11 states which previously formed part of the 'Soviet' bloc. The latter are currently referred to as 'economies in transition'. The rest of the world, comprising some 155 states, are the developing states which form the Group of 77. The Group of 77 often works as a single negotiating bloc within the framework of the UN. Within the UN system states are also arranged into regional groupings, usually for the purpose of elections to UN bodies. The five groupings are Latin America and the Caribbean Group; African Group, Asia Group; Western European and others group; and Central and Eastern European Group.

Frequently in environmental negotiations these rather simple distinctions tend to break down as states pursue what they perceive to be their vital national interests, including their strategic alliances, an issue which may be unrelated to environmental matters. The UNCED negotiations illustrated the extent of the differences which often existed between and among developed states and developing states on the particularly contentious issues: atmospheric emissions, conservation of marine mammals, protection of forests, institutional arrangements and financial resources.

1.3.2　International organizations　The international organizations involved in environmental matters make up a complex and unwieldy network at the global, regional, subregional and bilateral levels. It is unlikely that any international organization today will not have some responsibility over international environmental matters. The decentralized nature of international organizations in the environmental field makes it difficult to assess their role by reference to any functional, sectoral or geographic criteria. To help understand their activities and their interests they can, however, be divided into three general categories: global organizations under the auspices of, or related to, the UN and its specialized agencies; regional organizations outside the UN system; and organizations established by environmental and other international agreements.

International organizations perform a range of different functions and roles in the development and management of international legal responses to environmental issues and problems. International organizations fulfil each, or a combination, of roles of a judicial, legislative and administrative nature. The actual functions of each institution will depend to a very large extent upon the powers granted to it by its constituent instrument as subsequently interpreted and applied by the practice of the organization and the parties to it. Apart from very specific functions required of particular organizations, five separate but interrelated legal functions and roles are performed by international organizations.

First, they provide a forum for general cooperation and coordination between states on matters of international environmental management. Second, they play an informational role: they receive and disseminate information, facilitate information exchange, and provide for formal and informal consultation between states and between states and the organization. A third function is the contribution of international organizations to the development of international legal obligations, including 'soft law'. International organizations develop policy initiatives and standards, and may even adopt rules which establish binding obligations or which might reflect rules of customary law, including in relation to the development of procedural standards and the establishment of new and subsidiary institutional arrangements.

Once environmental and other standards and obligations have been established, institutions increasingly play a role in ensuring the implementation of and compliance with those standards and obligations. This may take a number of forms, including receiving information from parties or other persons on an informal and *ad hoc* basis, or it may entail the regular receipt and consideration of reports or periodic communications from parties to international environmental treaties as a means of reviewing progress in implementation. Assisting in implementation can also take place through the provision of formal or informal advice on technical, legal and administrative or institutional matters, including capacity-building. A fifth function is to provide an independent forum, or mechanism, for the settlement of disputes, usually between states.

1.3.3 Non-governmental actors (NGOs) Non-governmental actors have historically played an important role in developing international environmental law, and continue to play an influential role in a variety of different ways. They can identify issues which require international legal action; they may frequently participate as observers in international organizations and in treaty negotiations; and they can use a variety of efforts to ensure the national and international implementation of, and compliance with, standards and obligations which have been adopted at regional and global level. In the past two decades at least six different types of NGO have emerged as actors in the development of international environmental law: the scientific community; non-profit environmental groups and associations; private companies and business concerns; legal organizations; the academic community; and individuals. The Rio Declaration and Agenda 21 affirm the important partnership role of non-governmental organizations and call for their 'expanded role'.[2]

1.4 Defining the environment in international law
Legal definitions of the 'environment' reflect scientific categorizations and groupings, as well as political acts which tend to incorporate cultural and economic considerations. A scientific approach tends to divide environmental issues into 'compartments': these include the atmosphere, atmospheric deposition, soils and sediments, water quality, biology and humans. These scientific definitions are transformed by the political process into the legal definitions found in treaties, and although the term 'environment' cannot be said to have a generally accepted usage as a term of art under international law, recent agreements have tended to identify the various environmental media which are included in the term with a fair degree of consistency. Although the 1972 Stockholm Declaration does not include a definition of the environment, Principle 2 refers to the natural resources of the earth as including 'air, water, land, flora and fauna and ... natural ecosystems'. Those treaties which do refer to the environment and seek to include some form of working definition tend to adopt broad definitions. Under the 1991 Espoo Convention and the 1992 Transboundary Watercourses Convention the 'environment' which is defined by reference to impacts, includes 'human health and safety, flora, fauna, soil, air, water, climate, landscape and historical monuments or other physical structures or the interaction among these factors'.[3]

1.5 Sources of international environmental law
International law can be defined as those rules which are legally binding on states and other members of the international community in their relations with each other. The sources from which the binding rights and obligations of states and other members of the international community arise include:

- bilateral or multilateral treaties
- binding acts of international organizations
- rules of customary international law
- judgements of international courts or tribunals.

Additionally rules of 'soft law' which are not binding play an important role, by pointing to the likely future direction of formally binding obligations, by informally establishing acceptable norms of behaviour and by 'codifying' or reflecting rules of customary law.

In practice the most important sources are binding international agreements in the form of *treaties* (also referred to as conventions, protocols, agreements and so on) which can be adopted bilaterally (between two states), regionally (between states in a particular region geographically or politically defined) or globally (participation is open to all states). With more than 180 states now in existence, the number of bilateral environmental agreements runs into the thousands, supplemented by dozens of regional agreements and a smaller, but increasing, number of global treaties. European (in particular EC) and other industrialized countries have adopted a large body of regional environmental rules which frequently provide a basis for regional and global measures adopted in other parts of the world. Regional treaties are less well-developed in Africa, the Caribbean and Oceania, and virtually non-existent in Asia and the Americas. All industrial activity is, however, prohibited by treaty in the Antarctic.

The second principal source of international obligation arises from acts of international organizations. Almost all international environmental agreements establish institutional organs with the power to adopt certain acts, decisions or other measures. Such acts of international organizations, sometimes referred to as secondary legislation, can provide an important source of international law; they may be legally binding in themselves, or if they are not legally binding *per se* they may amend existing obligations, or they can authoritatively interpret treaty obligations. Non-binding acts, frequently referred to as soft law, can also, sometimes, contribute to the development of customary law. Binding acts of international organizations derive their legal authority from the treaty on which their adoption was based, and can therefore be considered as part of treaty law; some of the more far-reaching international decisions affecting the use of natural resources have been adopted in the form of acts of international organizations rather than by treaty. Many environmental treaties allow the institutions a choice of adopting acts with or without binding legal effects they establish. Those acts which do not have binding legal consequences could, however, subsequently be relied upon as reflecting a rule of customary international law.

The primary role of international environmental obligations adopted by treaty and acts of international organizations should not obscure the important, albeit secondary, role which is played by customary international law. Customary law rules fulfil a number of functions, by creating binding obligations and by contributing to the codification of obligations in the form of treaty rules and other binding acts. The significance of customary law lies in the fact that as a general matter it establishes obligations for all states (or all states within a particular region) except those which have persistently objected to a practice and its legal consequences. Establishing the existence of a rule of customary international law is made difficult by the need to provide evidence of consistent state practice, which practice will rarely provide any detailed guidance as to the precise context or scope of any particular rule. Article 38(1)(b) of the Statute of the International Court of Justice identifies the two elements of customary international law: state practice and *opinion juris* (the belief that practice is required by law).

These sources of binding obligation are supplemented by non-binding sources of 'soft law', reflected in guidelines, recommendations and other non-binding acts adopted by states and international institutions. These can provide evidence of state practice which might support the existence of a rule of customary international law, and often reflect trends which lead to the development of binding rules. The most important sources of 'soft law' are the 1972 Declaration of Principles of the 1972 Stockholm Conference, the 1982 World Charter for Nature and the 1992 Rio Declaration, which reflect 'to the extent any international instrument can do so, the current consensus of values and priorities in environment and development'.

The case law of international courts and tribunals, and arguments presented to such bodies, identify some general principles and rules of international environmental law. The importance of arbitral awards, in particular, in the development of international environmental law cannot be understated. Mention has already been made of the Pacific Fur Seal Arbitration, and before states had adopted many 'international statutes' important principles had been elaborated by Arbitral Tribunals in the *Trail Smelter Case* (concerning transboundary air pollution) and the *Lac Lanoux Arbitration* (concerning the use of a shared river). Judgments of the International Court of Justice have also contributed to the *corpus* of international environmental law, particularly in the *Icelandic Fisheries Cases* (on fisheries conservation) and the *Nuclear Tests Cases* (on the legality of atmospheric nuclear tests). The Court is currently faced with two potentially important environmental cases: the *Grabcikovo–Nagymaros Project Case* (concerning the construction of a dam on the Danube River) and the *World Health Organization Advisory Opinion* (concerning the legality of nuclear weapon use).

1.6   History

The development of international environmental law has occurred over four periods, responding to particular factors which influence legal developments. The emergence of principles and rules has often followed a catalysing event, such as an oil pollution or nuclear accident (the Torrey Canyon, Amoco Cadiz, Exxon Valdez and Chernobyl accidents each resulted in new international rules), or an initiative proposed by one or more governments, international organizations or non-governmental organizations. The principal factors influencing legal developments include industrial and technological developments that lead to increased demands on finite natural resources; improved scientific understanding of natural processes which have led to a greater recognition of ecological interdependence and the fact that many natural resources do not respect artificial, international legal boundaries; and individual accidents or incidents. More recently some states have sought to justify international measures by arguing that disparities in national environmental standards may lead to certain countries' industries not having to integrate environmental costs into production costs and thereby gaining competitive advantage in international markets. Until recently it was evident that international environmental law had arisen without a coordinated legal and institutional framework. The 1972 Stockholm Conference and then UNCED attempted to create such a framework.

1.6.1   To 1945
The first distinct period began with nineteenth-century bilateral fisheries treaties and the Pacific fur seal arbitration and concluded with the creation of the new UN family of international institutions in 1945. This period might be characterized as one in which states first acted internationally upon their understanding that the process of industrialization and development required limitations to be placed on the exploitation of certain natural resources (flora and fauna) and the adoption of appropriate legal instruments. National laws predated these international measures. Early efforts at international environmental regulation focused on international agreements to conserve wildlife, especially fisheries, birds and seals. International institutional arrangements were limited: until the UN was created in 1945 there was no international forum in which to raise environmental concerns, and most of the agreements adopted in this initial period did not create arrangements to ensure that legal obligations were complied with or enforced. Many initiatives grew from private activities by private citizens, an early harbinger of the more intensive activism of non-governmental organizations which marks international negotiations today.

The agreements which were adopted nevertheless established a pattern of precedents which are still relied upon today. In 1872 Switzerland proposed an international regulatory commission for the protection of birds, which led to the first multilateral birds' convention in 1902.[4] 1900 saw the first multilateral wildlife conservation agreement, in Europe's African colonies.[5] In 1909 the first treaty was adopted to prevent pollution of freshwaters.[6] 1916 heralded the first (bilateral) agreement to protect migratory birds,[7] and in 1940 the Americas became the home of the second regional arrangement to conserve wildlife generally.[8] These introductory, but rather vague and unenforceable, international rules reflected a growing awareness that the exploitation of natural resources could not proceed unchecked, that industrialization and technological developments brought with them pollution and associated problems, and that international measures were needed. Shortly before the Second World War the emerging consciousness was summarized thus:

> We have accustomed ourselves to think of ever expanding productive capacity, of ever fresh spaces of the world to be filled with people, of ever new discoveries of kinds and sources of raw materials, of continuous technical progress operating indefinitely to solve problems of supply. We have lived so long in what we have regarded as an expanding world, that we reject in our contemporary theories of economics and of population the realities which contradict such views. Yet our modern expansion has been effected in large measure at the cost of an actual and permanent impoverishment of the world.[9]

It was the creation of the UN in 1945 that began to put in place institutional arrangements to provide a more coherent basis for global action.

1.6.2   The creation of the UN: 1945–72   The UN introduced a second period, which culminated with the 1972 UN Conference on the Human Environment. Over nearly three decades a range of international organizations with competence in environmental matters were created, and legal instruments were adopted to address particular sources of pollution and the conservation of general and particular environmental resources. These included oil pollution, nuclear testing, wetlands, the marine environment and its living resources, the quality of freshwaters and the dumping of waste at sea.

The UN provided a forum for the discussion of the consequences of all this technical progress, and introduced a period characterized by two features: international organizations became involved with environmental issues, and those issues began to address the causes of pollution and environmental degradation. The connection was made on the relationship between economic development and environmental protection. However the UN Charter did not, and still does not, address environmental protection or the conservation of natural resources. Other members of the UN family, including the Food and Agriculture Organization (FAO), the United Nations Educational, Scientific and Cultural Organization (UNESCO) and the General Agreement on Tariffs and Trade (GATT), were granted a limited mandate over these matters. In 1949 the UN convened its first environmental conference, on the Conservation and Utilization of Resources. The Conference, which presaged the 1972 Stockholm Conference and the 1992 UNCED, addressed six main issues: minerals, fuels and energy, water, forests, land, and wildlife and fish. The main topics addressed included world resources and shortages (including their interdependence, use and conservation); the development of new resources by applied technology; education for conservation; the position of less-developed countries; and the integrated development of river basins.[10] Discussions also focused on the relationship between conservation and use, on the need to develop an appropriate standard to ensure conservation in human effort to meet human need, and on the relationship between conservation and development, but no recommendations or action plan were adopted.

The Conference was significant also because it recognized the UN's competence over environmental and natural resource issues. In 1954 the General Assembly convened a major Conference on the Conservation of the Living Resources of the Sea,[11] which led to the conservation rules adopted in the 1958 Geneva Conventions.[12] The following year it adopted the first of many resolutions on atomic energy and the effects of radiation,[13] which led to the 1963 Nuclear Test Ban Treaty[14] and, ultimately, the political context for Australia and New Zealand to bring to the International Court of Justice a case calling on France to stop all atmospheric nuclear tests.[15] These years also saw the adoption of the first global conventions on oil pollution prevention,[16] high seas intervention for clean-up,[17] and liability and compensation.[18] Other global agreements addressed high seas fishing and conservation and the protection of wetlands.

Noteworthy regional developments included the 1959 Antarctic Treaty limiting parties to peaceful activities in that region and prohibiting nuclear explosions or the disposal of radioactive waste; the EC's first act of environmental legislation, in 1967; the 1968 African Nature Convention, which aimed at the 'conservation, utilization and development of soil, water, flora and faunal resources in accordance with scientific principles and with due regard to the best interests of the people'[19] land, shortly before the Stockholm Conference, the first treaty to prohibit the dumping of a wide range of hazardous substances at sea.

By 1972 there existed an emerging body of rules establishing environmental obligations at the regional and global levels, and international organizations were beginning to address international environmental issues. These treaty and institutional developments were, however, adopted in a piecemeal fashion, and no international organization had overall responsibility for coordinating international environmental policy and law, and few had a specific environmental mandate.

1.6.3   Stockholm and beyond   The third period ran from the 1972 Stockholm Conference and concluded with UNCED. During this period the UN attempted to put in place a system for putting the task of addressing a growing range of environmental issues onto a more coordinated and coherent footing. A raft of regional and global conventions addressed new environmental issues, and new techniques of regulation were employed.

The 1972 Conference, convened by the General Assembly,[20] adopted three non-binding instruments: a resolution on institutional and financial arrangements; a declaration of 26 guiding principles; and an action plan setting forth 109 recommendations for more specific international action.[21] These represented the international community's first effort at developing a coherent strategy for the development of international policy, law and institutions to protect the environment. According to one commentator

> Stockholm enlarged and facilitated means toward international action previously limited by inadequate perception of environmental issues and by restrictive concepts of national sovereignty ... There were significant elements of innovation in (1) the redefinition of international issues, (2) the rationale for cooperation, (3) the approach to international responsibility, and (4) the conceptualization of international organizational relationships.[22]

Although the infusion of new international law was not dramatic, the trends leading to Stockholm were reinforced, particularly in relation to marine pollution, transboundary air and water pollution, and protection of endangered species. For international law the significant developments proved to be the creation of the United Nations Environment Programme (UNEP); the establishment of coordinating mechanisms among existing institutions; the definition of a framework for future actions to be taken by the international community; and the adoption of a set of general principles to guide such action, including Principle 21. UNEP has subsequently been responsible for the establishment and implementation of its Regional Seas Programme, including some 30 regional treaties, as well as important global treaties addressing ozone depletion, trade in hazardous waste and biodiversity.

Stockholm catalysed other global treaties adopted under the UN's auspices. These addressed, for the first time on global scale, the dumping of wastes at sea;[23] pollution from ships;[24] trade in endangered species;[25] and the protection of world cultural heritage.[26] The most important agreement, over time, may be the 1982 United Nations Convention on the Law of the Sea (UNCLOS). This establishes a unique, comprehensive framework for the establishment of global rules for the protection of the marine environment and marine living resources, including detailed and important institutional arrangements and provisions on environmental impact assessment, technology transfer and liability.[27] Its provisions have provided an influential basis for text subsequently adopted, even prior to its entry into force in November 1994.

Stockholm was also followed by other important regional developments, including environmental protection rules in the EC, and the creation of an Environment Committee at the OECD. New regional agreements addressed, in a more coherent and comprehensive fashion, the protection of migratory species;[28] the protection of habitats (as opposed to species);[29] land transboundary air pollution.[30]

Also in this period economic and financial institutions began to address environmental issues. In 1971 the GATT established a Group on Environmental Measures and International Trade (although it did not meet until 1991), and that organization began to be faced with countries adopting environmental measures which might affect international trade. In the face of increased public and governmental pressure, the World Bank and regional development sought to integrate environmental considerations into their loan-making processes. This led to the establishment of an Environment Department in the World Bank and the adoption of environmental impact assessment requirements in most multilateral development banks. The 1990 Articles of Agreement establishing the European Bank for Reconstruction and Development reflect changing times and values, including environmental obligations in that organization's fundamental objectives.[31] In 1990 the parties to the Ozone Convention created a Multilateral Fund to help developing countries meet certain incremental costs associated with implementing that agreement, and in 1991 the World Bank, UNEP and UNDP established the Global Environmental Facility to provide financial resources to support projects which benefited the global commons. Later that year the GATT decided to reactivate its long-dormant Group on Environmental Measures and International Trade. In the run-up to UNCED treaties were adopted to address an ever extending range of subjects, applying new techniques and approaches for environmental impact assessment;[32] the transboundary impacts of industrial accidents;[33] and the protection and use of international watercourses. Significantly the UN Security Council declared that ecological issues could constitute threats to international peace and security, and the UN General Assembly prohibited the use of driftnets.

'Soft law' instruments also proliferated, and three have particularly influenced new international laws: the 1978 UNEP Draft Principles on Shared Natural Resources, the 1981 Montevideo Programme of the UNEP Group of Legal Experts, and the 1982 World Charter for Nature. Non-governmental efforts resulted in comprehensive efforts which influenced binding legal developments. Particularly noteworthy was the work of the World Commission on Environment and Development which produced the Brundtland Report ('Our common future') and the accompanying Legal Principles and Recommendations on Environmental Protection and Sustainable Development prepared by an Experts Group on Environmental Law. Collaboration between IUCN, UNEP and WWF produced the 1980 World Conservation Strategy and its 1991 follow-up, 'Caring for the earth: a strategy for sustainable living'.[34]

By 1990, when preparations for UNCED formally began with General Assembly resolution 44/228, there existed a solid body of rules of international environmental law. States were increasingly subject to limits on the right to allow or carry out activities which harmed the environment. New standards were in place, a range of techniques sought to implement those standards, and environmental issues were intersecting with economic matters, especially trade and development lending. Perhaps most significantly, as part of the global bargain in the move towards global instruments, developing countries had succeeded in establishing the principle that financial resources should meet some of the costs of implementing obligations, and it had been accepted that not all countries should be bound by the same standards. New institutions addressed regional and global environmental issues, and old institutions were reforming themselves to begin to integrate environmental considerations issues into their activities. In spite of these relatively impressive achievements, environmental matters remained a peripheral matter for the international community.

1.6.4 UNCED and beyond   UNCED launched a fourth period for the 'greening' of international law, which might be characterized as the period of integration, requiring environmental concerns to be integrated into and fully taken account of by all relevant activities. In December 1987 the UN General Assembly had endorsed the Brundtland Report,[35] and the following year called for a global conference on environment and development.[36] UNCED was formally proposed in December 1989 by General Assembly Resolution 44/228, and after four preparatory negotiating sessions 176 states, several dozen international organizations and several thousand NGOs converged on Rio de Janeiro for two weeks in June 1992. The purpose of the conference was to elaborate strategies and measures to halt and reverse the effects of environmental degradation in the context of strengthened national and international efforts to promote sustainable and environmentally sound development in all countries. UNCED adopted three non-binding instruments: the Rio Declaration on Environment and Development (the Rio Declaration),[37] a Non-legally Binding Authoritative Statement of Principles for a Global Consensus on the Management, Conservation and Sustainable Development of All Types of Forest (the Forest Principles); and Agenda 21.[38] Two treaties were also opened for signature at UNCED: the Convention on Biological Diversity,[39] and the United Nations Framework Convention on Climate Change.[40]

It is still too early to fully judge UNCED's contribution to the progressive development of international law. Certainly it will lead to more international laws, but whether they will support or undermine efforts to protect the environment remains to be seen.

Nevertheless UNCED heralded a new stage of international environmental lawmaking. The UN General Assembly adopted five follow-up resolutions giving effect to UNCED recommendations, including negotiations for a convention on drought and desertification; the convening of a conference on the sustainable development of small island states; the establishment of the Commission on Sustainable Development; and a conference on straddling and highly migratory fish stocks.[41] Post-UNCED agreements updated earlier 'first generation' marine pollution agreements,[42] and introduced new rules on liability for oil pollution and for environmental damage generally.[43] New treaties are likely on nuclear safety and liability, desertification and drought, and the prevention of industrial disasters, and many existing agreements are being updated and modernized in the light of UNCED's new principles. The early entry into force of the Climate Change and Biodiversity Conventions suggested that such political will as existed at UNCED to adopt the instruments had been carried forward into the next phase.

2   Making international environmental law

How international law is made or brought about is important to understanding the nature of the existing regime. This section examines how international environmental policy and law is developed, under what circumstances and in what fora it is conceived.

2.1   Creating treaties

As noted before treaties are the most important source of international environmental law. There are no rules prescribing their form or how they should be developed, but the 1969 Vienna Convention on the Law of Treaties lays down rules for treaties concluded after 1980 on such matters as entry into force, reservations, interpretation, termination and invalidity. Treaties go by a variety of different descriptions, such as conventions, protocols, covenants, pacts or acts, but there is no legal significance associated with these different terms.

Negotiation of treaties has recently been following an increasingly standardized process. Often the need for a treaty is initially promoted by an international organization or a NGO. Negotiation formally begins within the framework of an existing international organization or with the establishment of an independent single purpose organization, often called an Intergovernmental Negotiating Committee (INC). Formal negotiations are often preceded by informal negotiations, where the parameters are determined and the preliminary positions of states are investigated. The initiative for these informal discussions and the formal negotiations most often comes from an international organization such as UNEP. Negotiations can take many years, for example, the negotiations for UNCLOS began in the 1960s, formally commenced in 1973 and were not concluded until 1982. In order to accelerate the process, negotiators are normally separated into several working groups which address separate issues simultaneously. Recent negotiations have also tended to allow substantial input from the NGO community, with some cases a NGO draft being used as the basic negotiating text for the INC (that is the 1991 Madrid Protocol to the Antarctic Treaty and the CBD).

The negotiation of a treaty is concluded by the adoption of the text of the treaty by the representatives of the relevant states. Unanimity in adoption of a treaty is not, however, always required. Indeed the custom for international treaties in some areas is for a two-thirds' majority of negotiating states to consent to the draft text. Each negotiation adopts its own rules of procedure which outline how adoption is to take place.

The full obligations or commitments in a treaty, however, do not become legally binding until a treaty has 'entered into force', although adoption does impose limited obligations on the parties. Traditionally a treaty did not come into force until all the negotiating states expressed their consent. This may be altered by agreement and it is now more usual to find that the treaty enters into force when it has been consented to by a specified number of states or states having certain characteristics. In such cases, however, the treaty is binding only between those states which have consented, though states which have adopted a treaty are expected, pending their consent, not to do anything which undermines its objects and purposes.

Consent may be expressed a number of ways, with the permitted ways of becoming a party to a particular treaty always being outlined in the text of the treaty itself. 'Signature' and 'ratification' are the most frequent means of expressing consent. The signature is that of the delegation negotiating the treaty and is sometimes the act of adoption as well. Ratification refers to the legislative and executive measures that a country is required by its constitution to undertake to be legally bound by a treaty (that is Act of Parliament). Another common way that a state can become a party to a treaty is by accession. Accession is the term used to refer to countries who join the treaty after it has entered into force. Accession is, however, only possible if it is provided for in the treaty or by agreement of all the parties to the treaty.

Treaties do not necessarily lay down clear or detailed rules capable of being acted upon without further clarification or elaboration; more often they are no more than a 'framework', laying down only very general requirements or guiding principles. The frequently cited prototypes are UNEP's Regional Seas Treaties and the 1985 Vienna Convention. The original text of the 1976

Barcelona Convention on the Protection of the Mediterranean Sea, the first Regional Sea Treaty, contained only the vaguest of guiding principles. These have subsequently been developed into much more specific and binding legal obligations through its accompanying protocols on cooperation in combating oil spills, dumping of wastes, protection of the marine environment from land-based sources of pollution, and protection of specially sensitive areas. In truth nearly all modern treaties are framework treaties. For example both of the treaties signed at UNCED are based upon the framework approach and envisage further protocols on a wide range of matters in order to develop the normative content of the convention.

2.1.1   Biodiversity convention   The multilateral negotiations for the CBD were typical of modern treaty development. Negotiations for the CBD began formally in 1987 with UNEP Governing Council Decisions 14/26 and 15/34, which called upon UNEP to set up a series of expert group meetings. Started in November 1988, the initial sessions were referred to as meetings of the 'Ad Hoc Working Group of Experts on Biological Diversity'. By mid-1990 sufficient progress had been made, including the completion of studies on various aspects of the issues, for several working groups to be established. For example the Sub-Working Group on Biotechnology was established to prepare terms of reference on biotechnology transfer. Other working groups examined issues such as *in situ* and *ex situ* conservation of wild and domesticated species; access to genetic resources and technology, including biotechnology; new and additional financial support; and safety of release or experimentation on genetically modified organisms.

The Governing Council of UNEP then created an 'Ad Hoc Working Group of Legal and Technical Experts' in mid-1990 to prepare a 'new international legal instrument for the conservation and sustainable use of biological diversity'. The legal and technical experts considered the reports of the various working groups in drafting the convention. The Executive Director of UNEP prepared the first formal draft Convention on Biological Diversity, which was considered in February 1991, by an 'Intergovernmental Negotiating Committee'. The first INC meeting was also known as the third session of the Ad Hoc Working Group of Legal and Technical Experts. Four subsequent sessions of the INC were held in the intervening two years, culminating in the adoption of the final text of the treaty in Nairobi, Kenya on 22 May 1992. On 29 September 1993, the Secretariat received the thirtieth ratification, which was the required number of ratifications for the Convention to enter into force, and the Convention entered into force three months later.

2.2 Institutions

After treaties the most important source of new international environmental policies and rules are the acts of international organizations. Not only do they often initiate multilateral negotiations for new treaties, they also produce policy, guidelines, codes of practice and resolutions which are largely voluntary and non-binding in strictly legal terms. These types of instrument are often referred to as 'soft' law. Despite the voluntary nature of many of these instruments, their role is important from a legal viewpoint as there is growing evidence that they have considerable influence on state practice and, in any event, they often eventually evolve into hard law. The important role that international organizations play in the development of policy and law was officially recognized at UNCED. Agenda 21 for instance not only devoted an entire chapter to the role of international organizations but also called for the establishment of the CSD to ensure that the UN and its agencies implement its obligations.

Although soft law is elusive and hard to define, it has an important contribution to make in establishing a new legal order in a dynamic field such as international environmental law. Soft law's advantage over hard law, and hence its importance, arises from its flexibility. The soft law approach allows states to tackle a problem collectively at a time when they do not want to completely shackle their freedom of action. With environmental matters this may be either because scientific evidence is not conclusive or complete but a precautionary attitude is required, or because the economic costs are uncertain or overburdensome. Such an approach does enable states to assume obligations that they would not otherwise assume, because these are expressed in vaguer terms, or conversely, in soft law form enable formulation of obligations in a precise and restrictive manner that would not be acceptable in a binding treaty. This flexibility is vital in securing the necessary compromises to develop policy and law in today's diverse international community.

International organizations also develop international environmental policy indirectly as a consequence of providing a permanent forum where negotiation of further rules and policy occurs. They thus facilitate and shape the compromises necessary to develop policy and law in a world consisting of different states with divergent interests and values. Their influence in this regard is through the provision of support services such as legal and scientific advice or secretarial services. For instance international organizations will often prepare the initial drafts of negotiating texts, drawing up preliminary agendas and commenting on proposals, and in this way they not only aid negotiations but have a substantive input into negotiations. In this sense they make a valuable contribution as part of the lawmaking process although they are not themselves technically involved in the process. The availability of their administrative machinery is an important part of the lawmaking process and should not be underestimated.

Most international organizations are involved in supervising, monitoring and prompting implementation of their codes and sometimes conventions. This is done more by reminder and comment than through active or binding enforcement measures. The key tasks that they perform in this context are those of collecting information and data, receiving reports on treaty implementation by states, facilitating independent monitoring and inspection and acting as a forum for reviewing the performance of states or for the negotiation of further measures and regulations. Supervision of this kind also often entails the negotiation and elaboration of detailed rules, standards, or practices, usually as a means of giving effect to the more general provisions of the treaty under which they are conducted. Not only does this give the treaties a dynamic character and allow the parties to respond to new problems or priorities, it is also a form of lawmaking. In some instances, this rule-making can have a legal significance beyond the immediate convention under which they were promulgated. For example the standards set by the IMO in safety and oil pollution discharges are accepted and implemented by countries not bound by them.

Recent developments foresee an even greater role in policy development and lawmaking. Both the Antarctic Mineral Resources Commission and the International Seabed Authority were delegated considerable power to manage the resources under their control. Crucially they both had the power to make binding decisions based upon a majority decision as opposed to relying upon unanimity. As experience with the international fishery commissions has illustrated, the latter type of voluntary agreement has proven to be incapable of making the tough decisions necessary for efficiently utilizing common property or arresting the 'tragedy of the commons'. Even though the Antarctic Mineral Resources Commission never came into existence and the future of the International Seabed Authority is uncertain, they indicate the type of power and control international organizations may be given in the future.

As we shall see international organizations also act as dispute resolution mechanisms which create rules and develop the law through clarification by 'judicial' interpretation of many of the vague rules of a convention. Finally, they provide a forum in which state practice, the basis of customary international law, can be developed and manifest itself

2.2.1   UN environmental programme   One of the more important and active international organizations for developing international environmental law over the last two decades has been UNEP. Created in 1972 to implement the results of the UNCHE, UNEP first spelt out its objectives for the development of international environmental law in 1975 when it stated that its intentions were: to contribute towards the development and codification of a new body of international law to meet new requirements generated by environmental concerns based on the Stockholm Declaration; to facilitate cooperation in developing the law on state responsibility in accordance with the principles of the Stockholm Declaration; to contribute to development of international law at national and regional levels; to promote protection of the international commons and their regulation from an environmental viewpoint; to establish guidelines and procedures for avoidance and settlement of disputes; and to study institutional structures related to the environment with the aim of devising efficient new mechanisms or improving old ones.

Central to their efforts to develop international environmental law has been the Programme for the Development and Periodic Review of Environmental Law, better known as the 'Montevideo Programme'. The Programme can be grouped loosely into three categories: (1) conclusion of international agreements; (2) development of international principles, guidelines and standards; and (3) provision of international assistance for national legislation and administration. Under each one of these headings, UNEP has developed a considerable body of documentation and a number of treaties. These include: the Regional Seas Treaties, the 1979 Bonn Convention, the 1985 Vienna Convention and the 1989 Basle Convention. Various guidelines have also been produced including: the 1978 Principle of Conduct in the Field of the Environment for the Guidance of States in the Conservation and Harmonious Utilization of Natural Resources Shared by Two or More States; the 1985 Montreal Guidelines for the Protection of the Marine Environment Against Pollution from Land-based Sources; the 1987 Cairo Guidelines and Principles for the Environmentally Sound Management of Hazardous Waste; and the 1987 Goals and Principles of Environmental Impact Assessment. UNEP has also provided considerable assistance in the drafting of national environmental legislation for both developed and developing countries.

Even though the normative content of the UNEP instruments tends to be weak and many are replete with ambiguities and contradictions, some of these instruments have developed into binding regimes. Notable examples of this hardening include the development of over 40 separate protocols under the Regional Seas Programme; the 1985 Vienna Convention which has been developed into one of the leading environmental treaties through several accompanying protocols, most notably the 1987 Montreal Protocol; and the transformation of the Cairo Guidelines and Principles for the Environmentally Sound Management of Hazardous Waste into the 1989 Basle Convention.

Although many of UNEP's initiatives have not so far been implemented effectively and despite the fact that it is not possible to judge whether they would have come about in the absence of UNEP, UNEP has undoubtedly played an important role in their development and influenced their substantive content.

2.3 Conference of the parties

All effective treaties provide a mechanisms whereby the parties can meet and consider how the purposes of the treaty are being met. Often these meetings are known as the Conference of the Parties or the COP. The COPs are the principal forum where the often general obligations found in many treaties are developed into meaningful commitments. They also provide for flexibility and adaptability within a convention. In a modern treaty COPs are held at regular intervals, typically every two years. The powers delegated to these bodies normally include: keeping under review the implementation of the convention; establishing the form and the intervals for the information transmittals required by the convention; considering such information as well as reports submitted by any subsidiary body; considering and, if necessary, adopting amendments to the convention, its annexes and protocols; establishing subsidiary bodies as deemed necessary; and coordinating the secretariat, the subsidiary bodies and executive bodies of other relevant conventions. Essentially COPs act as the legislative arm of a convention and, consequently, are the formal source of much international environmental policy and law.

Whereas early COPs were rather private affairs, involving only government delegations, excluding the public and receiving very little media attention, currently, most important COPs attract considerable attention from a wide range of interests and allow considerable public involvement in their decision-making process. For example, at the Eighth COP to CITES in 1992, there were over 1000 registered participants representing some 140 NGOs and a further 586 members of the press.

The importance of the role performed by the COP is perhaps most graphically illustrated by the absence of an effective COP, such as with the 1968 African Convention. Without a proper COP mechanism it has achieved very little in its 25-year history.

2.3.1 The Antarctica Treaty The important role of a properly functioning COP in developing policy and law and the politics involved in arriving at COP decisions are illustrated by the experience of the Antarctic Treaty System and its COP, the Antarctic Treaty Consultative Party Meetings (ATCMs). The 1959 Antarctica Treaty as originally adopted contained few concrete commitments and developed no institutional structure for its implementation (that is no convention 'secretariat' was established). In the absence of any institutional structure the Treaty has been almost entirely managed by the biennial meetings of its 'COP', the ATCMs. The purpose of these meetings, outlined in Article IX is 'to exchange information, consult on matters of common interest pertaining to Antarctica, and formulating and considering, and recommending to their Governments, measures in furtherance of the principles and objectives of the Treaty, including measures regarding:

(a) use of Antarctica for peaceful purposes only;
(b) facilitation of scientific research in Antarctica;
(c) facilitation of international scientific co-operation in Antarctica;
(d) facilitation of the exercise of the rights of inspection provided for in Article VII of the Treaty;
(e) questions relating to the exercise of jurisdiction in Antarctica;
(f) preservation and conservation of living resources in Antarctica.

ATCMs occur at a conference hosted and organized by one of the Consultative Parties and usually last for about two weeks. The first such meeting occurred in 1960. Although they used to occur every two years, since 1991 they have been held on an annual basis. The most recent was the XIXth ATCM held in Seoul in May 1995. The terms of the Treaty are developed through a variety of legal instruments which include ATCM or SATCM Recommendations, protocols to the Treaty or separate conventions. The most commonly used instruments are the ATCM Recommendations which are made consensual basis. To date there have been over 200 Recommendations made on a wide variety of subjects including; environmental protection, meteorology, telecommunications, transport and logistics, tourism and exchange of information. In addition to these regular meetings, special meetings are called from time to time to consider special issues; the most recent of these special ATCMs (SATCM) occurred in April 1991 in Madrid to finalize the Protocol on Comprehensive Environmental Protection for Antarctica.

The extent to which the ATCM has developed a detailed and elaborated Article X(f) is a paradigm of policy and rule-making by a COP. From this general obligation an elaborate management regime has been developed through additional recommendations, protocols and further conventions to provide comprehensive protection for the environment in Antarctica.

The development of Article X(f) began at the very first ATCM where rules governing the conduct of scientists working in the area, which had been developed by the Scientific Committee on Antarctic Research (SCAR), were issued to all Antarctic expeditions. These ideas were further discussed at the second ATCM (Recommendation II–II) and were developed into the Agreed Measures For The Conservation Of Antarctic Fauna And Flora (Recommendation III–XI).

As further threats to Antarctica became known, the ATCM has been the mechanism through which new regulations have been developed to control them. For instance when Norway expressed renewed interest in commercial exploitation of seals in 1964, it was suggested at the IIIrd ATCM in 1964 that national governments should regulate pelagic sealing on a voluntary basis. At the next ATCM a further step was taken with the Consultative Parties adopting Interim Guidelines for the Voluntary Regulations of Antarctic Pelagic Sealing (Recommendation IV–XXI). Finally, in 1972, the Consultative Parties adopted the Convention for the Conservation of Antarctic Seals, establishing a regime of protection for six species of Antarctic seals most threatened by sealing.

Similarly, when both Japan and the USSR began investigating the possibility of harvesting krill on a commercial scale in the late 1960s, the ATCM once again provided the framework within which a regime was developed to control and manage the marine resource. Negotiations were commenced at the IXth ATCM at London in 1977. After seven separate meetings and consultations the Convention on the Conservation of Antarctic Marine Living Resources (CCAMLR) was adopted. CCAMLR was an innovative document in that it contained a management regime based upon an ecological approach as opposed to a political one. This ecosystem approach meant that, instead of the jurisdictional boundaries of the Convention being determined by political parameters, it was defined by reference to the 'Antarctic Convergence', the natural biological frontier of the Antarctic marine ecosystem (which occurs where the warmer waters flowing south meet the Antarctic water). It also meant that unlike most other fishery agreements, which set quotas based upon maximum sustainable yields of the target species only, under CCAMLR equal consideration has to be given to the likely effects on non-target species and the marine ecosystem as a whole.

When the possibility of mineral exploitation arose, the Consultative Parties began negotiations for a treaty to regulate the development of the mineral resources of Antarctica in 1977 at the IXth ATCM. Recommendation (IX-3) established a moratorium on mineral resource activity in Antarctica (dependent on the 'timely conclusion of a convention on mineral resources activity') and the negotiations for an Antarctic Minerals Convention were commenced. By 1988 negotiations were completed and the Convention on the Regulation of Antarctic Mineral Resource Activities was adopted. The Convention created a regime proscribing all mineral resource activity unless and until the person who proposed such an activity proved, by extensive studies, that the activity in question would not cause damage to the Antarctic environment. Like CCAMLR, CRAMRA contained many innovative techniques never seen before at international level. Its most radical aspect was the amount of authority given to the Commission to manage Antarctica, mentioned before.

Many environmentalists felt that CRAMRA would stimulate mining interests as a result of the legal certainty which CRAMRA brought to mining rights in Antarctica. They argued that as the world's last pristine terrestrial environment, commercial exploitation of Antarctica was unthinkable: Antarctica should be preserved as a world park. As a result of intense political lobbying, the following ATCM, the XVth, was dominated by the fate of CRAMRA and environmental issues in general. The fate of CRAMRA was finally sealed by Recommendation (XV–7 and XV–8) which established a SATCM to consider the various proposals submitted by the Consultative Parties to declare Antarctica a world park.

The SATCM established at the XVth ATCM, over the course of a single year, negotiated a protocol to the Treaty which developed the disparate elements of the Antarctic Treaty System into a comprehensive environmental protection regime. The form and content of the Protocol were heavily influenced by NGOs with many of the government delegations containing NGO representatives.

The ATCM mechanism has not only developed a comprehensive regime for the protection of flora and fauna in Antarctica but has developed similarly comprehensive regulations governing every aspect of man's activities in the region. The comprehensiveness of this legal regime is probably the best example of international regulation of an international resource, and it is possibly one of the only examples of the successful international regulation of an international resource. The reasons for this are many and varied. The success of the system is, however, due in part to the fact that the Antarctic Treaty System has shown remarkable flexibility and adaptability in allowing the Antarctic Treaty System to meet the changing demands of its constituents. This dynamism has been due to the effectiveness of the Treaty's conference of the parties in developing the necessary policy and rules at an acceptable speed and within an acceptable fora for all the Consultative Parties: a success all the more remarkable given the absence of a secretariat for the Treaty.

The legal techniques developed by the ATCM have also influenced developments outside the ambit of Antarctica. The ecosystem approach first seen in CCAMLR has been adopted in the 1985 ASEAN Convention and is seen also in the Biodiversity Convention. In this sense the ATCM has therefore not only developed international law and policy by fleshing out the guiding principles of one treaty but it also has had a wider impact on the body of law as a whole.

The rise and fall of CRAMRA also illustrates how COPs have changed over recent years, becoming not only important sources of law and policy but also an important source of accountability. In addition the manner in which these rules and policy have been made illustrates the important role that NGOs and scientific bodies can have in their development.

2.4 Standing committees

Increasingly modern conventions are streamlining the decision-making process of the COPs. For example at most COPs several working groups are established to deal simultaneously with matters on the agenda. Only after agreement has been reached in the working group will the matter be presented to the plenary of the COP for formal approval. Another method beginning to emerge is the delegation of matters to a standing committee consisting of a restricted number of parties which will meet between the COP sessions. The Implementation Committee of the Montreal Protocol is an important example of a standing committee, with the authority to consider implementation of the Protocol. Furthermore the work of this Committee may have a wider effect in that it will be used as a precedent to help clarify similar obligations in other contexts.

The Multilateral Fund under the Montreal Protocol is also managed by a committee of elected members of the parties, known as the Executive Committee. In this case the Committee is made up of 14 members (seven from developing countries and seven from developed counties). Each Committee member represents a constituency of parties to the Protocol. Importantly decisions are made on the basis of a double majority, whereby it must be passed by members representing a majority of constituents and more than 50 per cent of the contributions of donors. The Committee is empowered to develop and monitor the implementation of specific operational guidelines and administrative arrangements for the purpose of achieving the objects of the Multilateral Fund under Article 10 of the Montreal Protocol. Even though its work will be primarily about financial matters and project approval, its interpretation of the meaning of 'incremental costs' has not only developed the meaning of Article 10 of the Montreal Protocol, but also has had important consequences for the other conventions using this term such as the CBD and the CCC. Furthermore without the requirement of unanimity in decision making, this will mean that the policy developed by the Committee will probably be innovative and, therefore, provide an important source of precedents for other fora.

This technique is most developed in the 1944 Chicago Convention on International Civil Aviation. Under Articles 37 and 54 of the Convention, international standards on aircraft noise and engine emissions have been developed by the Council of the International Civil Aviation Organization (ICAO). The ICAO is made up of 33 elected representatives of the parties to the Convention. Standards are adopted in the ICAO by a two-thirds' majority. Once adopted they become mandatory, without the need for ratification, for those states which do not notify the ICAO of their intention not to accept them. The authority of the ICAO is unparalleled in the environmental sphere and is probably the closest thing to an international legislature that exists today.

2.5 Secretariat

Although the COP is the repository of most of the formal authority to develop new rules and policy, the secretariat can also contribute to the development and application of policy. If the COP can be likened to the legislative arm of a convention then the secretariat is its executive. The influence of the secretariat in developing law is similar to that of an international organization, only more focused.

Secretariat functions normally include such matters as: making arrangements for sessions of the COP and its subsidiary bodies and providing the support for these conferences; compiling and transmitting reports submitted to it; helping the parties, particularly developing country parties, to compile the information required by the provisions of the convention; preparing reports on its activities and presenting this to the COP; and ensuring the necessary coordination with the international organizations or the secretariats of other conventions.

As with international organizations secretariats provide continuity and a forum through which exchange can occur. They also have an important influence on the activities of the COP in that they coordinate and organize the meetings of the COP, establish agendas, and, in some instances, can be delegated power to enact legislation.

An important example of lawmaking by a secretariat is found in the World Heritage Convention. Under this Convention the World Heritage Centre, the Secretariat of the Convention, is authorized to pronounce Operational Guidelines which develop the general commitments of the Convention into specific obligations. For instance, although the Convention provides that an area must be of 'outstanding natural beauty' for it to be a World Heritage Site, it is the guidelines that set out the precise features that a site must possess in order to be listed. Other examples of similar powers can be found in the development of international health regulations by the World Health Organization, the development of standard meteorological practices and procedures by the World Meteorological Organization or the development of international food standards of the Codes Alimentarius Commission.

2.6 Scientific/technical panels

The administrative structure of many modern environmental conventions consists not only of a secretariat but also contains scientific and technical panels, often referred to as the 'subsidiary bodies'. These subsidiary bodies are the engines for the development of policy. Although they come in many different guises, they are often either a permanent technical committee of an organization such as UNEP, the FAO or the IMO or an independent body established to help the convention itself (that is the IPCC for the CCC). A convention may have one or more subsidiary bodies. Ostensibly they are politically independent although this is rarely the case in practice. Their main function is to provide advice on a range of aspects: technical; scientific; policy; implementation; legal; and financial matters. Ultimately they are established to develop recommendations for the secretariat or the COP. They either meet at regular intervals or are in permanent session. They are normally open to participation by all parties. Typically they are constituted of government representatives competent in the relevant field of expertise. The work that they carry out is vital for effectiveness of a convention. In effect they provide the intellectual input to the secretariat. Typical responsibilities include: providing assessments of the relevant state of scientific knowledge; preparing scientific assessments on the effects of measures taken in the implementation of the convention; identifying innovative, efficient and state-of-the-art technologies and know-how and advice on the ways and means of promoting development and/or transferring such technologies; providing advice on relevant scientific research; and responding to scientific, technological and methodological questions that the COP may pose.

These bodies have a research, advisory and coordinating role rather than a managerial or lawmaking one. Though they have no regulatory role, they do come to conclusions and make recommendations, drawing attention to management and legislative needs, indicating whether species or pollutants should be added to regulatory annexes. In this indirect way they make a significant contribution to the development of policy and law.

2.6.1   SCAR and the Antarctic Treaty System   One of the longest standing examples of such a panel is found in the work of SCAR within the ATS. SCAR is a scientific committee charged with the initiation, promotion and coordination of scientific activity in Antarctica. SCAR was established contemporaneously and in parallel with the Antarctic Treaty. SCAR operates with a small secretariat, and holds regular meetings at which overall activities and priorities are discussed. Much of the detailed scientific coordination is handled through its permanent working groups of which there are 11, covering everything from biology to solid earth geophysics. SCAR operates in consultative party countries through national committees. Through these, and by direct relations with the agencies managing national scientific activities in Antarctica, national scientific expertise is harnessed. Members of its working groups need to be able to bring relevant professional knowledge to their deliberations and should not be appointed on political grounds or merely to attain a national presence.

SCAR has acted as a valuable vehicle for the development of policy and rules for the conservation of Antarctica. The agreed measures were initially prepared in consultation with the SCAR Working Group on Biology. Countries seeking membership of SCAR, which is usually a precursor to consultative party status under the Treaty, are required to give an undertaking that they will comply with the principles of protection of the environment recommended by SCAR. The development of the 1991 Madrid Protocol to the Antarctic treaty was heavily influenced by SCAR's Working Group on Biology and a Group of Specialists on Environmental Affairs and Conservation. SCAR's reports have also regularly been acted upon. Examples include: I–8 Conservation of Fauna and Flora, VIII–3 SSSIs; VIII–1 Man's Impact on the Antarctic Environment; VIII–13 Antarctic Environment; IX–5 Man's Impact on the Antarctic Environment; XIV Environmental Impact Assessment. The Antarctic Seals Convention invites SCAR to make recommendations on humane methods of killing and capture, which are required to be practised by those taking seals (section 5). Furthermore the Convention requires that the parties must notify SCAR annually of any steps that they have taken to implement the Convention during the previous year.

2.7   NGOs and private concerns

NGOs have proliferated in the last 20 years and are now a standard feature of many international environmental meetings. They make a vital contribution to the development of international environmental policy and law. Although the effectiveness of NGOs varies greatly, as a whole they have become increasingly effective. This has largely been achieved through their observer status at international and regional organizations and COPs. They are also a source of considerable numbers of scientific and technical papers presented to the COP which in some instances can be tabled directly, but in most cases have to be adopted by a party before they can be submitted formally.

Increasingly they are coordinating their activities in order to be more effective. For example at many COPs, NGOs meet daily to coordinate their policies and actions. At the INC meetings of the CCC or the CBD, not only were there daily coordination meetings but, prior to the COP, there were week-long conferences of the environmental NGOs to coordinate their policies and activities for the forthcoming INC. Some well-known examples of policy or legal developments directly attributable to NGOs are: the moratorium on whaling under the International Whaling Commission; the 1991 Protocol on Comprehensive Environmental Protection for Antarctica; and the listing of elephants on Appendix I of CITES.

The role played by NGOs was widely recognized at UNCED. Agenda 21 devoted a chapter to the role of NGOs and called upon the states and international organizations to improve access for NGOs to the processes of policy making and lawmaking.

2.7.1   The World Conservation Union (IUCN)   The activities of one of the most important NGOs, The World Conservation Union (IUCN), illustrates

the role that NGOs play in developing policy and law. The IUCN has partici-
pated in the drafting of many conventions on nature conservation. It even
initiated the preparation of CITES and the CBD. CITES had its origins in an
IUCN Resolution in 1963, before being concluded in 1973 and the CBD had
its origin in an IUCN Resolution in 1981. Other treaties in which the IUCN
has been involved in the elaboration or preparatory texts include: the 1968
African Convention; the 1986 Apia Convention; the 1979 Bonn Convention;
and the 1985 ASEAN Convention.

The IUCN has also played an important role in the implementation of
numerous conventions. It provided the secretariat for the CITES, until this
was taken over by UNEP. The World Heritage Convention expressly provides
for IUCN assistance in the deliberations of its World Heritage Committee, on
which it has consultative status. It also provides that the Committee should
call upon the IUCN to implement its programmes and projects. Finally the
World Heritage Convention provides that UNESCO should utilize the services of IUCN to prepare documentation for the Committee and for the execution
of its decisions.

The IUCN was the principal architect of both versions of the World Conservation Strategy. It also contributed to the drafting of the World Charter for
Nature, the initiative for which came from the President of Zaire, who proposed its elaboration, first at the 1975 IUCN General Assembly in Kinshasa.
The original text was drafted by the Legal Commission of the IUCN and then
examined by the General Assembly of the IUCN before being transmitted to
the UN where it was adopted by the General Assembly in 1982.

3   Basic principles of international environmental law

The relationship between environmental protection and international law has
thus been transformed in recent years. Previously marginal, international
environmental issues are now a central concern of the UN, GATT and other
international institutions, and to all governments. Scientific and political
concern about global and regional environmental issues is reflected in an
increase in the number of international agreements and acts relating to the
protection of the environment. At any time negotiations are in progress for
different instruments in different fora, making it virtually impossible for all
but the most highly resourced states to maintain effective, and consistent,
negotiating positions.

Despite these impressive achievements there is reason to doubt the impact
of this body of law on actual governmental and human behaviour. Limited
implementation and enforcement suggests that international environmental
law remains in its formative stages. Lawmaking is decentralized, with legislative initiatives being developed in literally dozens of different intergovernmental
organizations at the global, regional and subregional level. Coordination

between the initiatives is inadequate, leading to activities which are often duplicative and sometimes inconsistent. Moreover the lawmaking process tends to be reactive and somewhat *ad hoc* in nature, often depending upon the vagaries of political, economic and scientific events and findings.

Although no single international legal instrument establishes binding rules or principles of global application, the pattern of state behaviour has given rise to an emerging set of guiding principles and minimum standards of acceptable behaviour in relation to particular environmental resources. These principles and standards are considered in the following sections.

3.1   General principles

Several general principles and rules of international law have emerged, or are emerging, specifically in relation to environmental matters, as reflected in treaties, binding acts of international organizations, state practice and soft law commitments. They are general in the sense that they are potentially applicable to all members of the international community across the range of activities, which they carry out or permit to be carried out, and in respect of the protection of all aspects of the environment.

According to one view, principles and rules

> point to particular decisions about legal obligations in particular circumstances, but they differ in the character of the direction they give. Rules are applicable in an all-or-nothing fashion ... [A principle] states a reason that argues in one direction, but does not necessitate a particular decision ... All that is meant, when we say that a particular principle is a principle of our law, is that the principle is one which officials must take into account, if it is relevant, as a consideration inclining in one way or another.[44]

3.1.1   *Sovereignty over natural resources and the responsibility not to cause damage to the environment of other state or to areas beyond national jurisdiction*   The rules of international environmental law have developed in pursuit of two principles which pull in opposing directions: that states have sovereign rights over their natural resources, and that states must not cause damage to the environment. These objectives are now reflected in Principle 21 of the Stockholm Declaration and Principle 2 of the Rio Declaration, and provide the foundation of international environmental law. The first element (sovereignty) reflects the pre-eminent position of states as primary members of the international legal community. It is tempered by the second element (environmental protection), however, which places limits on the exercise of sovereign rights. In an environmentally interdependent world, where activities in one state are almost inevitably likely to produce effects in other states or in areas beyond national jurisdiction (such as the high seas), this aspect of Principle 21 and Principle 2 reflect changing international legal values. In the

form presented by Principle 21 and Principle 2, the responsibility not to cause damage to the environment of other states or of areas beyond national jurisdiction has been accepted as an obligation by all states; without prejudice to its applications on a case-by-case basis, Principle 21 is widely recognized to reflect customary international law, placing important international legal limitations on the right of states in respect of activities carried out within their territory or under their jurisdiction. The emergence of the responsibility of states not to cause environmental damage in areas outside their jurisdiction has historical roots which pre-date the Stockholm Conference. These relate to the obligation of all states 'to protect within the territory the rights of other states, in particular their right to integrity and inviolability in peace and war',[45] and the principle endorsed by the Arbitral Tribunal in the much cited *Trail Smelter* case, which stated that 'no state has the right to use or permit the use of territory in such a manner as to cause injury by fumes in or to the territory of another of the properties or persons therein, when the case is of serious consequence and the injury is established by clear and convincing evidence'.[46]

Saying that Principle 21 and Principle 2 reflect customary international law is not the critical issue however, and actually does not get anyone very far in support of a claim they might assert. Principle 21 and Principle 2 indicate the need to address other questions which need to be asked. What is environmental damage? What is the extent of environmental damage which is prohibited (any damage, or just damage which is serious or significant)? What is the standard of care applicable to the obligation (absolute, strict or fault)? What are the consequences of a violation (including appropriate reparation)? What is the extent of any liability (including measure of damages)? In practice few international claims have been brought alleging violations. More probably the significance of Principle 21 and Principle 2 lies in its reflection of a broad acceptance of the need to accept and adopt limits, and it has served as a basis for the adoption of many international agreements.

Closely related to the obligation not to cause damage to the environment of other states or of areas beyond the limits of national jurisdiction is the obligation to ensure that damage to certain environmental media does not occur. This obligation, sometimes referred to as the preventive principle, can be distinguished from the second element of Principle 21 and Principle 2 in two ways. First, the latter arise from application of respect for principle of sovereignty, whereas the preventive principle seeks to minimize environmental damage (and the protection of the environment) as an objective itself. This important difference of underlying rationale is related to the second difference: the preventive principle may require a state to prevent damage to the environment *within its own jurisdiction*,[47] including by taking appropriate regulatory, administrative or other measures. The preventive principle requires action to be taken at an early stage and, if possible, before damage has actually occurred, and is supported for a broad range of environmental objectives by extensive domestic and international legislation. It has been described as being of 'overriding importance in every effective environmental policy, since it allows action to be taken to protect the environment at an earlier stage. It is no longer primarily a question of repairing damage after it has occurred'.[48]

3.1.2 Good neighbourliness and international cooperation The principle of 'good neighbourliness', as enunciated in Article 74 of the UN Charter for social, economic and commercial matters, has been extended to environmental matters by rules promoting international environmental co-operation. It applies particularly where activities carried out in one state might have adverse effects on the environment of another state or in areas beyond national jurisdiction. The commitment to environmental cooperation is reflected in many international agreements and is supported by state practice. In general terms the obligation includes commitments to implement treaty objectives, or to improve relations outside a treaty or in relation to certain tasks. In specific terms the obligation can require information sharing, notification, consultation or participation rights in certain decisions, the conduct of environmental impact assessments, and cooperative emergency procedures, particularly where activities might be ultrahazardous. The construction of nuclear power plants on borders is an example where cooperatively obligations are particularly well-developed.

The extent to which this obligation has been complied with is a central issue in the dispute between Hungary and Slovakia over the construction of the Grabcikovo Dam and the proposed diversion of the Danube River, which was referred to the International Court of Justice in 1993. Hungary has claimed that Czecho–Slovakia (now just Slovakia) has violated its obligation to cooperate in good faith in the implementation of principles affecting transboundary resources, including the obligation to negotiate in good faith and in a spirit of cooperation, to prevent disputes, to provide timely notification of plans to carry out or permit activities which may entail a transboundary interference or a significant risk thereof, and to engage in good faith consultations to arrive at an equitable resolution of the situation.

3.1.3 Sustainable development An emerging principle requires states to ensure that they develop and use their natural resources in a manner which is sustainable. Although the ideas underlying the concept of 'sustainable development' have a long history in international legal instruments, the term has only recently begun to be used in international agreements. The ideas underlining 'sustainability' date at least to the Pacific Fur Seal Arbitration in 1893, when the USA asserted a right to ensure the legitimate and proper use of seals and to protect them, for the benefit of mankind, from wanton destruction.

What 'sustainable development' means in international law today is, however, a more complicated matter. Where it has been used it appears to refer to at least four separate but related objectives which, taken together, might comprise the legal elements of the concept of 'sustainable development' as used in the Brundtland Report.[49] First, as invoked in some agreements it refers to the commitment to preserve natural resources for the benefit of present and future generations. Second, in other agreements sustainable development refers to appropriate standards for the exploitation of natural resources based upon harvests for use; examples include use which is 'sustainable', or 'prudent, or 'rational', or 'wise' or 'appropriate'. Third, yet other agreements require an 'equitable' use of natural resources, suggesting that the use by any state must take account of the needs of other states and people. And a fourth category of agreements require that environmental considerations be integrated into economic and other development plans, programmes and projects, and that development needs are taken into account in applying environmental objectives.

The instruments adopted at UNCED reflect each of these four objectives, and translate them in Agenda 21 and the Rio Declaration into more specific proposals and principles to govern human activity.

3.1.4   Precautionary principle   The precautionary principle only emerged in international legal instruments in the mid-1980s, although it had previously been relied upon in some domestic legal systems. It aims to provide guidance to states and the international community in the development of international environmental law and policy in the face of scientific uncertainty and is, potentially, the most radical of environmental principles. It has generated considerable controversy. Some of its supporters invoke it to justify pre-emptive international legal measures to address potentially catastrophic environmental threats such as ozone depletion or climate change.[50] Opponents, on the other hand, have decried the principle for allowing overregulation and clamping down on a range of human activities. The core of this emerging legal principle, which has now been endorsed in a number of agreements, is reflected in Principle 15 of the Rio Declaration, which provides, *inter alia*, that 'Where there are threats of serious or irreversible damage, lack of full scientific certainty shall not be used as a reason for postponing cost-effective measures to prevent environmental degradation'.

3.1.5   Polluter-pays principle   The polluter-pays principle refers to the requirement that the costs of pollution should be borne by the person or persons responsible for causing the pollution and the consequential costs. The precise meaning, international legal status, and effect of the principle, remains open to question since international practice based upon the principle is limited. It is doubtful whether it has achieved the status of a generally applicable rule of customary international law, except perhaps in relation to states in the EC, the UN/ECE and the OECD. It has nevertheless attracted broad support and relates closely to the development of rules on civil and state liability for environmental damage, on the permissibility of state subsidies, and the growing acknowledgement by developed countries of the 'responsibility that they bear in the international pursuit of sustainable development in view of the pressures their societies place on the global environment', as well as the financial and other consequences that flow from this acknowledgment.[51] Supporting instruments include Principle 14 of the Rio Declaration, OECD Council Recommendations,[52] the EC Treaty and related instruments,[53] and the 1992 Agreement establishing the European Economic Area.[54]

3.1.6 Common but differentiated responsibility This principle has emerged from the application of the broader principle of equity in general international law, together with the recognition that the special needs of developing countries must be taken into account in the development, application and interpretation of rules of international environmental law if they are to be encouraged to participate in global environmental agreements. The principle is reflected in a handful of international environmental agreements, and is applicable in the Climate Change Convention to require parties to protect the climate system 'on the basis of equity and in accordance with their common but differentiated responsibilities and respective capabilities'. The principle of common but differentiated responsibility includes two important elements. The first expresses the common responsibility of states to protect certain environmental resources. The second element relates to the need to take account of differing circumstances, particularly in relation to each state's *contribution* to the creation of a particular environmental problem and its *ability* to respond to, prevent, reduce and control the threat. In practical terms the application of the principle of common but differentiated responsibility has certain important consequences. It entitles, or possibly requires, all concerned states to participate in international response measures aimed at addressing environmental problems. And it leads to the adoption and implementation of environmental standards which impose different commitments for states.

3.2 Topics and rules
As international environmental law has developed standards in relations to specific rules and topics have been adopted to address an ever widening range

of environmental resources. These standards tend to address particular resources, of which the most important have been, in roughly chronological order: flora and fauna; water quality; air quality; hazardous substances; and waste. Agenda 21, which was adopted at UNCED, identifies the priority environmental issues and divides them into two categories: those relating to the protection of various environmental media, and those relating to the regulation of particular activities or products. The first category addressed the priority needs for the protection and conservation of particular environmental media. These are:

- the protection of the *atmosphere*, in particular by combating climate change, depletion of the ozone layer and ground level and transboundary air pollution
- protection of *land resources*, by combating desertification and drought and protecting mountain ecosystems)
- halting *deforestation*
- the conservation of *biological diversity*
- the protection of *freshwater resources*
- the protection of *oceans and seas* (including coastal areas) and *marine living resources*.

The second category of major issues identified the products of human technological and industrial innovation which are considered to be particularly harmful to the environment and which require international regulation. These are:

- the management of *biotechnology*
- the management of *toxic chemicals*, including their international trade
- *agricultural* practice
- the management of *hazardous wastes*, including their international trade
- the management of *solid wastes* and sewage-related issues
- the management of *radioactive wastes*.

The difficulty with an approach which regulates sector by sector is that it has tended to transfer harm from one environmental medium to another, or to substitute one form of harm for another. Thus the prohibition on the dumping of radioactive wastes at sea may result in harm to land-based resources resulting from long-term storage. Efforts to address this problem of regulatory approach have led to the emergence of the concept of integrated pollution control, which requires states and other persons to consider and minimize the impact of activities on all environmental resources at each stage of the processes which make up that activity.

3.2.1 Protection of flora and fauna   The protection of flora and fauna was the subject of the earliest international environmental regulation and there are now widely accepted standards which prohibit interference with, in particular, endangered species. Important global instruments regulate wetlands,[55] trade in endangered species and, most recently, the conservation of biodiversity generally (also regulating the sustainable use of the components of biodiversity and the sharing of benefits arising out of the use of genetic resources). However efforts to adopt a forests' convention at UNCED proved to be fruitless in the face of sustained opposition from many developing countries. Regional rules adopted in Africa and the Americas are among the earliest examples of international environmental law. Apart from early fisheries conservation agreements, including the regulations adopted by the tribunal in the Pacific fur seal arbitration, regional conservation agreements were adopted as early as 1900 in Africa and 1940 for the Americas. Subsequent arrangements have been put in place in East Africa;[56] South East Asia;[57] Europe including the EC; the South Pacific;[58] and the Caribbean.

Acts adopted by international organizations have contributed significantly to the development of this area of international law. Notable examples include the 1982 decision by the International Whaling Commission to adopt a moratorium on commercial whaling, and the 1985 decision of the parties to the 1972 London Dumping Convention to adopt a moratorium on the dumping of radioactive waste at sea.

3.2.2 Protection of the marine environment   International law to prevent pollution of oceans and seas is now relatively well-developed at the global and regional levels. At the global level the 1982 UN Convention on the Law of the Sea, which enters into force in November 1994, establishes a comprehensive framework to address marine pollution from various sources, including dumping at sea; from land-based sources; from vessels; and from offshore installations, such as oil rigs. Apart from the instruments on intervention and liability and compensation for oil pollution, detailed obligations for these sources of marine pollution have been adopted both prior to and after UNCLOS. At the global level agreements regulate the dumping of waste at sea; on protection of the environment during salvage operations;[59] and oil pollution preparedness and response.[60] However no global agreement regulates pollution from land-based sources, which is particularly worrying since pollution from this source accounts for more than 70 per cent of the total.

At the regional level early instruments addressed dumping from ships[61] and pollution from land based sources.[62] These have since been supplemented by an extensive network of conventions adopted under the UNEP Regional Seas Programme which was initiated in 1975 and now includes programmes covering 10 regional seas: the Caribbean, East Asian, Eastern

African, Kuwaiti, Mediterranean, Red Sea and Gulf of Aden, South Asian, South Pacific, South-East Pacific, and West and Central Africa. More than 120 coastal states now participate in this UNEP Programme, and framework conventions and supplementary protocols are in force for eight regions: Caribbean, Kuwaiti, Mediterranean, Red Sea and Gulf of Aden, South-East Pacific, South Pacific, and West and Central Africa.[63] Additional commitments have been adopted for the EC and Antarctic regions.

3.2.3 Protection of freshwater resources   Freshwater resources include rivers, lakes and groundwaters. Many individual rivers and river systems are now subject to special rules governing their use and the maintenance of the quality of their waters. Noteworthy examples include the Rhine in Europe, the Zambezi in Africa, and the River Plate in South America, each of which has been subject to treaty protection for many years. More recently efforts have been made to develop rules which apply to all rivers in a particular region, or to all rivers globally. Lakes have also been subject to protective regimes, especially in North America[64] and other areas where acid rain deposits have threatened long-term damage. Protection of groundwaters remains less well-developed in international law.

3.2.4 Air quality   International law for the protection of the atmosphere addresses transboundary air pollution, ozone depletion and climate change. International measures now place limits on permissible atmospheric emissions of certain substances for many states, which have important implications for production patterns and, particularly, energy use.

A new area of international regulation, the first instrument was the regional 1979 UNECE Convention on Long-Range Transboundary Air Pollution, which has since been supplemented with protocols on sulphur dioxide,[65] nitrogen oxides[66] and volatile organic compounds.[67] The transboundary air pollution model has since been relied upon in the global efforts to protect the ozone layer with the framework 1985 framework Convention for the Protection of the Ozone Layer,[68] as supplemented by a 1987 Protocol subsequently amended in 1990 and 1992.[69] The 1992 framework Convention on Climate Change is also of global application. It entered into force in March 1994, aiming to limit emissions by developed countries of carbon dioxide and other greenhouse gases, and creating a framework for cooperation and general commitments to ensure that greenhouse gas concentrations in the atmosphere do not lead to dangerous anthropogenic interference with the climate system.

3.2.5 Waste   Binding international regulation of waste management is currently limited to regulating or prohibiting trade in certain wastes, as well as the provisions prohibiting the disposal at sea of certain hazardous wastes.

These measures encourage waste prevention and minimization by increasing costs, and are likely precursors to measures which might limit industrial wastes produced, including packaging.

Three recent instruments establish regulations and prohibitions on trade in hazardous waste. The only global instrument is the 1989 Basle Convention,[70] which aims to control traffic and trade in hazardous wastes by requiring importing countries to be notified of, and grant consent for, shipments before they occur (prior informed consent). The 1990 ACP–EEC Fourth Lomé Convention goes beyond Basle by prohibiting exports and imports between the EEC and certain African, Caribbean and Pacific countries.[71] And the 1991 Bamako Convention on the Ban of the Import into Africa and the Control of Transboundary Movement and Management of Hazardous Wastes within Africa, which also prohibits imports, redefines 'hazardous waste' to include all substances the use of which is banned in the exporting country.[72] Global regulation of radioactive waste movements is governed by a non-binding 1990 IAEA Code of Practice, which establishes regulatory guidelines and is far less stringent than any of the three agreements.[73]

3.2.6 Hazardous substances   The management of hazardous substances other than waste, including chemicals and pesticides, is not yet subject to any binding global legal instruments. Within the past few years, however, a large body of detailed, non-binding regulations and other instruments dealing with management of hazardous substances, including in particular international trade and chemical safety at work.[74] The OECD has developed a broad range of recommended practices which address product registration, dealer licensing, classification, packaging, labelling, advertising, international trade and transport.

3.3   Legal techniques
This section sets out the different legal techniques which are being used to implement environmental principles and standards at the regional and global level. Apart from the widespread reliance upon prohibitions and statutory regulations, including quality standards, the emerging, modern techniques relied upon in international environmental law include:

- environmental impact assessment requirements
- improving access to and dissemination of environmental information
- liability for environmental damage
- other economic approaches, including trade and competition rules, financial resources and intellectual property rights
- improved enforcement procedures and dispute settlement machinery.

These techniques supplement the general regulatory approach of setting standards and then ensuring that they are enforced (sometimes referred to as 'command and control'). This approach frequently regulates or prohibits activities, and recently the use of prohibitions has increased. Whereas a few years ago outright prohibitions established by international law were trade related, the 1987 Montreal Protocol and its 1990 Amendments marked the first time that the international community adopted measures to ban outright, within a specified time frame, the production and use of certain chemicals harmful to the ozone layer. The 1991 Environmental Protocol to the Antarctic Treaty extends the prohibition approach to commercial activity within a defined geographic region.

The regulatory approach is also taking new directions in unlikely areas such as advertising and corporate accounting. With regard to advertising, of particular note is the 1989 EC Directive on the pursuit of television broadcasting activities, which establishes minimum standards for, *inter alia*, television programme and advertising content, and provides that 'television advertising shall not ... encourage behaviour prejudicial to the protection of the environment'.

3.3.1   Environmental impact assessment   Environmental impact assessment (EIA) requires developers or regulators to assess the likely environmental impact of an activity before it is carried out with a view to determining whether the activity should be permitted. It generally requires alternatives to be considered, and provides a mechanism for ensuring that information on projects is disseminated and that citizens are allowed to participate in the decision-making process. EIA requirements are becoming an established feature of international environmental law. While no single global treaty establishes EIA obligations of general application, several regional or subject specific agreements include EIA provisions. Examples include the 1982 UNCLOS, the 1985 ASEAN Agreement on the Conservation of Nature and Natural Resources, the 1988 Convention on the Regulation of Antarctic Mineral Resource Activities,[75] and the 1992 Biodiversity Convention. EIA is also endorsed, as a national instrument, by the Rio Declaration.

Detailed modalities governing the conduct of EIAs have been adopted in 1985 by the EC,[76] and in a 1991 UN Economic Commission for Europe Convention, which adopts more stringent requirements, particularly in relation to the mitigation of transboundary impacts. It is also now increasingly common for multilateral development banks to incorporate EIA requirements into their project approval procedures.[77]

3.3.2   Environmental information   There is now broad recognition of the importance of ensuring broad and early access to information on matters relating to the environment. Environmental information objectives include improving the informational base upon which decisions are made, influencing the behaviour of consumers and other actors, and ensuring full participation of citizens in decision-making processes. A range of international mechanisms and techniques have been developed including:

- imposing international reporting requirements on international actors
- establishing international rights of access to information on the environment
- establishing independent international observation and monitoring programmes.

With varying degrees of success most international environmental agreements require state parties to provide certain information to national authorities, to other parties, or to international. The objective of improved public access to information on the environment is now reflected in various instruments adopted by the OECD,[78] EC[79] and, to a lesser extent, the World Bank.[80] The EC legislation, which has been followed by provisions in the other agreements, is intended to ensure free access throughout the EC to, and dissemination of, environmental information held by public authorities, to ensure greater environmental protection, and to remove disparities in member state laws which might create unequal conditions of competition. The legislative rationale is, therefore, both environmental and economic.

3.3.3 Liability for environmental damage   Liability for environmental damage is one way of integrating environmental costs into production processes. International treaties can impose liability upon a state or, as is more frequently the case, directly on the private actor engaged in the activity which cause environmental harm (these provide for civil liability rules at the national level). The early conventions of the 1960s, which established the liability of nuclear operators for certain damage resulting from nuclear accidents, were among the first to identify private corporations expressly in international agreements.[81] However they only established liability for damage to people and property, and it is only more recently that civil liability for environmental damage has been provided for in international instruments. Since then the number of international conventions establishing the liability of private actors has increased significantly and seems set to develop further. Recent instruments have addressed civil liability for environmental and other damage resulting from transport of dangerous goods[82] and from hazardous activities generally. Existing agreements are being amended in the light of new environmental concern, and new liability rules can be expected for waste trade and the Antarctic.

Developments in relation to state liability have proceeded more slowly, and to date no treaty rules of general applicability establish the liability of states for environmental damage, although specific treaties regulate liability for damage caused by space objects and in the Antarctic.

3.3.4   Other economic approaches, including trade and competition rules, financial resources and intellectual property rights   The limited effectiveness of traditional 'command-and-control' regulatory approaches has led to some support for the principle of increasing reliance upon economic and fiscal measures to protect the environment. Recent agreements and other international acts, including the Rio Declaration, encourage the use of such measures and there are some signs that the growing interdependence of international economic and environmental law may provide a framework for their increased use.

Economic agreements   Environmental issues have progressively permeated regional and global trade and economic cooperation arrangements. The GATT, EC and Canada–USA Free Trade Agreement have each had to address the situation where one state unilaterally adopts environmental protection measures which have the effect of limiting or prohibiting trade. In the GATT context the additional issue has arisen as to the compatibility of trade measures adopted by international environmental agreements (such as CITES and the 1987 Montreal Protocol) with the GATT. Although their institutions and tribunals have reached different conclusions on the appropriate balance between trade and environmental objectives, the general tendency has been to recognize that environmental requirements can, in certain circumstances, justify limitations on free trade. This issue is set to become increasingly contentious despite the *modus vivendi* which was reached at UNCED, and encapsulates all the conflicts surrounding the proper place of environmental concerns in an international legal order which seeks to accommodate the sometimes differing priorities of developed and developing countries. This led to the insertion of new provisions on environmental protection in the North American Free Trade Agreement (NAFTA).

Trade and competition rules   Multilateral prohibitions on trade in respect of endangered species and certain plant types have a long history pre-dating the GATT, dating back to at least 1940. Recently the use of trade prohibitions has been extended beyond nature protection to cover hazardous wastes and substances, such as those which deplete the ozone layer. More recently the 1987 Montreal Protocol and its 1990 Amendments adopt trade prohibitions and restrictions to limit production and consumption by non-parties, by:

- prohibiting the import of controlled substances from any state which is not a party to the Protocol
- providing for the eventual prohibition on the import from any non-party state of products *containing* controlled substances
- providing for the possible prohibition on the import from any non-party state of products *produced with*, but not containing, controlled substances.

Complex legal questions have been raised about the compatibility of measures such as these with free trade obligations under the rules of the EC, GATT and NAFTA. This has resulted in cases recently being brought before dispute settlement bodies, leading to conclusions as to the appropriate balance to be struck between free trade objectives and environmental protection objectives.

Economic instruments Many recent intergovernmental statements and declarations have called for the international use of economic and fiscal instruments as a tool of international environmental protection. Economic and fiscal policy instruments identified as potentially useful include taxes, emission charges and tradable emission permits. Many recent statements and declarations have endorsed the use of economic and fiscal instruments, but to date no binding international legal instruments establish or support taxes, charges or tradable permits. The most important development (which indicates the imminent introduction of laws making use of economic and fiscal instruments at the international level) is the EC Commission's proposal for a Community-wide tax 'based on an energy component and on a component based on carbon content', which is designed to limit use of fossil fuels to combat climate change.[83]

Like pricing and taxation policy, international regulation of subsidies and public investment remain at an early stage of development, with little tangible evidence of hard law outside the EC context. The EC has taken something of a lead in developing the law relating to subsidies to accommodate environmental needs, and the issue seems set to be addressed by the GATT following the Uruguay Round.

Financial resources The use of financial resources provided by the public sector to encourage environmentally beneficial activities and projects has become an increasingly important topic in international environmental law. It entails two essential aspects. First, ensuring that the multilateral development and lending institutions incorporate environmental considerations into their activities. And second, ensuring the availability of international public sector funds to assist poorer countries in meeting the costs associated with increasingly stringent international environmental protection requirements.

With regard to the former, all the multilateral development banks have recognized the need to address and integrate environmental concerns, and to varying degrees have adopted measures to achieve that objective. With regard to the latter, the most significant development in recent years has been the linkage made between the provision of financial resources by developed countries and the fulfilment of treaty commitments by developing countries. The 1990 Montreal Protocol amendment was the first agreement to make the fulfilment by developing countries of their obligations dependent upon the provision of finance by developed countries, and led to the establishment of a Multilateral Fund to meet certain incremental costs which arose under the Convention.

The Global Environment Facility was established in 1990 to provide grants or concessional loans on an additional basis to enable them to implement programmes that protect the global commons. The Facility is capitalized at over $1 billion, and is administered through a tripartite arrangement between the World Bank, UNEP and UNDP. The GEF allocates resources to projects addressing ozone depletion, climate change, biodiversity and the protection of international waters. Under the Climate Change and Biodiversity Conventions it will meet certain incremental costs incurred by developing countries in fulfilling their obligations. Other regional institutions, such as the EBRD, have also undertaken to commit a significant proportion of its funds in Central and Eastern Europe to 'environmental' projects.

Improved enforcement procedures and dispute settlement machinery   Finally, there is also now a recognition that it is not sufficient to adopt international environmental principles, standards and techniques: they must be implemented domestically by states and international institutions and enforced where non-compliance occurs, and tribunals and other bodies given an effective mandate to provide fora to address and settle disputes. Efforts to develop such mechanisms, including the potential role of NGOs and international secretariats in supplementing governmental efforts, are considered in the next section.

4   Compliance

Ensuring compliance by states and other members of the international community with their international environmental obligations has become a matter of increasing concern in recent years. This is evident from the attention which the issue of compliance received during the preparations for UNCED, and in the negotiation and implementation of recent environmental agreements, including in particular the 1987 Montreal Protocol, the 1992 Climate Change Convention and the 1992 OSPAR Convention. The response to those concerns has resulted in initiatives to develop existing mechanisms for implementation, enforcement and dispute settlement, and to develop new mechanisms.

Compliance has become increasingly important for several reasons. First, the nature and extent of international environmental obligations has been transformed in recent years as states take on more environmental commitments, under treaty and other obligations, which are increasingly stringent and with which they must comply. Second, the growing demands and needs of states and those subject to their jurisdiction for access to natural resources, coupled with a finite, and perhaps even shrinking, available resource base provide the conditions for increasing conflict over access to natural resources. And third, as international environmental obligations increasingly address fundamental economic interests and needs, states which do not comply with their environmental obligations are perceived to gain unfair, and perhaps unlawful, economic advantage from their environmentally harmful activities in relation to those states which are complying with their obligations.

Non-compliance limits the overall effectiveness of those treaties, undermines commitments which have been made under the international legal process, and can lead to conflict between states and instability in the international order. At UNCED, and in relation to the treaties mentioned above, attention has focused as much on the need to devise mechanisms to *prevent* disputes as on the development and application of procedures to resolve them peacefully when they arise. Recent efforts have also sought to ensure that, where possible, enforcement and the settlement of disputes are addressed in a non-contentious and non-adversarial manner.

Non-compliance can occur in a number of different ways, including the failure to give effect to substantive norms (for example to limit atmospheric emission of sulphur dioxide or greenhouse gases as required by treaty or to allow transboundary emissions of hazardous substances or gases in violation of any rules of customary law); the failure to fulfil procedural requirements which may be required by international law (for example to carry out an environmental impact assessment or consult with a neighbouring state on the construction of a new plant); or the failure to fulfil an institutional obligation (for example to submit an annual report to an international organization). From an international legal perspective, compliance raises at least three separate, but closely related, questions which relate to implementation, enforcement, and conflict resolution (or 'dispute settlement'). These are:

- What formal or informal steps must a state or international organization take to implement its international legal obligations?
- What legal or natural person may seek, or has the right, to enforce the international environmental obligations of a state or international organization?

- What techniques, procedures and institutions exist under international law to resolve conflicts or settle disputes over alleged non-compliance with international environmental obligations?

Over the years a range of techniques have been adopted to improve compliance, drawing upon developments in general international law. Since the *Pacific Fur Seal* arbitration of 1893, environmental disputes have since arisen, and been submitted to international dispute resolution arrangements, in the context of a variety of different issues, including: transboundary air pollution;[84] the diversion of the flow of international rivers;[85] conservation of fisheries resource;[86] the adoption of import restrictions in the name of environmental protection requirements to enforce domestic conservation standards; and responsibility for rehabilitation of mined lands.[87]

4.1   Implementation

States implement their international environmental obligations in three phases. First, by adopting national implementing legislation, policies and programmes; second, by ensuring that such national environmental legislation, policies and programmes are complied with by those subject to its jurisdiction and control; and third, by fulfilling any obligations to the relevant international organizations, such as reporting the measures taken to give effect to international obligations.

4.1.1   National law
Once a state has accepted an international environmental obligation it will usually need to develop, adopt or modify relevant national legislation, or give effect to national policies, programmes or strategies by administrative or other means. Some treaties expressly require parties to take appropriate measures to ensure the implementation of obligations,[88] or 'to take appropriate measures within its competence to ensure compliance with [the] Convention and any measures in effect pursuant to it'.[89] Others require parties to designate a competent national authority or focal point for international liaison purposes on domestic implementation.[90] The 1982 UNCLOS requires states to enforce their laws and regulations in accordance with the Convention and implement applicable international rules and standards.[91] Treaty obligations which have not been implemented into national law will generally be difficult to enforce in national courts, although the EU has developed particular rules on this matter.

4.1.2   National compliance
Once implemented into national law, the party to an international agreement must ensure that it is complied with by those within its jurisdiction and control. Some treaties expressly require this,[92] while others require the application of sanctions or punishment for viola-

tions.[93] Ensuring national compliance is a matter for the public authorities of each state. Recognizing that public authorities in many countries may not be particularly well-suited to ensuring compliance, either because of a lack of resources or a lack of commitment, and recognizing also the role which non-governmental actors can play in ensuring compliance, more and more states are allowing private enforcement of national environmental obligations before national courts through 'citizen suits'. Principle 10 of the Rio Declaration declares that '[e]ffective access to judicial and administrative proceedings, including redress and remedy, shall be provided'. The 1993 Council of Europe Civil Liability Convention, which addresses rules of civil liability for damage caused by waste, was the first international agreement to elaborate upon the rules governing access to national courts to allow enforcement of environmental obligations in the public interest.[94]

The question of which state may or must ensure implementation is difficult where the environmental obligation relates to the protection of a shared natural resource or the global commons. Some treaties allocate enforcement obligations to particular states. For marine pollution the 1982 UNCLOS includes detailed rules on the division of national enforcement responsibilities between the flag state, port state, or coastal states depending on where the pollution incident occurred.[95] Analogous jurisdictional provisions have been adopted in respect of activities on the moon and in the Antarctic.[96] In the absence of specific treaty provisions the rules governing enforcement jurisdiction for their environmental media remain subject to the general rules of international law concerning enforcement jurisdiction.

Given the failure of many states to implement their international obligations because of lack of financial and other resources, an important recent development is the linkage which has been made between the national implementation by developing countries of their treaty obligations and the provision to them of financial assistance by developed countries. The 1990 Amendments to the 1987 Montreal Protocol established an important precedent by establishing a mechanism to 'meet all agreed incremental costs' of developing country parties 'to enable their compliance with the control measures of the Protocol'.[97] The Climate Change Convention and Biodiversity Conventions also require developed country parties 'to meet the agreed full costs incurred by developing country parties in complying with their' reporting requirements and the 'agreed full incremental costs' needed by developing country parties for implementing their substantive obligations under the Convention.[98]

4.1.3 Reporting The third element of national compliance arises as a consequence of the requirement that states must usually report the measures which they have adopted to give effect to their international obligations to the relevant international institution responsible for implementing a particular treaty or other international act. The information to be reported will vary with each treaty or other obligation, but typically can include statistical information on production, imports and exports; information on the grant of permits or authorizations; including criteria; information on implementation measures which have been adopted; details of any relevant decisions which may have been taken by national authorities; scientific information; and information on breaches or violations by persons under the jurisdiction or control of the party.

These reports may be required on an annual or biannual basis, or according to some other time frame.[99] They provide a means for the international institution and the other parties to assess the extent to which, and how, parties are implementing their obligations. Many states are unable to fulfil even the basic obligation to provide a regular report. A report prepared for the United States Committee on Environment and Public Works recently considered, *inter alia*, six environmental treaties which require parties to submit periodic reports, and found wide variations in compliance with reporting requirements.[100] Under the Biodiversity and Climate Change Conventions financial resources will be made available to meet the incremental costs of developing countries of fulfilling their reporting requirements, and this should go some way towards improving compliance.

4.2   International enforcement

Once evidence has become available that a state, or a party to a treaty, has failed to implement an environmental obligation established by international law, the question arises as to which entities or persons may seek to enforce that international environmental obligation on the plane of international law. Enforcement means the right to take measures to ensure the fulfilment of international legal obligations or to obtain a determination by an international body that such obligations are not being fulfilled. The options which are available include international enforcement by states, by an international organization (including its secretariat), or by non-governmental actors. In practice international enforcement usually involves a combination of the three.

4.2.1   Enforcement by states   States have the primary role in enforcing rules of international environmental law. To be in a position to enforce a rule of international environmental law a state must, in the words of the International Law Commission, be an 'injured state'. This in turn means, according to Article 5 of the International Law Commission's Draft Articles on State Responsibility, that it is 'a state a right of which is injured by the act of another state'.[101]

For environmental injuries two situations need to be distinguished. The first involves the situations where one state is permitting activities which cause damage to the environment of another state. The second situation is where one state is permitting or causing damage to the environment in an area beyond national jurisdiction.

In situations involving damage to its environment a state will usually be able to argue that it is an 'injured state' and that it has standing to bring an international claim. In the Trail Smelter case the USA successfully claimed that it had, under the principles of international law as applied between it and Canada, a right not to be subjected to the harmful consequences of transboundary air pollution from sulphur emissions in Canada, and that as an 'injured state' it was entitled to bring a claim against Canada for having violated its rights.

Not all cases will be as straightforward as the Trail Smelter case, however. In the Nuclear Tests' cases, brought by Australia and New Zealand against France calling on the latter to halt its atmospheric nuclear testing in the South Pacific region, the claim raised an additional and rather more complicated legal question than the allegation of a violation of sovereignty by the deposit of radioactive fallout in its territory: did Australia and New Zealand have the right to bring a claim to the International Court of Justice on the basis of a violation of an obligation owed to all members of the international community to be free from nuclear tests generally or which were in alleged violation of the freedom of the high seas? As a general matter, where one party to a treaty or agreement believes that another party is in violation of its obligations under that treaty or agreement, it will have the right to enforce the obligations of the party alleged to be in violation, even if it has not suffered material damage.[102]

For alleged breaches of treaty obligations, the right of a state to enforce obligations will usually be settled by the terms of the treaty. Thus the EC Treaty allows a member state which considers that any other member state has failed to fulfil an EC obligation, including an environmental obligation, to bring the matter before the European Court of Justice.[103] Although this right has been relied upon on numerous occasions to threaten court proceedings, it appears to have resulted in a decision by the European Court of Justice on only one occasion, when France successfully brought proceedings against the UK for unlawfully having enforced domestic legislation setting a minimum mesh size for prawn fisheries.[104] The situation in general international law is less well-developed, although there may be a move in the direction taken by the EC under some recent environmental treaties. Thus a failure by one party to the 1987 Montreal Protocol to fulfil its obligations under that treaty would entitle any other party to the Protocol to seek to enforce the obligation by invoking the non-compliance or dispute settlement mechanisms under the Protocol, without having to show that it had suffered environmental damage as a result of the alleged failure. The 1989 Basle Convention similarly provides that any party 'which has reason to believe that another party is acting or has acted in breach of its obligations' under the Convention may inform the secretariat and the party against whom the allegations are made.[105] Most other environmental treaties are less explicit, establishing dispute settlement mechanisms which will settle the question of enforcement rights in accordance with the provisions available under that treaty or related instruments. Some treaties specifically preclude their application to the global commons. The 1991 Espoo Convention, for example, precludes parties from requesting an environmental impact assessment or other measures in respect of harm to the global commons.

Whether a state has, in the absence of a specific treaty right such as the Montreal Protocol, a general legal interest in the protection of the environment in areas beyond its national jurisdiction such as to allow it to exercise rights of legal protection on behalf of the international community as a whole (sometimes referred to as *actio popularis*) is a question which remains difficult to answer in the absence of state practice. The matter has been considered in passing by the International Court of Justice on at least two occasions, and by some of the judges in a third case. The matter remains inconclusive, although the tendency seems to favour the right of a state to bring an action in its capacity as a member of the international community to prevent significant damage from occurring to the environment in areas beyond its national jurisdiction.

The unwillingness of states to enforce obligations concerning the protection of the environment is evidenced by many examples. Perhaps the most notorious is the failure of any state to seek to enforce compliance by the former USSR with its international legal obligations arising out of the consequences of the accident at the Chernobyl nuclear power plant in 1986. Where the mere attempt to enforce obligations can establish a precedent which could subsequently bind the enforcing state, an increased enforcement role for international organizations, or other members of the international community, is increasingly being considered.

4.2.2   Enforcement by international organizations   While international organizations play an important legislative role in the development of international environmental law, their executive function in its enforcement is limited. States have been unwilling to transfer too much, if any, enforcement powers to international organizations and their secretariats, although there are some indications that this reluctance is being replaced by a limited willingness to grant more powers to international organizations.

Early examples of limited enforcement roles granted to international organizations include the right of the River Danube Mixed Commission to 'work out agreed measures' for the regulation of fishing in the Danube,[106] the right of certain international fisheries institutions to 'recommend' international enforcement measures or systems,[107] and the right of the International Commission for the Protection of the Rhine against Pollution to regularly compare draft national programmes of parties to ensure that 'their aims and means coincide'.[108] The CITES Secretariat, where it is satisfied that information it has received indicates that certain endangered species are being affected adversely by trade in specimens, may communicate that information to the relevant party or parties, which may then lead to the matter being reviewed by the next conference of the parties and 'which may make whatever recommendations it deems appropriate'.[109]

Developments in relation to the protection of the marine environment and the Antarctic environment foresee an enhanced enforcement role for international organizations. Under the 1971 Oil Pollution Fund Convention, the Fund may take enforcement proceedings before the national courts of Parties.[110] The 1982 UNCLOS also introduces innovative arrangements by endowing some of its institutions with a range of enforcement powers. Thus the Council of the International Seabed Authority has the power to 'supervise and coordinate the implementation' of Part XI of UNCLOS and 'invite the attention of the Assembly to cases of non-compliance'; to institute proceedings on behalf of the Authority before the Seabed Disputes Chamber in case of non-compliance; to issue emergency orders 'to prevent serious harm to the marine environment arising out of activities in the Area'; and to direct and supervise inspectors to ensure compliance.[111] And the Antarctic Mineral Resources Commission, which would have been established under the 1988 CRAMRA, would have been required to draw to the attention of all parties any activity which affects the implementation of the objectives and principles of CRAMRA or the compliance by any party with its obligations and any measures in effect pursuant to it, as well as of any activities by a state which is not a party which affects the implementation of the objectives and principles of the Convention.[112] It would also 'ensure the effective application' of the provisions in the Convention concerning, *inter alia*, notification, reporting of mineral prospecting, and keeping 'under review the conduct of Antarctic mineral resource activities with a view to safeguarding the protection of the Antarctic environment in the interest of all mankind'.[113]

The 1992 OSPAR Convention also goes some way towards establishing a role for the Commission it creates in ensuring compliance with obligations. Under Article 23, which is entitled 'Compliance', the Commission has two functions. First, it must 'assess' the compliance by parties with the Convention and the decisions and recommendations adopted thereunder on the basis of the reports submitted by the parties. Second, when appropriate the Commission may:

decide upon and call for steps to bring about full compliance with the Convention, and decisions adopted thereunder, and promote the implementation of recommendations, including measures to assist a Contracting Party to carry out its obligations.[114]

The EC Commission is required to ensure compliance by the EC member states of their environmental obligations under the EC law. Article 155 of the 1957 EEC Treaty requires the Commission to ensure that the provisions of the Treaty and the measures taken by the institutions are applied, and Article 169 of the EC Treaty provides that:

> If the Commission considers that a Member state has failed to fulfil an obligation under this Treaty, it shall deliver a reasoned opinion on the matter after giving the state concerned the opportunity to submit its observations.

In environmental matters the EC Commission has made frequent and often controversial use of its powers under Article 169. In 1982 the EC Commission commenced 16 infringement proceedings against member states under Article 169; by 1990 the number had risen to 217 infringement proceedings.[115]

4.2.3 Enforcement by non-governmental actors According to traditional rules of public international law non-governmental actors are not international legal persons except within the limited confines of international human rights law and its associated fields. In practice they play a central role in the development and application of international environmental law. In the enforcement process the role of environmental organizations can be formal or informal, and their primary role continues to be at the national level, through political means or by recourse to administrative or judicial procedures for enforcing national measures adopted by a state in implementing its international treaty and other obligations. Increasingly, however, non-governmental organizations are playing a role in enforcement of international obligations at the transboundary level and in other international contexts.

Many early environmental agreements sought to recognize and encourage their role, particularly where individuals were the victims of pollution or environmental damage in a transboundary context. These sought either to establish principles or rules governing equal access to national courts by victims of transfrontier pollution, or to establish the jurisdiction of courts in the event of transboundary incidents. The 1976 OECD Council Recommendation on Equal Right of Access in Relation to Transfrontier Pollution identified the constituent elements of a system of equal right of access,[116] including rights relating to access to information and participation in hearings and enquiries and 'recourse to and standing in administrative and judicial procedures' to prevent pollution, have it abated, and/or obtain compensation for the damage caused. These general rights were further elaborated the following year by a slightly more detailed OECD Council recommendation for the Implementation of a Regime of Equal Right of Access and Non-Discrimination in Relation to Transfrontier Pollution.[117]

The non-binding OECD instruments are supplemented by a range of treaty and other binding obligations which address equal access or the jurisdiction of courts over transboundary disputes. The 1974 Nordic Environmental Protection Convention allows any person who is affected or may be affected by a nuisance caused by environmentally harmful activities in another contracting state to bring before the appropriate court or Administrative Authority of that state the permissibility of such activities, including the question of measures to prevent damage and compensation.[118] An enforcement role for individuals is also envisaged by a number of the treaties establishing international rules on civil liability.

The other category of conventions assuring a role for individual enforcement of environmental laws are those establishing private international law rules allocating jurisdiction to national courts over a range of civil and commercial matters, including disputes arising out of the law of tort. These generally allow the victim a choice of courts. Under Article 5(3) of the 1968 Brussels Convention on Jurisdiction and Enforcement of Judgments in Civil and Commercial Matters (1968 Brussels Convention) it is provided that jurisdiction in matters 'relating to tort, delict or quasi-delict' is conferred on the courts of the place 'where the harmful event occurred'. In *Handelskwekerij GJ Bier* v. *Mines de Potasses d'Alsace* the European Court of Justice was asked for the first time to interpret the meaning of the words 'where the harmful event occurred' in a case in which the defendant was alleged to have discharged over 10 000 tonnes of chloride every 24 hours into the Rhine River in France but the damage was suffered by Dutch horticultural businesses in The Netherlands.[119] The Dutch plaintiffs wished to bring proceedings in The Netherlands rather than in France, and on an Article 177 preliminary reference request from the Appeal Court of The Hague the matter was referred to the European Court of Justice. The European Court held that Article 5(3) should be interpreted 'in such a way as to acknowledge that the plaintiff has an option to commence proceedings either at the place where the damage occurred or the place of the event giving rise to it'.

At the international level the formal opportunities for non-governmental actors to play an enforcement role are extremely limited. Under some of the regional human rights treaties individual victims, including non-governmental organizations, may bring complaints directly to an international body. Non-governmental organizations and individuals have played a particularly active role in supporting the enforcement role of the EC Commission, usually by submitting complaints to that institution concerning the non-implementation by member states of their environmental obligations. In 1991 more than 400 complaints were received by the EC Commission concerning non-compliance with environmental obligations, leading to a number of formal investigations by the Commission.

4.3   International conflict resolution (settlement of disputes)

A range of processes' and mechanisms' are available at the international level to assist in the pacific settlement of environmental disputes arising over non-implementation of international obligations. Article 33 of the United Nations Charter identifies the traditional mechanisms for the pacific settlement of disputes:

> the parties to any dispute, the continuance of which is likely to endanger the maintenance of international peace and security, shall, first of all, seek a solution by negotiation, enquiry, mediation, conciliation, arbitration, judicial settlement, resort to regional agencies or arrangements, or other peaceful means of their own choice.

These different techniques can be divided into two broad categories: diplomatic means according to which of the parties retain control over the dispute in so far as they may accept or reject a proposed settlement (negotiation, consultation, mediation, conciliation); and legal means which result in legally binding decisions for the parties to the dispute (arbitration and judicial settlement). Recourse to regional arrangements and international organizations as mediators and conciliators provide something of a middle way: the legal consequences of any decision taken by the institution will depend on the treaty establishing the institution. Many of the earliest environmental treaties did not provide for any dispute settlement mechanisms, whether of a diplomatic or legal nature, or of a voluntary or mandatory character. Initially the trend was towards the use of informal and non-binding mechanisms, such as negotiation and consultation, supplemented by the use of more formal mechanisms, such as conciliation, arbitration and judicial settlement. More recently there has been a move towards the development of new techniques which aim at establishing non-contentious mechanisms which allow the intervention of a third party in an international context. The practice of the most recent treaties has been to provide parties with a range of options for dispute settlement and encouraging implementation. A recent example of this approach, which is intended to provide maximum flexibility, is the 1992 Climate Change Convention, which envisages at least three mechanisms to assist in dispute resolution or non-implementation: a subsidiary body for implementation, which is intended to provide assistance in implementation; a multilateral consultative process for the resolution of questions regarding implementation in a non-confrontational way; and the settlement of remaining disputes in more traditional ways by reference to negotiation, or submission to arbitration or the International Court of Justice, or to international conciliation.[120]

4.3.1 Negotiation and consultation The technique of negotiation has been used to resolve a wide range of environmental disputes. In the *Fisheries Jurisdiction Case* the International Court of Justice held that the objective of negotiation should be:

> the delimitation of the rights and interests of the Parties, the preferential rights of the coastal state on the one hand and the rights of the Applicant on the other, to balance and regulate equitably questions such as those of catch-limitation, share allocations and 'related restrictions concerning areas closed to fishing, number and type of vessels allowed and forms of control of the agreed provisions'.[121]

The International Court also set out conditions establishing the basis for the conduct of future negotiations: they should be conducted 'on the basis that each must in good faith pay reasonable regard to the legal rights of the other ... thus bringing about an equitable apportionment of the fishing resources based on the facts of the particular situation, and having regard to the interests of other states which have established fishing rights in the area. It is not a matter of finding simply an equitable solution, but an equitable solution derived from the applicable law'.[122]

Environmental treaties refer, more or less as a matter of standard practice, to the need to ensure that parties resort to negotiation and other diplomatic channels to resolve their disputes before making use of other more formal approaches. Since negotiations of this type invariably take place behind closed doors it is difficult to identify specific examples involving the successful resolution of claims and disputes by negotiation. One example was the settlement between Canada and the USSR concerning damage caused by the disintegration over Canada of Cosmos 954, a nuclear-powered satellite launched by the USSR. The negotiated settlement was agreed to in the context of the USSRs consideration of the question of damage 'in strict accordance with the provisions' of the 1972 Space Liability Convention to which both countries were parties.[123]

Consultation between states is also encouraged by environmental treaties as a technique to avoid and resolve disputes and potential disputes between states. In the *Lac Lanoux Case* the arbitral tribunal held that France had a duty to consult with Spain over certain projects likely to affect Spain's interests, and that in this context:

> the reality of the obligations thus undertaken is incontestable and sanctions can be applied in the event, for example, of an unjustified breaking off of the discussions, abnormal delays, disregard of the agreed procedures, systematic refusals to take

into consideration adverse proposals or interests, and, more generally, in cases of violation of the rules of good faith.[124]

Specific examples of environmental treaties requiring consultation relate to numerous diverse situations, including the following non-exhaustive list: development plans which may affect the natural resources of another state; measures to prevent pollution of coastlines from oil pollution incidents on the high seas; prior to the grant of permission for ocean dumping in emergency situations; pollution from land-based sources of certain substances; on the permissibility of environmentally harmful activities; and generally problems in applying a treaty or the need for and nature of remedial measures for breaches of obligation.

4.3.2   Mediation, conciliation and international institutions   Where negotiation and consultation fail, a number of environmental treaties provide for the use of mediation[125] or conciliation[126] to resolve disputes. Mediation and conciliation involve the intervention of a third person. In the case of mediation the third person is involved as an active participant in the interchange of proposals between the parties to a dispute, and may even offer informal proposals of his or her own. In the case of conciliation, the third person assumes a more formal role and often investigates the details underlying the dispute and makes formal proposals for the resolution of the dispute.

Early examples of conciliation include the role of the International Joint Commission established by Canada and the USA in the 1909 Boundary Waters Treaty,[127] which fulfils a combination of quasi-judicial, investigative and recommendatory, and coordinating functions. GATT Dispute Settlement Panels perform a similar function. Under the 1985 Vienna Convention and the 1992 Biodiversity Convention, conciliation will be used if the parties to the dispute have not accepted compulsory dispute settlement procedures by arbitration or the International Court of Justice.[128]

The political organs of international institutions and regional agencies also play an important role in the settlement of disputes. Such organs may either be granted an express mandate to consider disputes between two or more parties to the treaty, or, as is more usually the case, seek to resolve disputes between parties absent a specific mandate to do so.

Some treaties established specialized subsidiary bodies to deal with compliance issues and disputes relating to non-compliance. An important model is the non-compliance procedure established under the 1987 Montreal Protocol and conducted under the auspices of an Implementation Committee first established by the Second Meeting of the Parties to the 1987 Montreal Protocol.[129] Under the non-compliance procedure any party which has reservations about another party's implementation of its obligations under the

Protocol may relate its concerns in writing to the secretariat, with corroborating information. The secretariat will then determine with the assistance of the party alleged to be in violation whether it is unable to comply with its obligations under the Protocol, and will transmit the original submission, its reply and other information to the Implementation Committee. The functions of the Implementation Committee, which now consists of 10 parties (originally five parties) elected by the Meeting of the Parties on the basis of equitable geographical distribution for a two-year period, is to receive, consider and report on submissions made by any party concerning reservations regarding another party's implementation of its obligations under the Protocol, and any information or observations forwarded by the secretariat in connection with the preparation of reports based on information submitted by the parties pursuant to their obligations under the Protocol. The Committee may, at the invitation of the party concerned, undertake information-gathering in the territory of that party, and will also maintain an exchange of information with the Executive Committee of the Multilateral Fund related to the provisions of financial and technical cooperation to developing country parties. The Committee is to try to secure 'an amicable resolution of the matter on the basis of respect for the provisions of the Protocol' and report to the Meeting of the Parties, which may decide upon and call for steps to bring about full compliance with the Protocol. The Fourth Meeting of the Parties also adopted an indicative list of measures that might be taken by a Meeting of the Parties in respect of non-compliance, which comprise:

(a) appropriate assistance;
(b) issuing cautions; and
(c) suspension (in accordance with the applicable rules of international law concerning the suspension of the operation of a treaty) of specific rights and privileges under the Protocol.[130]

Resort to the non-compliance procedure is without prejudice to the dispute settlement provisions available under Article 11 of the 1985 Vienna Convention.

4.3.3 Arbitration International arbitration has been described as having 'for its object the settlement of disputes between states by judges of their own choice and on the basis of respect for the law. Recourse to arbitration implies an engagement to submit in good faith to the award'.[131] Arbitral awards have played an important role in the development of international environmental law, and three in particular have contributed to the development of substantive rules on environmental protection and use of natural resources: the 1893 *Fur Seal Arbitration*, the 1941 *Trail Smelter Arbitration*, and the 1957 *Lac Lanoux Arbitration*.

Several environmental treaties establish detailed provisions, including annexes or protocols, providing for the submission of disputes to arbitration at the instigation of one party to the dispute[132] or both parties to the dispute.[133] And yet other treaties refer simply to the possibility of submitting disputes to arbitration without providing any details on the establishment of such a body or its working arrangements.[134]

4.3.4   International courts   The settlement of international disputes may also be referred to an international court, which is a permanent tribunal competent to deliver a legally binding decision. In relation to environmental disputes four international courts have played, and are likely to continue to play, a role: the International Court of Justice, the European Court of Justice, the courts established under the various regional human rights treaties, and the courts and tribunals established under the UN Convention on the Law of the Sea.

4.3.5   International Court of Justice   The International Court of Justice, sometimes referred to as the World Court or The Hague Court, is the principal judicial organ of the UN. It was established as a successor (although not formally the legal successor) to the Permanent Court of International Justice in 1945. Jurisdiction of the International Court of Justice over a particular dispute depends on whether the Court has been invoked in a contentious case between two or more states, or to give advisory opinions on questions of law at the request of states or certain international organizations.[135]

Many environmental treaties provide for possible recourse to the International Court of Justice (ICJ) to settle disputes. Occasionally they establish the compulsory jurisdiction of the International Court,[136] but more usually the reference of a dispute to the Court requires the consent, in each case, of all parties to the dispute.[137] In recent years the practice has developed in environmental treaties of allowing parties at the time of signature, ratification or accession, or at any time thereafter, to accept compulsory dispute settlement by recourse to arbitration or to the ICJ.[138] Few parties accept this option.

Contentious environmental cases could also get to the ICJ under Article 36(2) of the Statute (the 'Optional Clause') under which parties to the Statute of the Court may declare that they recognize the compulsory jurisdiction of the Court, in relation to other states accepting the same obligation, in all legal disputes concerning the interpretation of a treaty, any question of international law, the existence of any fact which, if established, would constitute a breach of an international obligation; and the nature or extent of the reparation to be made for the breach of an international obligation.[139] Acceptance of the jurisdiction of the Court under Article 36(2) may be made unconditionally, or on condition of reciprocity, or for a limited period of time.[140]

Additionally the practice of the Court has been to accept reservations or conditions to declarations made under the Optional Clause.

As set out in the text the Court has had an opportunity to consider several environmental issues, and in July 1993 it established a seven-member Chamber for Environmental Matters. This decision was taken in view of the developments in the field of environmental law which have taken place in the last few years and the need to be prepared to the fullest possible extent to deal with any environmental case falling within its jurisdiction.

The UN Charter also allows the General Assembly or the Security Council to request the ICJ to give an advisory opinion on any legal question, and allows other organs of the UN and specialized agencies authorized by the General Assembly to request advisory opinions of the Court on legal questions arising within the scope of their activities.[141] Advisory opinions are not binding in law upon the requesting body, although in practice they are accepted and acted upon by that body. Although no legal question on an environmental issue has been the subject of a request for an Advisory Opinion, this route could provide a useful and non-contentious way of obtaining independent international legal advice on environmental matters. If it considers that the circumstances so require, the International Court of Justice also has the power to indicate interim measures of protection to preserve the rights of the parties to a dispute.[142] The irreparability of environmental damage will make interim measures particularly important in cases concerning environmental protection. In the *Nuclear Tests Cases* the Court indicated interim measures of protection, asking that the parties to ensure that no action should be taken which might aggravate or extend the dispute or prejudice the rights of another party, and calling on France to 'avoid nuclear tests causing the deposit of radio-active fall-out on Australian territory'.[143]

4.3.6 European Court of Justice The European Court of Justice is the judicial institution of the EC and is required to ensure that in the interpretation and application of the EEC Treaty 'the law is observed'.[144] In 1988 a Court of First Instance was created. Environmental cases reach the European Court and/or the Court of First Instance in a number of ways. The most frequent route is under Article 169 of the EC Treaty, and since 1980 the EC Commission has brought more than 40 cases to the ECJ alleging the failure of a member state to comply with its EEC environmental obligations, in which it is usually successful. Under Article 170 of the EC Treaty a member state which believes another member state has breached its obligations has a similar right to bring a matter before the ECJ.

The ECJ has also considered environmental questions on the basis of its jurisdiction under Article 177, the 'preliminary reference procedure'. Under this provision the national courts of the EC member states may refer to the

ECJ questions concerning, *inter alia*, the interpretation of the EC Treaty and the validity and interpretation of acts of the EC institutions, provided that a decision on the question is necessary to enable the national court to give a ruling on the question. Preliminary references from national courts to the ECJ are used when a dispute before the national courts raise a complex question or questions of EEC law or where the dispute turns on the EEC point and no appeal lies against the decision of the national court. The Article 177 procedure has been used on several occasions to allow the EC to rule on matters of an environmental nature.

4.3.7 Human Rights Courts   The human rights courts established under the various regional human rights conventions (the European Court of Human Rights and the Inter-American Court of Human Rights) may also have jurisdiction over environmental matters, although so far only the European Court of Human Rights appears to have had an opportunity to address environmental issues. The European Court has jurisdiction over all cases concerning the interpretation and application of the European Convention provided that the party or parties concerned by the case have accepted its compulsory jurisdiction or, failing that, with their consent.[145] The Court may only deal with a case after efforts by the Commission to achieve a friendly settlement have failed.[146]

4.3.8 UNCLOS   Part XV of the 1982 UNCLOS contains detailed provision on compulsory dispute settlement, allowing states at the time of signature, ratification or accession or at any time thereafter to choose one or more of the following to decide disputes under UNCLOS: the International Tribunal for the Law of the Sea (established in accordance with Annex VI of UNCLOS), the ICJ; an arbitral tribunal (constituted in accordance with Annex VII); and a special arbitral tribunal (constituted in accordance with Annex VIII).[147] A state which does not designate one of these means is deemed to have designated arbitration in accordance with Annex VII.[148]

4.3.9 UNCED   Whereas the 1972 Stockholm Conference did not really address the compliance issue, the subject was clearly an important one for UNCED. Agenda 21 goes a little further in recognizing the limitations of existing arrangements, including the inadequate implementation by parties of their obligations, the need to involve international institutions and environmental organizations in the implementation process, and the existence of important gaps in the dispute settlement mechanisms. Chapter 39 of Agenda 21 addresses some of the needs. The whole of the international community is called upon to ensure 'the full and prompt implementation of legally binding instruments',[149] and parties to international agreements are instructed to 'consider procedures and mechanisms to promote and review their effective, full and prompt implementation', including through the establishment of 'efficient and practical reporting systems on the effective, full and prompt implementation of international legal instruments' and consideration of the ways in which international bodies might contribute towards the further development of such mechanisms.[150] The role of international institutions is recognized. UNEP is called upon to promote the implementation of international environmental law,[151] UNDP will play a lead role in support of the implementation of Agenda 21 and capacity-building at the country, regional, interregional and global levels;[152] and the UN Commission on Sustainable Development will 'consider, where appropriate, information regarding the progress made in the implementation of environmental conventions which could be made available by the relevant Conferences of the Parties'.

With regard to dispute settlement, the international community is called upon to study and consider:

> the broadening and strengthening of the capacity of mechanisms, *inter alia* in the United Nations system, to facilitate, where appropriate and agreed by the parties concerned, the identification, avoidance and settlement of international disputes in the field of sustainable development, duly taking into account existing bilateral and multilateral agreements for the settlement of such disputes.[153]

The functions of the UN Commission on Sustainable Development will include reviewing progress in the implementation of Agenda 21 commitments and 'to consider, where appropriate, information regarding the progress made in the implementation of environmental conventions, which could be made available by the relevant Conferences of the Parties'.[154]

Notes

1. (*Great Britain* v. *United States*), 1 Moore's International Arbitration Awards 755 (1893).
2. Chapter 38, paras 38.42 to 38.44.
3. Art. 1(vii) and Art. 1(2).
4. Convention to Protect Birds Useful to Agriculture, Paris, 19 March 1902, IV *IPE* 1615.
5. Convention destinee a assurer la conservation des diverses especes animales vivant a l'état sauvage en Afrique qui sont utiles a l'homme ou inoffensive, London, 19 May 1900, IV *IPE* 1607.
6. Treaty Relating to the Boundary Waters and Questions Arising Along the Boundary Between the United States and Canada, 11 January 1909, XI *IPE* 5704.
7. Convention Between the United States and Great Britain for the Protection of Migratory Birds in the United States and Canada, Washington, 7 December 1916, IV *IPE* 1638.
8. Convention on Nature Protection and Wild Life Preservation in the Western Hemisphere, Washington, 12 October 1940, 161 *UNTS* 193.
9. C.O. Sauer, 'Destructive exploitation in modern colonial expansion', *International Geographical Congress*, Amsterdam, Vol. III, Sect. IIIC, 494.
10. *Ybk UN* 1948–9, 481–2.
11. UN General Assembly resolution 900(IX) 14 December 1954. The Conference Report is at VIII *IPE* 3969.

12. Convention on the High Seas, Geneva, 29 April 1958, 450 *UNTS* 82; Convention on Fishing and Conservation of the Living Resources of the High Seas, Geneva, 29 April 1958, 559 *UNTS* 285; Convention on the Continental Shelf, Geneva, 29 April 1958, 499 *UNTS* 311.
13. UN General Assembly resolution 912(2), 3 December 1955.
14. Treaty Banning Nuclear Weapon Tests in the Atmosphere, in Outer Space and Under Water, Moscow, 5 August 1963, 480 *UNTS* 43.
15. Nuclear Test Cases (Australia v. France), 1974 *ICJ Reps* xxx; (New Zealand v. France), 1974 *ICJ Reps* 457.
16. International Convention for the Prevention of Pollution of the Sea by Oil, London, 12 May 1954, 327 *UNTS* 3.
17. International Convention Relating to Intervention on the High Seas in Cases of Oil Pollution Damage, Brussels, 29 November 1969, 9 *ILM* 25 (1970).
18. International Convention on Civil Liability for Oil Pollution Damage, Brussels, 29 November 1969, 973 *UNTS* 3; International Convention on the Establishment of an International Fund for Compensation for Oil Pollution Damage, Brussels, 18 December 1971, 11 *ILM* 284 (1972).
19. African Convention on the Conservation of Nature and Natural Resources, Algiers, 15 September 1968, 1001 *UNTS* 4.
20. UN General Assembly resolution 2398 (XXIII), 3 December 1968.
21. *Report of the U.N. Conference on the Human Environment, U.N. Doc.* A/CONF. 48/14 at 2–65, and Corr. 1 (1972); 11 *ILM* 1416 (1972). For an excellent account of the Conference and the Declaration see Louis B. Sohn, 'The Stockholm Declaration on the Human Environment', 14 *HarvILJ*. 423 (1973).
22. Caldwell, L. [CITE], 55, 60.
23. Convention on the Prevention of Marine Pollution by Dumping of Wastes and Other Matter, 29 December 1972, 1046 *UNTS* 120.
24. International Convention for the Prevention of Pollution by Ships, London, 2 November 1973, 12 *ILM* 1319, 1434 (1973); Protocol Relating to the Convention for the Prevention of Pollution by Ships, London, 17 February 1978, 17 *ILM* 246 (1978).
25. Convention on International Trade in Endangered Species, Washington, 3 March 1973, 993 *UNTS* 243.
26. Convention for the Protection of World Cultural and Natural Heritage, Paris, 16 November 1972, 11 *ILM* 1358 (1972).
27. United Nations Convention on the Law of the Sea, Montego Bay, 10 December 1982, 21 *ILM* 1261 (1982).
28. Convention on the Conservation of Migratory Species of Wild Animals, Bonn, 23 June 1979, 19 *ILM* 15 (1980).
29. Convention on the Conservation of European Wildlife and Natural Habitats, Berne, 19 September 1979, *UKTS* 56 (1982), Cmnd. 8738.
30. Convention on Long-Range Transboundary Air Pollution, Geneva, 13 November 1979, 18 *ILM* 1442 (1979).
31. Agreement Establishing the European Bank for Reconstruction and Development, London, 29 May 1990, 29 *ILM* 800 (1990).
32. Convention on Environmental Impact Assessment in a Transboundary Context, Espoo, 25 February 1991, 30 *ILM* 802 (1991).
33. Convention on Transboundary Effects of Industrial Accidents, Helsinki, 17 March 1992, 31 *ILM* 1330 (1992).
34. Convention on the Protection and Use of Transboundary Watercourses and International Lakes, Helsinki, 17 March 1992, 31 *ILM* 1312 (1992).
35. UN General Assembly resolution 42/187, 11 December 1987.
36. UN General Assembly resolution 43/196, 20 December 1988.
37. 31 *ILM* 801 (1992).
38. 31 *ILM* 812 (1992).
39. 31 *ILM* 822 (1992).
40. 31 *ILM* 849 (1992).

41. UN General Assembly resolutions 47/188, 47/189, 47/192 and 47/191, 22 December 1992.

42. Convention for the Protection of the Marine Environment of the North East Atlantic, Paris, 22 September 1992, 31 *ILM* 750 (1992).

43. Convention on Civil Liability for Damage Resulting from Activities Dangerous to the Environment, Lugano, 21 June 1993, 32 *ILM* 674 (1993).

44. R. Dworkin, *Taking Rights Seriously*, 24, 26 (1977).

45. Permanent Court of Arbitration, Palmas Case (1928), 2 H.C.R. p. 84, at p. 93.

46. *United States* v. *Canada*, 3 RIAA, p. 1907 (1941); citing Eagleton, *Responsibility of States*, 1928, p. 80.

47. See Judge N. Singh, Foreword, in D. Munro and H. Lammers, *Environmental Protection and Sustainable Development: Legal Principles and Recommendations*, 1986, xi–xii.

48. L. Kramer, *EEC Treaty and Environmental Protection*, (1990), 61.

49. Original Hungarian Application, 22 October 1992, paras. 27, 29 and 30, in P. Sands, R. Tarasofsky and M. Weiss, *Basic Documents in International Environmental Law* (1994), xx.

50. See e.g. the support for the precautionary principle by low lying AOSIS countries in the climate change, which is put as follows: 'For us the precautionary principle is much more than a semantic or theoretical exercise. It is an ecological and moral imperative. We trust the world understands our concerns by now. We do not have the luxury of waiting for conclusive proof, as some have suggested in the past. The proof, we fear, will kill us.' Ambassador Robert van Lierop, Permanent Representative of Vanuatu to the United Nations and Co-Chairman of Working Group 1 of the INC/FCCC, Statement to the Plenary Session of the INC/FCCC, 5th February 1991, at 3.

51. 1992 Rio Declaration, Principle 7.

52. OECD Council Recommendation C(72)128 on 'Guiding Principles Concerning International Economic Aspects of Environmental Policies', 26th May 1972; 14 *ILM* 236 (1975); Council Recommendation C(74)223, 14 November 1974, 14 *ILM* 234 (1975); OECD Council Recommendations on the Application of the Polluter-Pays Principle to Accidental Pollution (C(89)88 (Final), 25 July 1989, 28 *ILM* 1320.

53. Council Recommendation 75/436/Euratom, ECSC, EEC of 3 March 1975, Annex, para. 2; *OJ* L 169, 29.6.1987, p. 1; Treaty establishing the European Community (as amended), Art. 130r(2).

54. Agreement on the European Economic Area, 20 May 1992, Art. 73(2).

55. Convention on Wetlands of International Importance, Ramsar, 2 February 1972, 996 *UNTS* 245.

56. 1985 Nairobi Protocol concerning Protected Areas and Wild Fauna and Flora in the Eastern African Region, 21 June 1985, *IELMT* 985: p. 47.

57. 1985 ASEAN Agreement on the Conservation of Nature and Natural Resources, Kuala Lumpur, 9 July 1985, 15 *EPL* 64 (1985).

58. Convention for the Protection of the Natural Resources and Environment of the South Pacific Region, Noumea, 24 November 1986, 26 *ILM* 38 (1987).

59. International Convention on Salvage, London, 28 April 1989, *IJECL* 300.

60. International Convention on Oil Pollution Preparedness, Response and Co-operation, London, 30 November 1990, 30 *ILM* 733 (1991).

61. Convention for the Prevention of Marine Pollution by Dumping from Ships and Aircraft, Oslo, 15 February 1972, 932 *UNTS* 3.

62. Convention for the Prevention of Marine Pollution from Land-Based Sources, Paris, 4 June 1974, 13 *ILM* 352 (1974).

63. See generally, UNEP, Status of Regional Agreements Negotiated in the Framework of the Regional Seas Programme, Ref. Point 2, August 1990.

64. Agreement between the United States and Canada Concerning the Water Quality of the Great Lakes, Ottawa, 15 April 1972, 11 *ILM* 694 (1972).

65. Protocol on the Reduction of Sulphur Emissions or their Transboundary Fluxes by at Least Thirty Percent, Helsinki, 8 July 1985, 27 *ILM* 707 (1987).

66. Protocol Concerning the Control of Emissions of Nitrogen Oxides or their Transboundary Fluxes, Sofia, 31 October 1988, 28 *ILM* 214 (1988).
67. Protocol on the Control of Emissions of Volatile Organic Compounds and their Transboundary Fluxes, Geneva, 18 November 1991, 31 *ILM* 568 (1992).
68. Vienna, 22 March 1985, 26 *ILM* 1529 (1987).
69. Protocol on Substances that Deplete the Ozone Layer, Montreal, 16 September 1987, 26 *ILM* 1550 (1987); amended in 1990 and 1992.
70. Convention on the Control of Transboundary Movements of Hazardous Wastes and Their Disposal, Basle, 22 March 1989, 28 *ILM* 649 (1989).
71. Lome, 15 December 1989, 29 *ILM* 783 (1990), Articles 39 and 40.
72. Convention on the Ban of Import into Africa and the Control of Transboundary Movement and Management of Hazardous Wastes within Africa, Bamako, 30 January 1991, 30 *ILM* 775 (1991).
73. IAEA Doc. GC(XXXIV)/920, 27 June 1990, 1 *YbkIEL* 537 (1990).
74. Convention Concerning Safety in the Use of Chemicals at Work, Geneva, 24 June 1990, 1 *YbkIEL* 295 (1990).
75. Wellington, 2 June 1988, 27 *ILM* 868 (1988), Articles 4, 15, 26, and 53.
76. 1985 Council Directive 85/337 on the Assessment and Effects of Certain Public and Private Projects on the Environment, *OJ* 1985 L175/1.
77. See e.g. World Bank Operational Directive 4.00, Annex A: Environmental Assessment, 21 September 1989. Other MDBs requiring EIA include the European Investment Bank; the European Bank for Reconstruction and Development; the African Development Bank; the Asian Development Bank; the Caribbean Development Bank; and the Inter-American Development Bank.
78. Council Decision-Recommendation Concerning the Provision of Information to the Public and Public Participation in Decision-Making Processes Related to the Prevention of, and Response to, Accidents Involving Hazardous Substances, 28 *ILM* 277 (1988).
79. EC Council Directive on Freedom of Access to Information on the Environment, 7 June 1990, *OJ* 1990 L158/56.
80. Operational Directive 14.70 on Involving Non-Governmental Organizations in Bank Supported Activities (1990).
81. OECD Convention on Third Party Liability in the Field of Nuclear Damage, Paris, 29 July 1960, 956 *UNTS* 251; Convention on Civil Liability for Nuclear Damage, Vienna, 29 May 1963, 1063 *UNTS* 265.
82. Convention on Civil Liability for Damage Caused during Carriages of Dangerous Goods by Road, Rail and Inland Navigation Vessels, Geneva, 10 October 1989.
83. Communication from the Commission to the Council: A community strategy to limit carbon dioxide emissions and to improve energy efficiency, EC Commission Doc. XI/626/91, 22 September 1991, paras. 19 to 28, at para. 25.
84. Trail Smelter Arbitration (*Canada* v. *United States*) (1941).
85. Lac Lanoux Arbitration (*France* v. *Spain*) (1957). Gabcikovo-Nagymaros Project Case (*Hungary/Slovakia*).
86. Fisheries Jurisdiction case (*United Kingdom* v. *Iceland*) (1974).
87. Certain Phosphate Lands in Nauru case (*Nauru* v. *Australia*) (1992).
88. 1972 London Convention, Art. VII(1); 1989 Basle Convention, Art. 4(4).
89. 1988 CRAMRA, Art. 7(1).
90. 1989 Basle Convention, Art. 5.
91. 1982 UNCLOS, Arts. 213, 214, 216, 222 and 235(2).
92. 1972 Oslo Convention, Art. 15(1); 1973 CITES, ART. VIII(1); 1974 Paris Convention, Art. 12.
93. 1972 London Convention, Art. VII(2); 1989 Basle Convention, Art. 4(4).
94. Art. 10.
95. 1982 UNCLOS, Arts. 217 to 220.
96. 1969 Moon Treaty, Arts. 12(1) and 14(1); 1988 CRAMRA, Art. 8(10).
97. Art. I(T) replacing Art. 10 of the 1987 Montreal Protocol.
98. 1992 Climate Change Convention, Art. 4(3) (the Convention states that the 'extent to

which developing country Parties will effectively implement their commitments under the Convention will depend on the effective implementation by developed country Parties' of their financial commitments, Art. 4(7)); 1992 Biodiversity Convention, Arts. 20(1) to (4).

99. See e.g. 1992 Climate Change Convention, requiring initial reports to be submitted within six months of entry into force by OECD countries, within three years of entry into force or upon the availability of financial resources by developing countries, and at their discretion by least-developed countries: Art. 12(5).

100. See United States General Accounting Office, *International Environment: International Agreements Are Not Well Monitored*, Report to Congressional Requesters, GAO/RCED–92–43 (1992).

101. ILC Draft Articles on State Responsibility, Pt 2, Art. 5(1) Report of the ILC to the United Nations General Assembly, UN Doc. A/44/10 (1989), 218.

102. See e.g. *The Wimbledon* (1923) PCIJ, Series A, No 1.

103. 1957 EEC Treaty, Art. 170.

104. Case 141/78 *France* v. *United Kingdom* (1979) ECR 2923.

105. 1989 Basle Convention, Art. 19; the information is then to be submitted to the Parties.

106. 1958 Danube Fishing Convention, Art. 12(1).

107. 1982 Convention for the Conservation of Salmon in the North Atlantic Ocean, Art. 4(2).

108. 1976 Rhine Chemical Convention, Art. 6(3).

109. 1973 CITES, Art. XIII.

110. 1971 Oil Pollution Fund Convention, Art. 2(2).

111. 1982 UNCLOS, Art. 162(2)(a), (u), (v), (w) and (z).

112. Art. 7(7) and (8).

113. Art. 21(1)(f) and (x).

114. Art. 23(b).

115. See EC Commission, *Eighth Report to the European Parliament on the Enforcement of Community Law* (1991).

116. OECD C(76)55 (Final), 18 May 1976.

117. OECD Doc. C (77) 28 (Final), 23 May 1977.

118. 1974 Nordic Environmental Protection Convention, Art. 3.

119. Case 21/76, [1976] *ECR* 1735.

120. 1992 Climate Change Convention, Arts. 10, 13 and 14. See also 1985 Vienna Convention, Art. 11; 1989 Basle Convention, Art. 20; 1992 Biodiversity Convention, Art. 27 and Annex II.

121. Icelandic Fisheries Case (*United Kingdom* v. *Iceland*) 31.

122. *Ibid.*, 33.

123. By a Protocol dated 2 April 1981 the USSR agreed to pay, and Canada agreed to accept, Canadian $3 000 000 in a final settlement of the claim.

124. Lac Lanoux Arbitration, see above.

125. 1968 African Nature Convention, Art. XVIII (referring disputes to the Commission of Mediation, Conciliation and Arbitration of the OAU); 1982 UNCLOS, Art. 284 and Annex V, Section 1; 1985 Vienna Convention, Art. 11(2).

126. 1974 Paris LBS Convention, Art. 21 (conciliation by the Commission); 1985 Vienna Convention, Art. 11(4) and (5) (providing for the establishment of a conciliation commission); 1992 Biodiversity Convention, Art. 27(4) and Annex II, Part 2; 1992 Climate Change Convention, Art. 14(5) to (7).

127. 1909 Boundary Waters Treaty, especially Arts. VIII and IX.

128. 1985 Vienna Convention, Art. 11; 1992 Biodiversity Convention, Art. 27.

129. See Decision II/5 (Non-compliance), Report of the Second Meeting of the Parties to the Montreal Protocol on Substances that Deplete the Ozone Layer, UNEP/OzL.Pro.2/3, 29 June 1990; see now Decision IV/5 and Annexes IV and V, adopting the non-compliance procedure; Report of the Fourth Meeting of the Parties, UNEP/OzL.Pro.4/15, 25 November 1992, 32 *ILM* 874 (1993).

130. Fourth Meeting of the Parties to the 1987 Montreal Protocol, Decision IV/5.

131. 1907 Hague Convention on the Pacific Settlement of International Disputes, Art. 37.

132. MARPOL 73/78, Art. 10 and Protocol II; 1988 CRAMRA, Arts. 55 to 59 and Annex; 1992 OSPAR Convention, Art. 32(2).
133. 1980 CCAMLR Art. XXV and Annex; 1983 Cartegena Convention, Art. 23 and Annex; 1986 Noumea Convention, Art. 26 and Annex.
134. 1985 Vienna Convention, Art. 11.
135. In relation to contentious cases it is important to recall that 'only states may be parties in cases before the Court', United Nations Charter, Art. 34(1).
136. 1963 Vienna Convention, Optional Protocol Concerning the Compulsory Settlement of Disputes, Art. I (not in force).
137. 1959 Antarctic Treaty, Art. XI(2); 1974 Baltic Convention, Art. 18(2).
138. 1985 Vienna Convention, Art. 11(3); 1989 Basle Convention, Art. 20(3); 1992 Climate Change Convention, Art. 14(2); 1992 Biodiversity Convention, Art. 27(3); 1992 Industrial Accidents Convention, Art. 21; 1992 Watercourses Convention, Art. 22.
139. Statute ICJ, Art. 36(2). As of 1 January 1992 51 states have accepted the Optional Clause.
140. Art. 36(3).
141. Art. 96. ECOSOC, the Trusteeship Council and 15 of the specialized agencies have been authorized by the General Assembly, as has the IAEA, the Interim Committee of the General Assembly and the Committee for Applications for Review of the UN Administrative Tribunal. UNEP and UNCSD have not been so authorized by the General Assembly.
142. Statute ICJ, Art. 41.
143. (*Australia* v. *France*), Order re Interim Measures, ICJ Rep 1973, 99; (*New Zealand* v. *France*), Order re Interim Measures, ICJ Rep 1973, 135.
144. 1957 EEC Treaty, Art. 164. The ECJ also has competence in relation to the interpretation and application of the 1950 ECSC and 1957 Euratom.
145. 1950 ECHR Arts. 44, 45 and 48. All the Parties to the Convention have accepted the compulsory jurisdiction of the Court. Protocol No. 2 to the Convention confers upon the Court competence to give advisory opinions: Strasbourg, 6 May 1963, in force 21 September 1970.
146. Art. 47.
147. 1982 UNCLOS, Art. 287(1).
148. Art. 287(3).
149. Agenda 21, Chapter 39, para. 39.3(e).
150. Para. 39.7.
151. Para. 38.22(h).
152. Para. 38.24 and 38.25(a).
153. Para. 39.3(h).
154. GA Res. 47/191 (institutional arrangements to follow up the UNCED), 22 December 1992, paras. 3(c) and (h).

Bibliography

Anderson, K. and Blackhurst, R. (eds) (1992), *The Greening of World Trade Issues*, Harvester Wheatsheaf: London.

Anderson, J. and Hazell, P. (1989), *Variability in Grain Yields*, World Bank: Washington, D.C.

Arrow, K. and Fisher, A. (1974), 'Preservation, uncertainty and irreversibility', *Quarterly Journal of Economics*, **87**, 312.

Atkinson, R. and Tietenberg, T. (1991), 'Market failure in incentive-based regulation: the case of emissions trading', *Journal of Environmental Economics and Management*, **21**, 17.

Baldwin, R. (1995), 'Does sustainability require growth?', in R. Goldin and A. Winters (eds), *The Economics of Sustainable Development*, Cambridge University Press: Cambridge.

Barbier, E. (1995), *Economics and Ecology*, Chapman & Hall: London.

Barbier, E., Burgess, J. and Folke, C. (1994), *Paradise Lost?*, Earthscan: London.

Barbier, E., Burgess, J., Swanson, T. and Pearce, D. (1990), *Elephants, Economics and Ivory*, Earthscan: London.

Barnett, H. and Morse, C. (1963), *Scarcity and Growth: The Economics of Natural Resource Availability*, Johns Hopkins University Press: Baltimore.

Barrett, S. (1990), 'Global environmental protection', in D. Helm (ed.), *Economic Policy Towards the Environment*, Blackwell: Oxford.

Barrett, S. (1994), 'Self-enforcing international environmental agreements', *Oxford Economic Papers*, **46**, 878.

Baumol, W. and Oates, W. (1988), *The Economics of Environmental Policy*, Cambridge University Press: Cambridge.

Beckerman, W. (1994), *Small is Stupid*, Blackwell: Oxford.

Beltratti, A., Chichilnisky, G. and Heal, G. (1995), 'The green golden rule', in R. Goldin and A. Winters (eds), *The Economics of Sustainable Development*, Cambridge University Press: Cambridge.

Birnie, P. (1985), *International Regulation of Whaling*, Oceana Publications: London.

Boulding, K. (1992), 'The economics of the coming spaceship Earth', in A. Markandya and J. Richardson (eds), *Reader in Environmental Economics*, Earthscan: London.

Braden, J. and Kolstad, C. (1991), *Measuring the Demand for Environmental Quality*, Elsevier: Amsterdam.

Broome, J. (1992), *Counting the Costs of Global Warming*, White Horse: Cambridge.

Caldwell, L. (1990), *International Environmental Policy*, Duke University Press: Durham.

Carraro, C. and Siniscalco, D. (1997), 'The international protection of the environment', in P. Dasgupta, K.-G. Maler and Vercelli, D., *The Economics of Transnational Commons*, Oxford University Press: Oxford.

Cervigni, R. (1998), 'Incremental cost under the biodiversity convention', *EARE*, (forthcoming).

Cheung, S. (1973), 'The fable of the bees', *Journal of Law and Economics*, v. 15: 26–42.

Chichilnisky, G. and Heal, G. (1993), 'Global environmental risks', *Journal of Economic Perspectives*, **7**(4), 65.

Chichilnisky, G. (1994), 'North south trade and the global environment', *American Economic Review*, **84**(4), 851.

Churchill, R. and Lowe, V. (1988), *The Law of the Sea*, Manchester University Press: Manchester.

Cline, W. (1991), 'Scientific basis for global warming', *Economic Journal*, **101**(47).

Cline, W. (1992), *The Economics of Global Warming*, Institute of International Economics: Washington, D.C.

Conrad, J. (1980), 'Quasi-option value and the expected value of information', *Quarterly Journal of Economics*, **94**, 813.

Costanza, R. (ed.) (1991), *Ecological Economics – the Science and Management of Sustainability*, Columbia University Press: New York.

Daly, H. (1992a), 'The economic growth debate', in A. Markandya and J. Richardson, *Reader in Environmental Economics*, Earthscan: London.

Daly, H. (1992b), *Steady State Economics*, Earthscan: London.

Daly, H., Ehrlich, P., Mooney, R. and Ehrlich, A. (1991), 'Greenhouse economics: learn before you leap', *Ecological Economics*, **4**(1).

Daly, H. *et al.* (1992), *Toward a Steady-State Economy*, (second edn), Island Press: Washington, D.C.

Dasgupta, P., Maler, K.-G. and Vercelli, D. (1997), *The Economics of Transnational Commons*, Oxford University Press: Oxford.

Diamond, J. (1989), 'Overview of recent extinctions', in 'Population, resources, and the environment in the twenty-first century', in D. Western and M. Pearl, *Conservation for the Twenty-first Century*, Oxford University Press: Oxford.

Ecological Economics (1994), Special Issue: Trade and the Environment, **9**(1).

Ehrlich, P. (1986), 'The loss of diversity: causes and consequences', in E.O. Wilson (ed.), *Biodiversity*, National Academy of Sciences: Washington, D.C.

Ehrlich, P. and Ehrlich, A. (1981), *Extinction*, Random House: New York.

Escapa, M. and Gutierrez, M. (1997), 'Distribution of potential gains from international environmental agreements: the case of the greenhouse effect', *Journal of Environmental Economics and Management*, **33**, 1–16.

Esty, D. (1994), *Greening the Gatt*, Institute for International Economics: London.

Freeman, A.M. (1979), *The Benefits of Environmental Improvement*, Johns Hopkins: Baltimore.

Grossman, G. (1995), 'Pollution and growth: what do we know?', in R. Goldin and A. Winters (eds), *The Economics of Sustainable Development*, Cambridge University Press: Cambridge.

Grossman, G. and Krueger, A. (1992), 'Environmental impacts of NAFTA', Princeton University discussion paper.

Hanley, N. and Spash, C. (1993), *Cost Benefit Analysis and the Environment*, Edward Elgar: Cheltenham.

Hardin, G. (1968), 'The tragedy of the commons', *Science*.

Hartwick, J. (1977), 'Intergenerational equity and the investing of rents from exhaustible resources', *American Economic Review*, **67**(5), 972–84.

Harsanyi, J. (1989), 'Bargaining', in J. Eatwell *et al.* (eds), *The New Palgrave: Game Theory*, Macmillan: London.

Hart, O. and Moore, J. (1990), 'Property rights and the nature of the firm', *Journal of Political Economy*, **98**: 1119–58.

Hartwick, J. and Olewiler, N. (1986), *The Economics of Natural Resource Use*, Collins: New York.

Helm, D. (1991), *Economic Policy Toward the Environment*, Blackwell: Oxford.

Hoel, M. (1991), 'Global environmental problems: the effect of unilateral actions', *Journal of Environmental Economics and Management*, **25**, 56–75.

Holz-Eakin, D. and Selden, R. (1994), 'Stoking the fires', *Journal of Public Economics*.

Howarth, R. and Norgaard, R. (1995), 'International choices under global change', in Bromley (ed.), *The Handbook of Environmental Economics*, Blackwell: Oxford.

Johansson, P.O. (1987), *The Economic Theory and Measurement of Environmental Benefits*, Cambridge University Press: Cambridge.

Johnstone, N. (1996), 'Trade and environmental degradation', in T. Swanson (ed.), *The Economics of Environmental Degradation*, Edward Elgar: Cheltenham.

Keen, E. (1988), *Ownership and Productivity of Marine Fishery Resources*, McDonald: Virginia.

Klaasen, G. (1996), *Acid Rain and Environmental Degradation*, Edward Elgar: Cheltenham.

Klaasen, G. and Nentjes, A. (1997), 'Creating markets for air pollution in Europe and the USA', *Environmental and Resource Economics*, **10**(2), 125.

Krutilla, J. (1967), 'Conservation Reconsidered', *American Economic Review*, **57**.

Krutilla, J. and Fisher, A. (1980), *The Economics of Natural Environments*, Resources for the Future: Washington, D.C.

Leader-Williams, N. and Albon, S. (1988), 'Allocation of resources for conservation', *Nature*, **336**, 533–5.

Libecap, G. (1989), *Contracting for Property Rights*, Cambridge University Press: Cambridge.

Lovejoy, T. (1980), 'A projection of species extinctions', in G. Barney (ed.), *The Global 2000 Report to the President*, Council on Environmental Quality: Washington, D.C.

Lucas, R., Wheeler, D. and Hettige, H. (1992), 'Economic development regulation and the international migration of toxic industrial pollution: 1960–1988', Background Paper for the *World Development Report 1992*, World Bank: Washington, D.C.

Luxmoore, R. and Swanson, T. (1992), 'Wildlife and wildland utilization and conservation', in T. Swanson and E. Barbier (eds), *Economics for the Wilds: Wildlands, Wildlife, Diversity and Development*, Earthscan: London.

Lyster, S. (1985), *International Wildlife Law*, Grotius: London.

Maler, K.-G. (1991), 'International environmental problems', in D. Helm (ed.), *Economic Policy Toward the Environment*, Blackwell: Oxford.

Maler, K.-G. (1992), 'Incentives in international environmental problems', in H. Siebert (ed.), *Environmental Scarcity*, JLB Mohr: Tubingen.

Markandya, A. and Richardson, J. (1992), *The Earthscan Reader in Environmental Economics*, Earthscan: London.

Marks, S. (1984), *The Imperial Lion*, Westview: Boulder.

Mason, R. and T. Swanson (1994), 'Joint implementation of the Second Sulphur Protocol - final report to UN ECE'.

McGuire, M. (1982), 'Regulation, factor rewards, and international trade', *Journal of Public Economics*, **17**, 335.

McNeely, J., Miller, K., Reid, W., Mittermeier, R., and Werner, T. (1990), *Conserving the World's Biological Diversity*, IUCN: Gland, Switzerland.

Merrifield, J. (1988), 'The impact of selected abatement strategies on transnational pollution: the terms of trade and factor rewards', *Journal of Environmental Economics and Management*, **15**, 259.

Misiolek, W. and Elder, H. (1989), *Using Surveys to Value Public Goods*, Resources for the Future: Washington, D.C.

Mitchell, R. and Carson, R. (1989), *Using Surveys to Value Public Goods*, Earthscan: London.

Murdoch, C. and Sandler, T. (1997), 'The voluntary provision of a pure public good: the case of reduced CFC emissions and the Montreal Protocol', *Journal of Public Economics*, **63**: 331–49.

Newbery, D. (1992), 'Acid Rain', *Economic Policy*, **10**, 110–32.

Norgaard, R. (1989), 'The case for methodological pluralism', *Ecological Economics*, **1**, 37–58.

Nordhaus, W. (1991), 'Economic approaches to global warming', in R. Dornbusch and J. Poterba (eds), *Global Warming: Economic Policy Responses*, MIT: Cambridge.

Nordhaus, W. (1991), 'To slow or not to slow', *Economic Journal*, **101**(47).

Nordhaus, W. (1992), 'Lethal model 2: the limits to growth revisited', *Brookings Papers on Economic Activity*, no. 2.

Nordhaus, W. (1993), 'Reflections on the economics of climate change', *Journal of Economic Perspectives*, **7**(4), 11.

Olsen, M. (1970), *The Logic of Collective Action*, Schoken: New York.

Pearce, D., Markandya, A. and Barbier, E. (1989), *Blueprint for a Green Economy*, Earthscan: London.

Perrings, C. (1987), *Economy and Environment*, Cambridge University Press: Cambridge.

Prescott-Allan, R. and Prescott-Allan, C., (1983), *Genes from the Wild*, Earthscan: London.

Rauscher, M. (1994), 'On ecological dumping', *Oxford Economic Papers*, **46, 822**. *Ecological Economics*, Special Issue: *Trade and the Environment*, **9**(1).

Reid, W. and Miller, K. (1989), *Keeping Options Alive*, World Resources Institute: Washington, D.C.

Repetto, R. and Gillis, M. (1988), *Public Policies and the Misuse of Forest Resources*, Cambridge University Press: Cambridge.

Robison, H. (1988), 'Industrial pollution abatement: the impact of balance of trade', *Canadian Journal of Economics*, **21**(1), 187.

Rothschild, M. and Stiglitz, J. (1976), 'Equilibrium in competitive insurance markets', *Quarterly Journal of Economics*, **90**(4), 629–49.

Rubinstein, A. (1988), 'Perfect equilibrium in a bargaining game', in K. Binmore and P. Dasgupta, *The Economics of Bargaining*, Cambridge University Press: Cambridge.

Sagoff, M. (1988), *The Economy of the Earth*, Cambridge University Press: Cambridge.

Sandler, T. (1967), *Global Challenges*, Cambridge University Press: Cambridge.

Sandler, T. and Murdoch, D. (1997), 'The voluntary provision of a pure public good: the case of reduced CFC emissions and the Montreal Protocol', *Journal of Public Economics*, **63**, 331.

Schotter, A. (1986), *The Economics of Institutions*, Cambridge University Press: Cambridge.

Selden, T. and Song (1995), 'Environmental quality and development: is there a Kuznets curve for air pollution?', *Journal of Environmental Economics and Management*, **22**, 37.

Siebert, H. (ed.) (1991), *Environmental Scarcity: The International Dimension*, J.C.B. Mohr: Tubingen.

Smith, K. (ed.) (1979), *Scarcity and Growth Reconsidered*, Resources for the Future: Washington (especially chapters by Stiglitz, Daly and Barnett).

Solow, A. (1991), 'Is there a global warming problem?', in R. Dornbusch and J. Poterba (eds), *Global Warming: Economic Policy Responses*, MIT: Cambridge.

Solow, R. (1962), 'Technical progress, capital formation and economic growth', *American Economic Review*, papers and proceedings (May).

Solow, R. (1974a), 'The economics of resources or the resources of economics', *American Economic Review*, **64**, 1–12.

Solow, R. (1974b), 'Intergenerational equity and exhaustible resources', Review of Economic Studies, Symposium Issue on Depletable Resources, 37–48.

Solow, R. (1992), 'Economics of resources or the resources of economics', in R. Dornbusch and E. Dornbusch.

Swanson, T. (1989), 'Policy options for the regulation of the ivory trade', in S. Cobb (ed.), *The Ivory Trade and the Future of the African Elephant*, Ivory Trade Review Group: Oxford.

Swanson, T. (1990), 'The international regulation of oceanic resources', in D. Helm (ed.), *Economic Policy Towards the Environment*, Blackwell: Oxford.

Swanson, T. (1991), 'Conserving biological diversity', in D. Pearce (ed.), *Blueprint 2: Greening the World Economy*, Earthscan: London.

Swanson, T. (1992), 'Wildlife utilization and other policies for biodiversity conservation', in T. Swanson and E. Barbier (eds), *Economics for the Wilds*, Earthscan: London.

Swanson, T. (1992), 'The economics of a biodiversity convention', *Ambio*, **18**, 72.

Swanson, T. (1993), *The International Regulation of Extinction*, Macmillan: London.

Swanson, T. (1994), 'The economics of extinction revisited and revised', *Oxford Economic Papers*, **24**, 85.

Swanson, T. (1996), 'International regulation for environmental protection: the case for CITES', *Economic Affairs*, **10**, 1.

Swanson, T. (1996), *The Economics of Environmental Degradation*, Edward Elgar: Cheltenham.

Swanson, T. (1997), *A Framework for International Cooperation on Biodiversity*, Earthscan: London.

Swanson, T. (1998), 'Key economic concepts and the role of market structure in benefit sharing', OECD experts group discussion paper.

Swanson, T. and Barbier, E. (eds) (1991), *Economics for the Wilds*, Earthscan: London.

Swanson, T. and Barbier, E. (eds) (1992), *Economics for the Wilds: Wildlands, Wildlife, Diversity and Development*, Earthscan: London.

Swanson, T. and Mason, R. (1998), 'The impact of the Montreal Protocol', paper presented for the UNEP.

Swanson, T. and Pearce, D. (1989), 'The international regulation of the ivory trade – the ivory exchange', paper prepared for the International Union for the Conservation of Nature: Gland.

Tietenberg, T. (1984), *Emissions Trading*, Resources for the Future: Washington, D.C.

Tietenberg, T. (1985), *Emissions Trading*, Resources for the Future: Washington, D.C.

Tietenberg, T. (1992), 'Economic instruments for environmental regulation', in D. Helm (ed.), *Economic Policy Toward the Environment*, Blackwell: Oxford.

Thirlwall, A. (1982), *Growth and Development*, Macmillan: London and Basingstoke.

Tobey, J. (1990), 'The effects of domestic environmental policies on patterns of world trade', *Kyklos*, **43**(2), 191.

TRAFFIC International (1991), 'Asian boneytongue exports from Indonesia', *TRAFFIC Bulletin*, **12**(1/2).

Underdahl, A. (1980), *The Politics of International Fisheries Management*, Universitetsforlagt: Oslo.

Vitousek, P., Ehrlich, P. and Matson, P. (1986), 'Human appropriation of the products of photosynthesis', *Bioscience*, **36**(6), 368–73.

Western, D. (1989), 'Population, resources, and environment in the twenty-first century', in D. Western and M. Pearl, *Conservation for the Twenty-first Century*, Oxford University Press: Oxford.

Whalley, J. (1991), 'The interface between environmental and trade policies', *Economic Journal*, **101**(2), 180.

Whalley, J. and Wigle, R. (1991), 'The international incidence of carbon taxes', in R. Dornbusch and J. Poterba (eds), *Global Warming: Economic Policy Responses*, MIT: Cambridge.

Wijnstekers, W. (1988), *The Evolution of CITES*, Secretariat of the Convention on International Trade in Endangered Species: Lausanne.

Williamson, P. (1986), *The Economic Institutions of Capitalism*, Free Press: London.

Wilson, E.O. (1988), *Biodiversity*, National Academy of Science: Washington, D.C.

Witt, S. (1985), *Biotechnology and Genetic Diversity*, California Agricultural Lands Project: San Francisco.

World Bank (1990), *World Development Report*, Oxford University Press: Oxford.

World Bank Memorandum (1992), 'Let them eat pollution', *Economist*, 8 February, 66.

World Conservation Monitoring Centre (WCMC) (1992), *Global Diversity*, Chapman & Hall: London.

World Resources Institute (1990), *World Resources 1990–1991*, Oxford University Press: Oxford.

Young, O. (1989), 'The politics of international regime formation: managing natural resources and the environment', *International Organisation*, **43**(3), 1–37.

Index

abatement 115
abstention loophole 174
acceptance 162
accession 219
accident experience rate 172
acid rain 107–14, 151, 153, 154, 155
Act of Parliament 219
Ad Hoc Working Group of Experts on
    Biological Diversity 220
Ad Hoc Working Group of Legal and
    Technical Experts 220
adjudicative function 205
Administrative Authority 255
administrative function 204–5
adverse selection 137, 141
A.E.G. 146
Africa 57, 70, 71, 182
    Convention on International Trade in
        Endangered Species and trade
        regulations 192, 196, 199
    East 239–40
    environmental law principles 207,
        210, 213, 239, 240, 241
    sub-Saharan 189
    West 240
    see also Central
African Convention 224, 232
African elephant 174–84, 193, 196, 198,
    200
African Nature Convention 214
Agenda 21 206, 207, 209, 217, 221, 236,
    238, 262, 263
Agreed Measures for the Conservation
    of Antarctic Fauna and Flora 225
agriculture 16, 57–61, 238
air pollution 127
air quality 240
Albon, S. 192
alternative instruments and alternative
    distributions 101–3
American Tropical Tuna Commission
    171
Americas 210, 213, 239

see also Latin America; North
    America; South America
Anderson, J. 60, 62
animal benefactor motive 50
Antarctic 210, 240, 243, 249, 253
    Convergence 226
    Mineral Resources Commission 222,
        253–4
    Minerals Convention 226
    Treaty 214, 219, 224–7, 231, 242
        Consultative Party Meetings 224–5,
            226, 227
        System 227, 230–31
Apia Convention 232
Appeal Court of the Hague 255
Arbitral Tribunal 203, 211, 234
Arrhenius 33, 37
Arrow, K. 48
Articles of Agreement 216
ASEAN Agreement on the Conservation
    of Nature and Natural Resources
    242
ASEAN Convention 227, 232
Asia 57, 60, 207, 210
    East 239
    South 240
    South East 92, 189, 239
Asian bonytongue 195–6
Atkinson, R. 121
Australia 55, 214, 251, 261
Austria 150, 156

Bamako accord/Convention 70, 241
Bangladesh 60, 61
bans 103–4
Barbier, E. 86, 196, 200
Barcelona Convention 219–20
bargaining 162
    bilateral 113, 138
    concepts 124
    distribution as barrier to cooperation
        118–19
    frontier 122

277